CW01638198

ISE

Frontispiece: Thomas Johnes of Hafod 1748—1816
(engraved by Engleheart)

Peacocks in Paradise

Elisabeth Inglis-Jones

Golden Grove Editions

This edition published in 1988 by
The Golden Grove Book Company Limited
Golden Grove House, 10 Quay Street,
Carmarthen, Dyfed, SA31 3JT. Dyfed, Wales

© Elisabeth Inglis-Jones 1988

First published in 1950 by Faber & Faber
Second edition 1960
Paper edition 1971 by Service Publications
for Galloway & Morgan

Printed on acid-free paper

All rights reserved. No part of this publication may be reproduced, stored in a retrieval system, or transmitted, in any form or by any means, electronic, mechanical, photocopying, recording or otherwise, without the prior permission of The Golden Grove Book Company Ltd.

Printed and bound in Wales by J D Lewis & Sons Ltd.
Gomer Press, Llandysul, Dyfed, Wales

To E.N.H.

By the same author

STARVED FIELDS (1929)
CRUMBLING PAGEANT (1932)
PAY THY PLEASURE (1939)
THE LOVING HEART (1942)
LIGHTLY HE JOURNEYED (1946)
AUNT ALBINIA (1948)
THE STORY OF WALES (1955)
THE GREAT MARIA (1959)
A Portrait of Maria Edgeworth
THE LORD OF BURGHLEY (1964)
AUGUSTA SMITH OF SCILLY (1969)

ACKNOWLEDGEMENT

It is melancholy to record that while these words are being written, the total demolition of Hafod has reached the final stages. For their assistance in placing at my disposal much valuable material that has made it possible to compile this history of that romantic place, my grateful thanks are due to Sir William Ll. Davies, Librarian of the National Library of Wales; to Mr. Spencer Savage, Librarian and Assistant Secretary, The Linnean Society of London; and to Mr. H. J. McLachlan, Librarian of Manchester College, Oxford, for permission to quote from the Shepherd correspondence.

I am also greatly indebted to Mr. Lloyd-Johnes, of Dolaucothi and Holland Park, W., for his kindness in allowing me to reproduce family portraits in his possession; to Major H. J. Lloyd-Johnes, of Summerleas, Monmouth, for his tireless exertions in supplying papers, pictures and information; to Lord Croft for interesting facts respecting Croft Castle and the Knights; to the Rev. Daniel Thomas, Vicar of Caio, Carmarthenshire, for transcribing long lists of entries in his parish registers, relating to the Johnes family; and to Mr. Gwynn Evans of Llanfairfawr, near Lampeter, for showing me the site of the old manor-house of Llanfair.

For services of various descriptions my thanks are also due to Mr. H. J. Bruce, Mr. Ralph Dutton, Mr. Geoffrey Grigson, Miss Evelyn Lewes, The Royal Society of Arts, Sir R. George Stapledon, the late Mr. Herbert M. Vaughan, and Miss Ela Wingfield.

I have throughout adhered to the contemporary spelling of place-names.

CONTENTS

ILLUSTRATIONS

The illustrations that appear in this edition of *Peacocks in Paradise* are provided from the private collection of Thomas Lloyd, with the exception of the following to whom the publishers acknowledge their indebtedness—3, National Museum of Wales; 12, Victoria & Albert Museum; 15, Lady Lever Art Gallery; 24, 25, Endpiece, National Monument Record for Wales.

Tracing copyright-holders of the other original negatives has proved difficult, sometimes impossible. Where the copyright-holders believe they have a claim, the publishers invite them to make application to them so that proper arrangements can be made and full acknowledgment granted to them in any future editions.

*Dolaucothi

Preface

'Ha! Cardiganshire you say you come from, do you? Cardiganshire!' A crow of excited recognition lifted the strident tones of the talkative old gentleman—his appearance suggested a retired schoolmaster—who had rattled off question after question, like a salvo of bullets, through the roar of the train. 'Dear me, it's a great many years since I was there, but strangely enough I saw one place in Cardiganshire that I've never forgotten. Why, I sometimes find myself wondering about it even now—it was such a phenomenal sight! However, I daresay you'll be able to tell me what I've long puzzled my head over. It was miles off the beaten track, among the mountains to the north, not far from the Radnorshire borders from what I can recall—a property called Hafod.

'What do you say? Have I been there? Well, not actually, but I passed close to it twenty-odd years ago and, as I've been telling you, it stuck in my mind. And now, as I can see that you know it, perhaps you could give me some information on the subject and tell me about Thomas Johnes. . . . Oh, I heard of him from a road-mending fellow who happened to come along. Well, as there's no particular hurry, we've another two hours' run at least before the train gets in, I may as well explain how I happened to find myself in that out-of-the-way part in the first instance, and afterwards you can tell me what it was all about, for the place must have a history. I had never been to Wales in my life until that summer, though I've always been fond of scenery and in those days usually spent the holidays cruising about the country or abroad, having a look round. But that year some friends had taken a small house on the Cardiganshire coast for a few weeks, and invited me to stay. The village had an unpronounceable name that entirely escapes me. I never saw a wilder stretch of coast in my life. All very well for a week or two in summer, but my word, I wouldn't have liked to live there.

'From there I went on to Herefordshire. I made rather a roundabout journey of it on purpose, to see a bit more of the Welsh country as I didn't think, somehow, I'd be likely to go that way again. As a matter of fact, in a way I was rather taken with it. It was certainly very different from any other part of Britain I'd seen, and the coast was fine. So were the valleys I passed through on my way inland—lovely little spots! But after I'd been heading north for a while, the scenery seemed to change for the worse—I can't say I liked the drab, desolate look of those hills. Besides, the weather had deteriorated too. It had been nice and bright when I started, but after a couple of hours or so it had clouded over and one of those heavy summer storms seemed to be coming on. Well, it broke, I remember, just after I'd left the main road and was climbing up a narrow by-road that would take me across the mountains and in time, I hoped, bring me on to the road for Rhayader and England. And what a benighted stretch of country it seemed—I never saw anything more desolate and depressing, though I must admit that the conditions I saw it under were pretty bad, with the rain pelting down and my old car pulling as badly as she could up that infernal hill which never seemed to end.

'What with the rain and the blind corners, I scarcely knew where I was heading next. Luckily there wasn't much traffic—all I met was a farm-cart and a few labouring chaps with bits of sacking thrown over their heads and shoulders to keep the rain off, poor devils. The cottages I saw looked wretched too—altogether it struck me as the most poverty-stricken and unprepossessing area, if you'll excuse my saying so, and the farther I went the worse it seemed to become, from what I could make out through the downpour. Then, on top of everything else, my windscreen wiper nearly conked out, and it was all I could do to see the bit of road in front of me. Owing to that, I didn't notice when the scenery began to change, though I remember thinking how much darker everything got.

'Well, as I remember, after some time I crossed a bridge over what looked like a deep gully and took a sharp turn to the right, up another steep hill, and then I did notice a large wood running parallel with the road on my right inside an old wall, covered with ferns and moss. But by now my car was pulling so badly I thought she might break down at any minute, and it was all I could do to get her up to the top. Luckily we made it in the end, and when we came out into the light again, leaving the wood behind us, the rain had quite cleared off and the sun was trying to break through. I pulled into the side and got out, meaning to look at the engine, but as I set foot on the road the sun shone out with all its might. I never saw such a sight in my life as I saw then—it quite took my breath away. For I found myself standing at the top of the world, so it seemed, and facing me for miles and miles around were mountains covered with the most splendid woods I ever saw in my life, fairly glittering with the sunshine on the wet leaves. To find trees like those in the middle of that barren wilderness struck me at once as most extraordinary, all the more since it was obvious that they had been planted by a master hand. They fitted those hills like a perfectly tailored garment, or that's how they looked to me.

'I was just standing stock still, staring at that glorious and unexpected sight, when an old fellow with a pick on his shoulder came along, and it was he who told me that was Hafod.'

'And what else did he tell you?'

'Not much at first, but after he'd helped himself from my pouch and lighted his pipe he became quite conversational. He said there was a big mansion down below among the trees and pointed out a glimpse of the roof among the woods. I'd have liked to see more, I must own. And he told me the trees had been planted long ago by this Mr. Johnes who was a very good man, and that crowds of visitors, Americans and others, came to see some wonderful monument in the church he had built. He was very anxious I should see it, but I was pressed for time and his instructions were not very clear as to where it was. And that's about all, I think, except that the house had changed hands many times since and some very old gentleman was living in it then. And he hinted that people didn't like to stay there now, that the servants left almost as soon as they arrived. . . . Well, that did not seem very surprising to me. I never saw a more lonely house buried in that valley. An astonishing situation for a house altogether, and in the old days it must have been even more cut off from the world than it was when I saw it twenty years ago. Rum sort of fellow Johnes must have been to settle down in such a forlorn sort of place. I take it he built the house? He must have thought a lot of it, too; one could tell that from those beautiful woods of his—an almost continuous forest which must have cost something to plant even in those days. It's a funny thing how often I've remembered those trees and seen them as I saw them that day in wave upon wave of shining green, though I don't suppose I've ever mentioned it to a soul. It just crops up every now and then, for no particular reason. However, perhaps you can enlighten me a little about that strange place, and first of all can you explain what brought him there?'

As very inadequately I attempted to satisfy his curiosity, I had to admit that although I had known Hafod all my life, and the name of its founder was familiar because of his trees and many other activities, I knew little more than the barest facts. It was this that set me wondering and finding out what the true story of Hafod had really been. Gradually, from one source and another, the history was built up that is related in the following pages.

CHAPTER I

Introducing 'A Beggarly Estate'

From the days of Queen Elizabeth there had been a house of some importance locally at Hafod. At that time its loneliness and inaccessibility must have been extreme, for all through the winter it was almost entirely isolated from other parts of the country, the tracks leading up to it from the valleys being often impassable for many weeks together. This did not prevent it all the same from being at the hub of all kinds of stirring and often violent episodes, for the history of those forlorn regions was wild and eventful, and must have brought a strange diversity of characters at different times to Hafod. For near at hand were some of the richest of the north Cardiganshire mines; and this provides the explanation why a house should have been built there in the first instance.

The reputation of all that part was so bad in the old days that it was regarded with fear as a savage land inhabited by a savage race. Travellers, when circumstances compelled them to pass that way, did so with great uneasiness of spirit and their lives in their hands. 'I was putte in great feare how I should passe the Vpper parte of Cardigansheir,' wrote one who succeeded in coming through it unmolested, 'for it was towlde me that I must pass a place called Coomystwyth, where many Theeves that lived as outlawes, and some not outlawed indeed, made their abode, and that they lived by open Robbyinge; but God be thanked I escaped their handes, and they said that place and thereaboutes is never ffree from such persons.'

Wild and dangerous though it was, abounding with terrifying ravines and perilously green bogs where every trace of a body could easily be disposed of, some were drawn to settle themselves there, tempted by the fortunes they might make. From time immemorial, Cardiganshire had been rich in minerals, and nowhere more than in these mountains. The ancient Britons had competently worked the copper, silver and lead mines and had fought fiercely to preserve them from the predatory Romans. The early Welsh understood the use of metals, and it was owing to their good application of these resources that they were able to keep the English invaders at bay for so long. But after their final surrender to Edward I, mining activities ceased, largely owing to the fact that the Crown claimed possession of all mines and minerals in England and Wales. The industry did not revive until several centuries later when Queen Elizabeth imported experienced German mineralogists to work the mines in both countries 'for their sole use and profit' though rendering to the Crown a tithe of all gold and silver ores. These patentees had the power to divide their tenures into shares, which they sold. 'The original patentees, therefore, under the three grants, with these subsequent purchasers, were incorporated by the style of 'The Governor, Assistants, and Commonalty, of the Mines Royal.' William, Earl of Pembroke, who was already hereditary manager of the Queen's property in Wales, was appointed Governor.

After this, the Cardiganshire mines figured prominently in English history. In the time of James I, every penny of the princely fortune which Sir Hugh Middleton, who had farmed the principal mines, made out of them he spent in providing the City of London with a water-supply—the New River at Islington. His successor, Mr. Bushell, who was 'allowed singular privileges' by Charles I, even to the extent of setting up his own mint at Aberystwyth Castle to coin silver to pay his labourers, at the time of the Civil Wars clothed the whole of the King's army at his own expense. He furnished the King besides with a loan of £40,000, and raised a regiment among his miners which he maintained at his own expense until nearly the end of the wars.

By the time the Civil Wars were over, the house at Hafod had been standing for nearly a century and had been occupied by several generations of the family whose founder, Morgan Herbert, had built it when, 'having embarked upon some mining adventure in the neighbourhood', he settled there. He was probably connected with that branch of the great Welsh Herbert family of which Lord Pembroke was head, and thus had obtained a lease of the mines near Hafod from his powerful kinsman. However that may have been, he established his line there and prospered. His descendants rose to a place of importance in that part of the country, entertained hospitably at Hafod and married into some of the best Cardiganshire houses. Otherwise very little is known about them, except that they planted oaks and other forest trees to shelter their land, and that in 1620, in an attempt to reform the local inhabitants whose behaviour 'had become desperate, lawless and dangerous', William Herbert of Hafod built a chapel upon his estate and installed a clergyman to instruct the people in the rudiments of religion. Almost certainly the Herberts contrived to preserve their right to work the mines, otherwise they could scarcely have flourished in that barren locality as they are said to have done, or have been satisfied to remain there.

Throughout the seventeenth century fresh veins of minerals were constantly being discovered to enrich the leaseholders and infuriate the unfortunate landlords upon whose properties they were situated, for they were not entitled to profit from them in any way. Nothing was more unjust or better calculated to stir up bitter quarrels and ill feeling between all parties. But as the century drew towards its close, better times for the landowners were dawning. In 1693 'a most glorious act' was passed in

Parliament which empowered all subjects of the Crown henceforth to enjoy and work their own mines. A Cardiganshire gentleman, Sir Carbery Pryse, whose own estate teemed with riches, is said to have ridden from London to Cardiganshire in the record time of forty-eight hours to spread the joyful news.

This *volte-face* in mining affairs cannot seriously have affected the position of the Herberts, who were themselves large landowners by then. Besides, in 1693 their line was rapidly drawing to its close. Scarcely more than ten years later a tablet was put up in the chapel, built by his ancestor, recording that: 'Here lyeth the Body of William Herbert of Havod Ychtryd Esquier, who having married his only Daughter to Thomas Johnes of Llanvair Clydoge Esquier departed this life the 13th. day of June Anno Domini 1704 aged 47 years.'

Jane Herbert who married Thomas Johnes was an only child and the heiress of her father's estate. She did not long survive her marriage and at her death Hafod descended to her husband, to be added to the already considerable list of his lands in west Wales. He lived in the old manor-house of Llanfair, pleasantly situated on the banks of the river Teify and a great many miles away from the Herberts' desolate abode which tempted him not at all. Llanfair was much more propitiously placed, in a sheltered valley in the south-western extremity of the county, not far from the market town of Lampeter. Its lands were rich and profitable and the manor was surrounded with valuable lead mines as well as by fertile acres. For the next fifty years, practically nothing is known of Hafod which seems to have been occupied by a succession of humble tenants.

Jane Herbert's widower lived till 1734. Although he had married again, he left no descendants behind him and at his death bequeathed his estates to his cousin, Thomas Johnes of Penybont. Penybont was a farm placed on the lower slopes of a bleak range of hills at the edge of a vast and desolate bog. Like many other members of younger branches of the old families, this Thomas Johnes, who now became head of the clan and lord of Llanfair

Manor, had hitherto lived very simply and probably not much better than an ordinary yeoman farmer. He was married to the daughter of a Radnorshire gentleman and had two sons and two daughters.

The removal from the farm to the spacious and dignified manor-house and the fortune attached to it, was a wonderful lift up in their position. To the elder of the two boys, another Thomas who at the time was aged about thirteen, it must have been particularly delightful. The pomps and the vanities were always dear to his heart; besides this it was a much livelier neighbourhood with young companions within easy reach. At another mansion, Peterwell, just beyond Lampeter, there were his cousins, John and Herbert Lloyd, whose father was Attorney-General for the counties of Cardigan, Carmarthen and Pembroke. Mr. Attorney Lloyd's daughter was already married to Sir Lucius Christianus Lloyd whose seat, known in English as Millfield, was also close by Lampeter.

These Lloyds of Millfield were an intemperate and uproarious lot and the same riotous kind of life persisted there that had gone on for a hundred years. Then they had brought down upon their heads the malediction of a saintly hymnologist, Vicar Pritchard of Llandovery, whose only son was said to have been murdered by one of the Lloyds following a drunken orgy at Millfield.

May God with heavy curses chase
All Maesyfelin's villain race,
For they have drowned in Teifi's flood
Llandovery's flower and Cymru's pride.

Sir Lucius with his young brothers-in-law, and when he grew older their cousin from Llanfair, made the countryside rock with their wild behaviour. The passion for gambling which had such a hold on the rich and leisured classes all over England was just as strong in this remote corner of Wales. Drinking, dicing and whoring provided the chief pleasures that enlivened the little country houses buried in the deep valleys and perched on exposed hillsides. Generally the distances that divided them were immense, thus Llanfair was unusually favourably placed, being not far away from a town with two important properties adjoining it. Young Thomas Johnes was thus at an early age initiated into the pleasures of manhood by his cousins, who a little later on introduced him in London.

For the young bloods of Cardiganshire did not remain hidden behind their hills. Both John and Herbert Lloyd had matriculated at Oxford and both were called to the Bar—John later succeeding his father as Attorney-General for the three counties. Where Thomas Johnes received his education is not clear, but when he grew up he was certainly not content to stay at home. His father gave him the means to cut a figure in the fashionable world of London, where it is said that he frequented all the gay and popular haunts and associated with some of the foremost rakes of the day. There must have been something about the young Welshman which attracted men older than himself; men, moreover, who held high places in the world of fashion and politics towards which young Johnes was drawn. They paid him the compliment of enduring the hazards and discomforts of the tedious journey down to Cardiganshire to stay at his father's house. For weeks at a time, it is said, he entertained at Llanfair Manor that 'polished courtier, the votary of wit and fashion', Sir Charles Hanbury Williams, whom Horace Walpole praised as the model *par excellence* for the gilded youth of his time; and Sir Charles's friend, the dark-faced, dissipated politician Henry Fox who was later created Lord Holland. A younger member of the party was the parvenu Richard Rigby of Mistley Hall in Essex, grandson to a linen draper, who had attached himself to Frederick, Prince of Wales, to whom he politely lost money at the gaming-table. Unfortunately, no such delicacy of feeling prompted his conduct towards his Welsh host, whose cousin John Lloyd also made one of the party. Night after night, till the chilly dawn came creeping through the shutters to supplement the dwindling candlelight, they sat over their cards and wine, Fox and Rigby nearly always proving the winners. In the end, according to a contemporary account, 'the country gentlemen were cut up,' though each of the young men soon repaired his fortune by making a rich marriage.

By the time he was twenty-six, Thomas Johnes had married Elizabeth Knight, the only child and heiress of Richard Knight of Croft Castle, Herefordshire. It was a very great match indeed, for she brought him a dowry of £70,000. She was two years his senior and a woman of determined character, who enjoyed fashionable society and had no intention of exchanging the glories of her father's fine castle and all the grand company he entertained there for an old-fashioned manor-house in uncivilized Cardiganshire. Her bridegroom, whose strong worldly streak had nearly been his undoing, surely needed little persuading before he agreed to live at Croft Castle with his bride's parents. So from the date of his marriage he never again lived in Cardiganshire, though he visited it several times a year, and not very long after he left it was appointed Custos Rotulorum for the county.

For this advancement he had to thank the powerful friends he made in Herefordshire, the Earl of Oxford who lived at Eywood, and Viscount Bateman at Shobden. He found it infinitely congenial and profitable, to live in the imposing old Border Castle in the midst of a fine deer-park. His life could never have prospered thus had he remained in his native county, whose proverbial barrenness earned for it in ancient times the nickname of 'The Devil's Grandmother's jointure'. He was more enterprising and ambitious than most of his friends and cousins there, for though they made occasional sorties to London and elsewhere they always returned with relief to their petty autocracies conveniently hidden behind the mountain ranges.

The Cardiganshire landowners were a very rough lot altogether and a law unto themselves. They virtually ruled the countryside, interpreting the law of the land at the local Court Leet to their own advantage for there was little risk of their findings being questioned. Each in his own orbit was a little potentate, while as for the peasants, their lot was scarcely more fortunate than that of the serfs of an earlier epoch. The farmers in most cases leased their holdings from the squires, a circumstance that necessarily bridled them since their welfare was largely dependent upon their landlord's favour. Magistrates had almost boundless opportunities for enriching themselves at the expense of the poor and the unscrupulous did not hesitate to take advantage of it. In the towns, the stocks and the whipping-post were conspicuous objects, serving as salutary warnings to the refractory.

One of the most blackguardly characters was the Custos of Cardiganshire's cousin, Herbert Lloyd. In appearance he was a magnificent man, tall as a giant, with shapely limbs and a small, proud head that gave an impression of avian cruelty and cunning—a sparrow-hawk's rather than an eagle's. His hot blood was as violent and untamed as everything else in his forceful, selfish nature. The same year that he was called to the Bar he married a Miss Bragge of Essex, and instead of pursuing his legal career he hastened back home with his bride and her £15,000. His father presented him with a small manor in a remote mountain village and there he continued to live, lording it over the villagers and brawling and fighting with all who resisted him.

The scales were weighted heavily in his favour. Being a Justice of the Peace he could bring to book all who dared oppose him. Many a poor fellow was 'Committed to the County Gaol for insulting and abusing Herbert Lloyd, Esq. . . . and calling the said Herbert Lloyd, then sitting in Court, a *scoundrelly dog* and making use of other *indecent expressions*.' They stood no chance against the tyrant, though a few were high-spirited enough to put up a fight. On one occasion a yeoman of the village was 'committed to the custody of the Gaoler, for uttering several menaces against Herbert Lloyd, Esquire, and threatening to Run him through the Body with a Pitchfork at ye time of Quarter Sessions'. Wherever mischief brewed, there Herbert Lloyd was to be found. The Cardiganshire mines provided a never-ending source of trouble and quarrels between the landowners and the Crown, and in these affairs he played a conspicuous part.

Although the glorious Act of 1693 gave the landlords full rights over the minerals on their estates, the Crown laid claim to all the mines situated on the Crown lands. Fresh veins were always being found and in many cases gave rise to bitter disputes which as often as not culminated in pitched battles on the hillsides between the natives and the King's representatives. Much to the disgust of the Welsh gentry, English manorial law had been applied to their country, and among other detested doctrines was the presumption that all unenclosed land was the waste of the lordship or manor in which it was situated and therefore the property of the Crown. Landowners of all degrees strenuously opposed this claim, asserting that although they were unenclosed, these lands still formed part of their freehold estates. They fought desperately to preserve their rights and the lot of the Crown's agents whom the landlords regarded as their natural enemies was far from being enviable.

At this time the Deputy Steward of the Crown Manors in Cardiganshire was Lewis Morris, a native of Anglesey. 'Thank God that you are in a country where all the people are not mad and wicked,' he wrote on one occasion to his brother there, meaning every word of it. His constitution was not particularly robust and his tastes were peaceful; he was renowned as an antiquarian and a poet. Still he did his utmost to serve the King faithfully, very often at the peril of his life. It was his dangerous task to lay claim to the wastes and commons and to hold them for the Crown, besides working any mines that might happen to be there for the Crown's benefit. This he did, while the neighbouring landlords watched him like a pack of hungry foxes, waiting for an opportunity to descend upon his preserves and carry off the ore. Lewis Morris believed that, if they were properly developed, the mines could still be sources of immense wealth, but unfortunately none of the owners had either the intelligence or diligence to manage them competently. His opinion was certainly justified in the case of Mr. Johnes of Croft Castle, who was in constant trouble over his mines at Llanfair, losing money on them every year and having the greatest difficulty in disposing of his ore. Finally, sick of the whole business, he leased them to one Chauncey Townsend, whom he saw at a glance 'had a thorough spirit of mineing and seems very ready and understanding in the business'. Townsend's understanding was so great that he quickly discovered large quantities of silver at Llanfair, made a fortune, and became one of the most important figures in the mining history of South Wales.

It is the discovery of a mine that carries the story back in the direction of Hafod.

It was known as the Esgair y Mwyn lead mine, and was discovered by Lewis Morris himself in the mountains a few miles from Hafod. It lay north of Crosswood, the ancient seat of the Vaughans, and Viscount Lisburne, who was head of the family, lived there. He was one of Morris's most powerful enemies. The mine turned out to be exceptionally rich, and before very long Lord Lisburne and his neighbour, Thomas Powell of Nanteos, both of whose estates extended there, laid claim to it. Lord Lisburne as Lord Lieutenant of the county commanded many supporters, and so did his friend, Mr. Powell. Neither spared himself in stirring up popular indignation at the Crown's action and the atmosphere grew more and more unhealthy for the King's servants. The bellicose Mr. Powell and his reverend brother complained loudly to the Deputy Steward how cruel a thing it was for the Government to fall upon a private gentleman as it had done to them. Although Morris spoke up manfully in defence of King George, he was driven to declare that 'the insolence of these people is Intolerable, and I am sure that if some care be not immediately taken about the King's rights in Wales, it will be all sunk in a few years'.

But the Viscount and the Squire were not satisfied merely with grumbling and allowing the matter to rest there. They were determined to fight in order to get possession of what they continued to insist was their property. Lord Lisburne was, however, somewhat awkwardly placed. Since he was Lord Lieutenant, the King's official representative in Cardiganshire, it was not really possible for him openly to lead the mob who would attempt to seize and imprison His Majesty's Steward. He was therefore compelled to keep out of sight and to put the responsibility of raising and leading an army into the willing and capable hands of Herbert Lloyd, who was certainly promised a fat reward.

Herbert Lloyd was now brother-in-law to Powell of Nanteos, for his first wife had died within a year and he had subsequently married the pious and well-provided-for widowed sister of Thomas Powell. He lost no time in collecting together a great band of belligerents and prepared to take the mine by storm. Even the Sheriff of the county was induced to ride at the head of the mob with Herbert Lloyd and Powell one bitter February day, when the unfortunate Lewis Morris, busy at his work, suddenly espied a huge crowd advancing towards him over the mountains. It was a wild and noisy gang, several hundreds strong; some were brandishing fire-arms, others had cudgels, pitchforks and scythes. They yelled and swore as they pressed forward towards the banks of Esgair y Mwyn, while the terrified miners rushed to take shelter among the slag-heaps and behind the cranes and pulleys. The insurgents poured down upon them, threatening not only the life of Lewis Morris but also the lives of his agents and miners if the mine was not immediately handed over to them. And Herbert Lloyd, then in the full flowering of his strength and good looks, presented a cocked pistol at the unhappy Steward's head and threatened to shoot him dead, while his men surrounded him with fire-arms and seizing him carried him off in triumph to Cardigan gaol. There

Lewis Morris remained in a cell for six weeks until the Lord Chief Justice admitted him to bail, to appear later at the King's Bench when the question of the ownership of the mine was thrashed out in court.

The Deputy Steward, although an honest man, fared badly. Before the matter ended he was ousted from his post as agent and superintendent of the mine which he had himself discovered and opened, in spite of the fact that the Crown successfully proved its title to it. Herbert Lloyd, on the other hand, came out of the business not one whit worse off and continued in his capacity as Justice of the Peace. In many other respects also this was a fortunate period for him. When his brother John died childless in 1755, he succeeded to his estates which had been considerably augmented by the addition of the Millfield property which Sir Lucius Lloyd (who also had died without an heir some years earlier) had bequeathed to his brother-in-law in consequence of a will made 'in a frolicsome humour'. Thus Herbert, who had been glad formerly to play the part of hired assassin to Lord Lisburne, became a powerful landlord and Lord of the Manor of Lampeter: an exalted position that none could challenge.

In 1757, when the Crown granted a lease of Esgair y Mwyn to the Earl of Powis, the whole bitter brew boiled up again and once more Herbert Lloyd was well to the fore, working against the King's men. He 'decoyed into a snare' a distant and disreputable cousin and namesake of the Custos, who was also a Cardiganshire landowner and magistrate. Indeed, he was the magistrate who only a short while previously had given to the Crown's representative repossession of the mine. This important personage was none other than the crafty Lord Lisburne whose claim to it was said to have cost the Government several thousands of pounds. Having successfully hoodwinked this other Thomas Johnes by pretending to be his 'bosom friend', Herbert Lloyd caused his band of a hundred men to capture and carry him off to gaol, where soon the prisoner's partisans pursued him in an attempt to release him. It was a terrible time in the country. The rebellious gentry and their adherents were all under arms and ready at any moment to set on the friends of the Government. The riots and brawls waxed fiercer than ever amidst orgies of drunkenness and corruption, anonymous threats and hand-to-hand struggles. It was wise to reach home by daylight and to stay quietly there behind locked doors, for there was no knowing what fate might be lying in store for those who travelled the roads by night.

For years the Crown's agents had been begging in vain for military aid, and now at long last it was sent down from London, to preserve the King's rights and to settle the rioters. It was the duty of the Custos to lead the troops, an impressive business and far from disagreeable to Mr. Johnes. In splendour and triumph he rode across the hills at the head of a contingent of Scots Greys mounted on horseback, and a gallant array they must have made with their scarlet coats and clanking swords and the merry jingle of bit and bridle as they trotted along the rugged tracks across the dun-coloured mountains. It was a sight that struck terror in the hearts of the poor people and even sobered down their betters. It was a bad time for the country, for the soldiers of those days were a drunken, disorderly lot who played havoc in the farms and ale-houses where they were quartered until peace was restored. As for the Custos, he had his lodging ready for him at Hafod, where he invariably put up when he came to that part of the world to collect his rents and attend to his business there.

The reputation that locality bore was still as bad as ever. According to a clergyman who not long before this had been sent to minister at the little church, but who had very quickly fled away from a cure fraught with such fearful perils, they were 'a dangerous banditti, and a disgrace to human nature . . . they laid open the chapel, and turned it into a receptacle for riotous meetings and all kinds of debauchery, insomuch that it is in vain, and dangerous, for a minister to perform divine service.'

Not a soul had cared about the place or the welfare of the people since the Herberts long ago. The only interest Hafod had for Mr. Johnes was the wretchedly small rental he accrued from this 'beggarly estate' as he called it. It cost him many an arduous and sometimes dangerous journey to reach it, being buffeted by storms as he crossed the open mountains and threatened with drowning as his tired horse struggled through the flooded rivers. The house was a poor old place, falling to pieces. Only the trees were fine and worth a good deal in timber, and this was the best thing that could be said for it. Being like the majority of his class and era, of an eminently commonsensical and materialistic turn of mind, the grandeur and variety of the scenery was the last thing he would have observed. All he saw at Hafod was a broken-down old house in a miserable wilderness, and the sooner he got away from it and back to Croft Castle the better.

Added to all its other drawbacks, it had lately had the sinister reputation of being haunted by a poltergeist, known as the *Bwgan yr Hafod*. There was no end to the tricks this creature played, harrying the old couple who lived in the house out of their lives. Potatoes jumped out of their baskets 'as you have seen maggots jump out of a cheese in hot weather', Lewis Morris reported to his brother. Heavy tables flew up to the ceiling and down again, chairs dressed themselves up in their master's clothes, and a heavy oak coffer laid itself across his legs as he lay in bed. Appropriate tools were proffered by invisible hands, and tubs of oatmeal threw themselves on to the kitchen table without spilling a grain. When in despair the farmer implored a parson to come and exorcise it, the reverend gentleman had no sooner arrived than the ghost attacked him and broke open his head till the blood ran. Even if the Custos knew of all this, he was certainly far too sensible to allow such superstitious nonsense to disturb his rest.

Maybe the farmer was finally frightened away by the ghost, or perhaps he died. Whichever way it was, two years later, in 1759, Mr. Johnes let the house on a life-lease to another strange and violent character, John Paynter. This was the man who had contrived to overthrow Lewis Morris and now was Lord Powis's manager at Esgair y Mwyn.

Paynter had been in the mining business in Cardiganshire for a number of years. Clever, ruthless and full of vanity, he had pushed himself steadily upwards and had managed to get himself accepted on terms of friendship with many of the most important people. He was constantly at Crosswood with Lord Lisburne and at the other leading houses, and himself gave lavish entertainments in Aberystwyth, where he dispensed large quantities of liquor and picked up a great many secrets. According to a contemporary, he was 'cutting a most astonishing figure in Cardiganshire, building, taking great farms, &c., in short driving ten times hotter than Jehu'. When Lord Powis appointed him as manager, he immediately built himself a residence close to the mine. Near the house he made 'a great pool of water, which he calls Pwll dialedd, i.e. the pool of punishment . . . it is contrived to frighten Bailiffs or any persons that have the confidence to come and demand money of the agent, or that have otherwise affronted him. Several persons have been threatened with it, and even carried to ye brink of it by a body of miners, by Mr. P's order. . . .' And another writer described how on one occasion when Paynter had 'ordered that we should come up on a Sunday and make up our account . . . instead of settling, his servant, when I went to the door, threw the stool at my face, and, hearing of a noise, Mr. Paynter asked what was there, his servant answered "that Rogue Charlton"; with that Mr. P. came out with his stick and begins to beat me as hard as ever he could, instead of settling accounts. Then his lady came with a stick and begins to beat me . . . they set on throwing stones as hard as ever they could and told me they would murder me . . . they sent for the pumpers out of the works and followed me down below Cricklas to Marchnat, Mr. Paynter and all of them bareheaded.'

The rumbustious agent had not used his new house and his ducking pool very long when he fell in love with the beauties of Hafod. His passionate admiration for romantic scenery was an entirely unsuspected side to his curious character. From the moment he first saw it he did everything he could to induce Mr. Johnes to let it to him, and on the strength of being paid 'a great advanced rent', Mr. Johnes finally gave him a life-lease. Although he was strongly opposed to Paynter, he was glad enough to get some money for Hafod at last, though his satisfaction very soon turned to anger when he learnt that his cunning tenant, who had undertaken to repair the house, had cut down above £100 worth of timber for the purpose.

From Hafod, Paynter played a vigorous part in county affairs. He served as High Sheriff and as Steward of the local Court Leet it was sometimes his agreeable duty to impose large fines on his enemies 'for uttering abusive language towards the Steward'. He rode down to Lampeter to attend Quarter Sessions, where he sat on the bench with Herbert Lloyd, the Custos and others of the elect. For a short while he even interested himself in the little church at Hafod, and writing to the Bishop of St. David's he promised to 'take uncommon pains to get [it] into repair'. He further suggested that should His Lordship wish to come into the neighbourhood to confirm, 'I may flatter myself with hopes of entertaining you and your retinue at Hafod. . . . If your Lordship is fond of fossils, and other curious productions of that kind, you will be entertained, and the more so at seeing my little hotel surrounded with woods, rocks, caves, cataracts, and rivers, which are neither frightful nor inconvenient. They are indeed quite otherwise. They serve to excite an admiration of God's miraculous works, while they furnish me with health, recreation, and numberless conveniences of life.'

As Paynter's habits were the reverse of monogamous and his household a notably disreputable one, it was scarcely a suitable place for an eminent ecclesiastic to visit. But the invitation was not taken advantage of any more than the church was mended. Another most unwelcome expense suddenly confronted the new

Hafod in 1792 by 'Warwick' Smith

Party from Hafod visiting the Robbers' Cave 1792
(by 'Warwick' Smith)

Sir Herbert Lloyd, Bart. of Peterwell 1719—1769
(attributed to Zoffany)

tenant which well may have made him unwilling to spend elsewhere. Before he had been at Hafod long, the poltergeist started its pranks again. It was even more obstreperous than formerly and had developed besides many amorous propensities. What with the way it hugged and kissed the girls in the dark, many were inclined to believe that the *Bwgan* was none other than Paynter himself. But when it materialized in the form of a beautiful woman anxious to be embraced by him, and then, turning into a pig, rubbed against his legs, this assumption was quite disproved. Indeed no one was more frightened by the ghost than the blustering agent, who finally sought out a Breconshire wizard who agreed to lay it for a fee of £100. After that nothing more was seen of it.

And now, with the ghost disposed of and Paynter in peaceful occupation of Hafod, we will follow Mr. Johnes into Herefordshire. How fortunate it was for him that he could not foresee the part his wife's great fortune would some day play in the destiny of these arid mountains which he always left behind him with thankfulness.

CHAPTER II

The Custos, the Captain, and an Infamous Baronet

The thought of how well he had succeeded in life must often have been uppermost in Mr. Johnes's mind as he rode back into Herefordshire from Wales, and welcomed with relief the cornucopian abundance of its orchards and hop-gardens, the warm red earth laden with vegetation that appeared all the richer after the sickly fields he left behind him. It was a sight to cheer his heart and lift it in acknowledgment of the manifold well-deserved mercies that had fallen to his share. A tide of good fortune had swept him steadily upwards from the day that his father exchanged his farm on the edge of a bog for Llanfair Manor. Later, the change from the manor-house to Croft Castle had been even more spectacular, for Croft was not only vast and imposing in itself, with its battlements, towers and magnificent surroundings, but made even more splendid by the great fortune of old Richard Knight.

In the portrait that Hoare of Bath painted of the Cardiganshire Custos, a comfortable self-satisfaction pervaded every inch of his broad, plump face, with its wide-set, calculating grey eyes and full, smooth lips. He chose to be represented sitting at his desk, with a sheaf of important documents propped up in front of him, a quill pen in his hand, interrupted it would appear in the very act of inscribing words of moment upon the paper spread in readiness. He looked what he knew himself to be; a man of public importance and one of the largest landed proprietors in west Wales. Added to this, his family tree which he had carefully worked out was quite exceptional, for he could trace his lineage back, without a single break, to the first prince of the ancient Britons who had flourished five centuries before the birth of Christ. It is likely that this wonderful pedigree was sometimes a useful weapon against the purse-proud members of the rich industrial family he had married into. With his lineage and his wife's money, he had ensured for his posterity a high place among the great English landed proprietors. He never suspected the relentless swiftness with which the winds of time would scatter his schemes in the dust or that to-day the principal interest attached to his stout bewigged figure, handsomely dressed in mulberry velvet and fine lawn and lace, is the link he forms between two periods. If we substitute for the panelled chamber at Croft where he sat the sombre background of his own Cardiganshire, we see him uniting two eras in its social history—the dark age of tyranny and lawlessness with the dawning of a better.

The Knights were of a different breed. They had been iron-masters, a Richard Knight of Madely in Worcestershire having been engaged in the iron trade at the time of the Commonwealth. His son and namesake derived immense wealth from the business and settled at Downton in Herefordshire, where he lived until his death in 1745 when his large fortune was divided between his four sons. He was Elizabeth Johnes's grandfather; her father, Richard Knight, being his eldest son. Of the other three, Thomas who became Rector of Bewdley inherited Downton, married late in life and was the father of two distinguished sons who were christened respectively Richard Payne and Thomas Andrew. Edward, the third brother, settled himself at Wolverley Manor in Worcestershire, while Ralph established his line at Henley Hall.

How Croft Castle, the property of Sir Archer Croft whose

family had held it for eight centuries, came into Richard Knight's hands has never been explained though the impoverished baronet was undoubtedly financially involved with the Knights. Richard Knight, who had studied law in his youth and had married Elizabeth Powell of Stanage Park, Radnorshire, was as eager as most men whose fortunes were founded in industry, to acquire a fine house and large estates which would enhance his importance in the county. The way he tricked his nephew and ward later on,* shows him to have been quite unscrupulous when it came to getting what he wanted. Richard Powell at thirteen inherited Stanage Park from his father, who as a younger son had gone into trade at Liverpool, and had remained in business after he succeeded his brother, hoping to improve the family fortunes. The widow and her son lived on at Liverpool, Richard Knight taking care of the Stanage property which was close to Croft. As soon as the young heir came of age, his guardian hurried to Liverpool and persuaded him to sell him his inheritance at a low price, without employing an attorney to act for him. Afterwards it was Richard Knight's great joke that 'the young man forgot the timber'.

His daughter, Elizabeth Johnes, appears to have been as astute over money as her father, very unlike her easy-going husband who with idle good-nature was generally willing to agree to a loan or a lease. But physically Mr. Johnes was full of vigour and energy, undertaking his long rides quite undeterred by fears of fatigue and the gouty attacks that sometimes beset him when he was traversing the lonely Welsh moorlands, far from the solace afforded by 'great shoes' and buskins. All through the winter he hunted the fox with four different packs. On his own declaration he was 'a most firm fox-hunter', rising in the icy darkness morning after morning and travelling incredibly long distances to attend the meets. Mr. Johnes's brother had inherited the family indolence to a far greater degree, giving in to it and fostering it in every way possible.

Although his grand wife made no secret of her contempt for

*From information supplied by Capt. T. F. Powell, Sharow Hall, Ripon.

his stormy country and dowdy, rustic relations, the Custos was always exceedingly fond of his younger brother Jack. John Johnes had been in the army as a young man, but had 'quitted a Military Life' with the rank of captain a year or two after his marriage to a Carmarthenshire young lady, Miss Jane Rees of Court Pembrey. He had settled down at Dolecothy, a small estate seven miles from Lampeter across the Carmarthenshire border, which appears to have belonged jointly between the brothers. There he farmed in a dilatory sort of way, keeping a sleepy eye on his brother's affairs and informing him of all that went on in his county. On his way into Cardiganshire Mr. Johnes usually spent the night at Dolecothy, and this provided an excellent excuse for a convivial family reunion.

Around the flaccid figure of 'the Captain', as he was called, a heavy miasma of discouragement clings. His thin, puce, bleary-eyed countenance, stamped with the gloom that permeated his spirit, peers at us to-day from a miniature—a sadly different person from his vigorous, successful brother. The humid, relaxing air of the narrow glen where Dolecothy was placed, its inordinately heavy rainfall dripping from the trees which pressed against the house, shrouding the rugged hills which towered above it, rising in ghostly vapours from the river at its doors, was altogether too much for him. There was nothing to help him withstand it, for he had no interest in any outdoor sport or exercise which might have saved him from the inertia that his brother vainly tried to rally him out of. Even in his youth he had been an excessive drinker and at the time of his marriage Mr. Johnes had been constrained to express the hope that 'my sister will be able to prevail with you to take more care of yourself and that you will not push the glass quite so brisk'. But not even the blandishments of a young wife could stay the Captain's hand. 'I wish you would use more exercise out of door and less over the Bottle': all down the years the Custos peppered his letters with similar admonishments, though to no avail. The Captain's potations grew steadily heavier as the years dragged by, while he paid dearly with attacks of torturing gout.

An agreeable feature of the brothers' friendship was the regular exchange of presents which took place between Dolecothy and Croft. Gaunt-featured, hairy-looking carriers, as wild in their ways and appearance as their shaggy cobs, used to arrive at the Castle from Wales laden with all kinds of delicacies—dried salmon from the river Cothi, oaten bread and specially well fatted poultry. Sometimes more exotic gifts surprisingly came from that isolated valley, miles away from anywhere and completely out of touch, one would have thought, with anything as exquisite as the fine French silks Mrs. John Johnes occasionally sent to her sister-in-law and the two young ladies at Croft Castle. The Dolecothy family were on amicable terms with the smugglers who infested the little coves all along the dangerous coast. In return for these attentions, the carriers went back to Wales packed up with haunches of venison, bags of hops, and 'great Potts' which contained as many as nine-dozen bottles of port wine for the Captain, which his brother recommended as being far more wholesome for him than the 'Malt liquour' to which he was fatally addicted.

The Welshmen were frequently inclined to be troublesome and to resent having to make the return journey encumbered with more bulky packages. Sometimes they rose before daybreak, stuffed their pockets with bread and cheese and anything else they fancied in the larder, filled their horses' nosebags to the brim, and vanished, leaving 'potts' and parcels behind them. As a rule when they arrived at Dolecothy, several bottles were missing—broken on the way, the carriers declared, though Mr. Johnes was inclined to suspect that they had revived themselves with the contents on the journey: 'they generally taste of everything.' The pleasures of the table played a highly important part at Croft Castle, and the tasty fare that arrived from Dolecothy was always joyfully welcomed. On one occasion we catch a glimpse of that formidable lady, Mrs. Johnes, being so much carried away by the excellence of the Dolecothy fish and ducklings that at the end of the meal, when they had already eaten and drunk their fill, she insisted on calling for more wine and toasting each member of the Captain's family in bumpers.

Nevertheless, it was fifteen years before she was persuaded to visit Dolecothy, and although she made herself vastly civil to the Captain and his delicate, provincial wife, praising everything with the condescending exaggeration of a lady of fashion, she was far from pleased by the mean little house on the river, where fires had to be kept going all through the year to combat the wet that streamed down its walls. When she desired a change of scene she was accustomed to rent a house in London or visit a fashionable spa. She had nothing whatever in common with these well-meaning country bumpkins. She and her husband belonged to quite another world, and this she instilled into her four children from a very early age. For these children great things were hoped and planned. The eldest, Thomas, should make a name for himself, marry well and reign some day at Croft. Elizabeth and Anne were also intended to make advantageous alliances, while a suitable profession would be found for little Samuel.

Their father's country must often have tantalized the imaginations of these children and puzzled their little heads, as with noses flat against the window-panes they watched his short, sturdy figure in his heavily skirted riding coat, his pistols in their holsters, disappearing down the drive. It must have seemed as though he were riding off into quite another sphere; a mysterious, alarmingly exciting place to which their mother's unconcealed disapproval gave an added spice. Then there were the periodical visits of the carriers; and rough old drovers who appeared on their way to sell their cattle in Birmingham with messages from Mr. Johnes's farms; and members of the quality like Herbert Lloyd who would come clattering up in his great travelling coach on his way to London, or Paynter *en route* for Lord Powis's at Oakley Park. Croft Castle was a regular port of call for travellers from west Wales, who whether they liked it or not could not help being impressed as they climbed the hill to the castle, looming with grim magnificence among the waving plumes of the oaks and beech trees for which it was famed. No other Cardiganshire gentleman, not even Lord Lisburne himself, had anything as grand to show. Though Herbert Lloyd may have had Croft in his mind when he planned the fine new house which he built at Peterwell.

Peterwell threw a baneful shadow with long tentacles creeping up and down the land, for, firmly entrenched there, its dissolute lord ruled the surrounding country like a despot with none daring to oppose him. He had erected his house on very favourable terms to himself, paying the builders '6d. per day only for labour without diet', and when it was finished it was the wonder as well as the terror of the people, for nothing to match it in size and grandeur had ever been seen before.

Standing at the end of an avenue, half a mile beyond the town and within easy view of the public highway, it presented a most striking appearance, with its four great towers crowned with domes and a fine flight of steps leading up to its vast oak doors. Those doors were frequently approached with dread of what might be lying in store behind them, for when Herbert Lloyd was too impatient to wait till the next Quarter Sessions his house was often used as a court of justice. Many a malefactor was dragged up that fine avenue to be tried, with little hope of mercy to steady his quaking limbs. As for the bailiffs whose duty it was to serve writs upon the spendthrift lord of the manor, they approached it every whit as fearfully, for he generally met them brandishing his heavy riding whip, and while the lash whistled round their heads, he would compel them to swallow the bit of blue paper in front of his eyes.

Although his lawless cousin was a perpetual thorn in the flesh of the Custos, he usually stayed at Peterwell when he came to attend the court in Lampeter. They rode about the county together and stayed at Hafod with Paynter, where on one occasion at least Lord Powis was also a guest. The ambitious agent must nearly have burst with pride at housing such a distinguished party at his little hotel. Mr. Johnes averred that it was principally for the sake of their mutual relations that he kept on good terms with Lloyd and closed his eyes to much that went on. It is probable, however, that he was not really interested. He attended Court Leet at Lampeter as a matter of form, but did not worry himself that the measures that were regularly passed to improve the town were never carried out. His home and interests lay far away, and it was wiser to have as little as possible to do with that contumacious country as long as his own concerns there were not seriously interfered with. Lampeter had nothing to do with him; it was entirely Herbert Lloyd's province and the less the Custos meddled the better.

Lloyd was surrounded by a band of retainers as dishonest as himself, whom he was careful to see filled all the important posts in the town such as Port Reeve and Steward of the Court Leet, over which he himself presided. It was a reign of terror that the defenceless inhabitants were powerless to resist, and those who might have protected them would not for fear of incurring the tyrant's enmity. He levied fines, extorted forced labour and stole a large part of the Common where the horses and cattle of the townsfolk had freely grazed for centuries. Yet when he came riding down the cobbled street they stood humbly aside, doffing their caps and curtseying. When he travelled back from London, his tenants were ordered to supply relays of horses and oxen at various points along the road to help forward his travelling coach and baggage waggons. He rewarded them by carrying off the stock from their farms, and on one occasion he even plundered a tenant of the Custos's, whose indignation does not seem to have impelled him to take punitive measures. His career of crime continued for a number of years, and carried him to a seat in Parliament and brought him a coveted title.

In 1761, and not on the strength of his popularity, he was

returned as Member for Cardigan Borough; a constituency which comprised the four chief towns in the county. Only burgesses of these towns had the right to vote, though this did not necessarily mean that they were either freeholders or residents. There were burgesses of Lampeter living all over South Wales. Burgess-making was a regular feature of the Leets, and before Herbert Lloyd's election the Court sat for fifteen days swearing in scores of burgesses presented by a jury composed of his partisans. All the menservants at Peterwell, from the butler to the ploughman, were admitted to the freedom of the borough. The Port Reeve was Lloyd's infamous agent, Oakley Leigh, whose bastards over-ran the town, who had his own methods of extorting votes for his master. And it was as the Member for Cardigan Borough that the following year (two years after George III had ascended the throne) he drove up to London carrying a loyal though somewhat belated address of congratulation to the monarch, on behalf of his constituents. For this service he was rewarded with a baronetcy, an ill-deserved honour which aroused great indignation and was neatly lampooned by a Cardiganshire wit.

A would-be member brought of late
From borough little known,
In an address of early date
His incense to the Throne.

Soon tidings came where Teify flows,
Through the rent-harassed land,
That Lloyd to envied honours rose
And kissed the royal hand.

Oh, had our gracious Sovereign's touch
But cur'd him of his evil,
I'd own St. George ne'er boasted such
A triumph o'er the devil.

The writer was said to be a local nonconformist minister, whose indignation must often have been roused by the extravagance and evil living that went on at Peterwell, which from the first made havoc of the new baronet's fortune. Nonconformity at that time was rapidly gaining ground in Cardiganshire. The religious revival was at its height; itinerant preachers were travelling up and down the country delivering their message, burning with a holy zeal to rouse their benighted countrymen out of the pits of spiritual darkness in which an idle and often absentee clergy had left them to founder. The response was eager. The people came flocking down the hills and along the valleys in crowds, to listen. The spirit swept across the land like a gale, bringing them forth from every hole and cabin to meet together in barns and fields. The air was filled with fiery tongues of praise, the hills resounding with the sweet wild notes of a thousand voices whose natural expression was song. At last hope was dawning, to alleviate the black despair in which they had wallowed for centuries.

The squires as a rule were strongly opposed to Methodism and its missionaries who were loud and tireless in condemning impurity, intemperance and frivolity, and did their utmost to suppress them. Like the Apostles of old, the preachers were stoned and beaten, but curiously enough Herbert Lloyd was never among their persecutors. On the contrary, in his younger days, influenced perhaps by his pious wife, he had entertained the ministers who came to his mountain village, and to Peterwell he invited the celebrated Whitefield to preach to the inhabitants of Lampeter. Occasionally, too, he drove over to Llangeitho to listen to the preaching of another celebrated revivalist, Daniel Rowlands, and as likely as not accompanied Whitefield there, who afterwards recorded that he was appalled with wonder at the scenes he had witnessed. 'I have seen', he said, 'at 7 in the morning, some 10,000 people breaking forth into the most ecstatic strains in the middle of a sermon, shouting "glory" and "hallelujah" and jumping with a lively joy, under the Divine power. . . .'

The power and pathos of Rowlands's exhortations were said to eclipse that of every other evangelist, and there is a tradition that it was while he was listening to Rowlands at Llangeitho that Handel first conceived the Hallelujah Chorus. The great musician was on terms of close friendship with that 'elect lady' the Countess of Huntingdon, who founded the nonconformist college at Trevecca in Breconshire. She had such veneration for Daniel Rowlands that she even kept a carriage for him, and it is well within the bounds of possibility that Handel did accompany her to Llangeitho. But what unappeased longings gnawing at his choleric spirit drove Herbert Lloyd to these meetings will never be explained, for he certainly did not apply their ethics to his own conduct. One tale of his infamy has been handed down, which illustrates again the unhappy plight and powerlessness of the peasants: it is of the terrible doom Herbert Lloyd inflicted upon an honest old freeholder, whose only crime was that he had the courage to resist him.

Among the glories of Peterwell was a roof-garden where on fine summer evenings it pleased the great man to cool himself of his wine, while he enjoyed the prospect of his broad acres with the Teifi flowing through them. And from there he could see, besides, the farms and hovels of the poor, who dwelt like beasts of the field under the shadow of his great house. His greedy heart rejoiced that as far as his eyes could see all belonged to him, with one sole exception. This was an eighteen-acre field plumb in the middle of the Peterwell estate, which was a source of constant exacerbation. It was the proud possession of Shon Philip whose family had owned it from time immemorial. The old farmer was as obstinate as a mule and, although Herbert Lloyd had made frequent offers to buy it, no money would induce Shon Philip to part with it.

The lovely field sloping down to the banks of the river was the pride of his heart, and in it from morning till nightfall he laboured, helped by his good old wife. The gold pieces the squire jingled in his pockets while he tried to persuade him to sell meant nothing to him. The wheat and roots off his field, his pig and his cow, provided all his simple wants. Thus, though Lloyd argued and bargained repeatedly, Shon Philip remained adamant and nothing Lloyd could offer would induce him to part with his property.

Herbert Lloyd decided to see what effect liquor might have in breaking the old man's resistance and gave orders that at every opportunity Shon Philip should be invited to the Peterwell kitchens, and given a good supply of strong home-brewed ale. But wary Shon Philip would scarcely touch it, and was sober and stubborn as ever when Herbert Lloyd waylaid him with fresh offers, on his way home. Early in the winter of 1762, he came to the end of his patience and evolved a plan that would settle the matter once and for all. A rumour was spread about the place that a valuable black ram belonging to him had either strayed or been stolen from his flock, and his servants were sent searching for it all over the country. One moonless night, two of his men removed the animal from its hiding-place. They carried it across the fields to Shon Philip's cottage and, clambering with it on to the roof, dropped it down the open chimney. Then they scuttled back to Peterwell to inform their master that his instructions had been successfully carried out.

In spite of the hour, it was then three o'clock, Lloyd sent at once for the parish constable, and informing him that he had every reason to believe that Shon Philip had stolen the ram, he gave him a warrant and ordered him forthwith to search the cottage. Shon Philip was held in such high esteem that the constable argued violently that such a thing was impossible and finally set off on his distasteful mission most unwillingly.

Tired with their day's work and probably a little deaf besides, the old couple had slept soundly through the descent of the ram down their chimney and were only awakened by the constable's loud drubbing on the door. Bewildered and half-blind with sleep, as they groped their way across the floor, perhaps they took the awkward black creature bounding ahead of them to be some figment of the night—a creature of their dreams. But if they did, the illusion was rudely dispelled by the astonished constable. In vain did they protest, declaring their innocence. The proof was there, black and living, impossible to refute. The poor old people stared hopelessly at one another with terrified, uncomprehending eyes, as the constable read the warrant for Shon's arrest. Then he was dragged away from his weeping wife and marched off to Peterwell where Herbert Lloyd awaited them.

Although the unfortunate old man doggedly persisted that he had never touched the ram and was innocent, Lloyd refused to listen to him, reminding him instead that he would undoubtedly hang for his crime. Then he promised to forget and forgive the whole business if Shon would agree to sell his field, but Shon's passionate pride of possession and his native obstinacy made him continue to shake his head. Finally the furious squire ordered his men to remove him and keep him safe until they could get him to gaol. He spent the rest of that night and half next day in the stocks, until a large band of men armed with staves fetched him and took him off to the county gaol at Cardigan.

There he lay until the following March, while his persecutor pursued his life of pleasure, dicing and drinking with his friends and making his great journey to London to receive his new title. In March Shon Philip was brought before the Assizes. Sir Herbert's case was presented by the Attorney-General, but the prisoner was undefended, all the local attorneys being too timid to speak for him. Nearly every member of the jury was one of Lloyd's men, thus the outcome of the case was inevitable. Shon Philip was condemned to death and hanged outside the town, and a few days later a deed of conveyance was forthcoming that purported to bear his mark, giving the new baronet possession of the field.

This easy method of acquiring property appealed to him so much that a few years later he tried it again. This time his servants dropped a piece of valuable tapestry down a farmhouse chimney but, luckily for them, the owners were still awake, gathered round the hearth listening to the music of a travelling harpist. They saw the bundle come hurtling down, knew at once it boded no good, and probably remembering the fate of poor old Shon, they stoked up the fire, poked it in, and by the time the constable appeared not a trace of it was left.

Success no longer smiled on Sir Herbert's undertakings. At the time of the elections for the new Parliament in 1768, he announced his intention of standing for the county. The account of what befell him was written by the identical minister who had lampooned his baronetcy, in a letter to his clergyman brother.

'Sir Herbert intended to stand for ye county, but a general meeting last autumn declaring in favour of Lord Lisburne, he was oblig'd to decline it, but at ye same time declared himself a candidate for ye Town [Cardigan] In order to which he endeavoured to get a friend of his (Ben Davies of Glancuch, whose daughter Sally you have kiss'd formerly) to be chosen mayor. But Lewes ye bookseller of Carmarthen being elected by a great majority, Sir Herbert notwithstanding got his own Mayor sworn in, so that for some time ye Town was doubly officered. This caus'd a King's Bench suit, which was determin'd at Hereford in favour of Lewes. Mr. Campbell had some time before declar'd and supported by . . . a great Majority of ye county Gentlemen. Sir H. however determined to stand a poll, and order'd down his Lampeter Burgesses, who amounted to upwards of 2000 [sic]. But Ben Davies meeting him on ye Road and refusing to act as returning officer, ye Bart himself being apprehensive of Writs to take him, he return'd home, and left his men to shift for themselves, so that his antagonist had ye field entirely to himself.'

The end was now not far off. Riddled with debt and rotten with disease, Sir Herbert had little left to live for. According to the story that has been handed down, one fine Sunday the following summer some whim took him to his parish church, where he listened to the vicar preaching from a text whose import may well have struck terror in his heart. 'Brethren, be not deceived. God is not mocked, for whatsoever a man soweth that shall he also reap.' A few days later he set out for London for the last time, ostensibly to attend to business, though his chief motive was gambling in a den near Brook Street which he and his familiars frequented. And it was there that the ugly story of his life came to a fitting close, for one grey dawn following many nights of disastrous play, found him in the little garden at the back of the premises where he had gone to take the air. He was lying across the seat shot through his temple, his face ghastly in the pallid light, his pistol on the ground beside him where it had dropped.

By dint of a good many lies, and the exchange of a good many guineas, a verdict of accidental death was obtained, and, packed up in a big crate labelled 'Valuable Furniture' for fear of his creditors, his servants brought his body back to Peterwell. But even this was not quite the end, for, in spite of precautions, the bailiffs managed to slip into the house and pin their blue paper on the coffin as it lay in state in the hall, keeping guard beside it day and night. According to the law, the corpse of a debtor was denied burial until his debts were paid in full. The money was not to be had. August turned into September, the weather was warm, and each day the situation became more intolerable, though nothing would move the bailiffs. Finally the butler solved the problem by serving them one night with heavily drugged ale. The instant they lapsed into unconsciousness, he locked them up tight and hurried the coffin out of the house. Tenants bearing lighted torches were waiting without to carry their tyrant to the churchyard and there, at dead of night, his body was buried.

In all the little homesteads round about the curse of the old vicar of Llandovery was recalled, for stones from Millfield had gone into the building of Peterwell. Farther away, at Croft Castle, the Custos of Cardiganshire was horror-stricken. A fortnight after that nocturnal burial he wrote to the Captain: 'I can

Thomas Johnes (senior) of Croft Castle 1721—1780

John Johnes of Dolecothi (1768—1815)

now mention the Bart, though it is still disagreeable, when I first heard of his death . . . it made me quite sick and I could not bear to think of the villain with any degree of temper. . . . I had seen him so often in the jaws of death that I imagined it had no power over him.'

It gave him plenty to ruminate on. At the age of fifty, Herbert Lloyd, having squandered his health and fortune, had killed himself. Thomas Johnes, having taken care of both, was at forty-eight very satisfied still with his life which continued to unfold and develop satisfactorily. Croft Castle had belonged to his wife for several years, as the old gentleman had died. Their two elder children were now grown up—his son Thomas was at present making the fashionable Grand Tour in Europe, while before very long his daughter Elizabeth would please them all by marrying John Hanbury Williams of Coldbrook Park, whose own excellent fortune had been considerably augmented when he had inherited his uncle's, for he was nephew and heir of Mr. Johnes's old friend Sir Charles. As quickly as possible the Custos forgot about his kinsman and the many wretched matters connected with him. His own prospects presented nothing to worry him, and now his thoughts were mainly occupied with his clever son, of whom he expected great things.

CHAPTER III

The Silver Spoon

The heir to Croft Castle and extensive estates in Herefordshire, besides vast tracks of land in West Wales, for he was the sole heir of his grandmother Knight as well as of both his parents, was born with a silver spoon in his mouth if ever a lad was. It looked as though there would be little in life that he could not command. Mr. Johnes, very ambitious for this son of whom he was inordinately proud, and warned by his own early follies, was determined that he should not lead an idle, aimless life. The young man, although of many excellent parts, already showed signs of that hereditary indolence which the spoiling of his mother and grandmother encouraged in every possible way. The prudent father bought a commission in the army for him, which his son should take up as soon as he returned from his travels abroad. A few years of military discipline and responsibility would be of infinite service to stiffen up his somewhat volatile and irresponsible nature. Otherwise, with too much money and nothing particular to occupy him, he might easily become nothing but a bookworm like his cousin Dick Knight at Downton. Two years younger than Thomas Johnes, the cousins had always been great friends, as they were with another rich young neighbour and contemporary, Uvedale Price of Foxley. There was no question of either of these youths following a profession, and both of them were a great deal too much preoccupied with the arts for the sturdy taste of Mr. Johnes. But he flattered himself that his son was of a more robust constitution and a few years of regimental life would successfully dispose of any of the new-fangled aestheticism that he might have picked up on the Continent. Content in this assurance he sat back and waited.

We only know the barest details of the young man's early life, though we can safely assume that nothing was thought too good for him. All that the silver spoon implies surrounded him from his cradle; an opulence that grafted the first shoots of grandeur in the willing soil of his young mind which were to flourish with such disastrous abundance all through his life. Not that he was particularly pampered, for he was packed off to a dame-school at Ludlow when he was seven and then to the free grammar school at Shrewsbury, where his schoolfellows were drawn from every walk in life, from butcher's shop and baronial hall.

He was happy at Shrewsbury, boarding at the house of one of the masters whose kindness he never forgot. This was characteristic, for all his life he was peculiarly vulnerable to the kindness or unkindness of others, his impetuous open-heartedness sparing him nothing as it plunged him headlong into friendships. This fieriness of spirit was part of his Celtic heritage. The Knights were of an altogether cooler temperament, though it was from them that he derived his instinctive taste for learning and the arts; the romantic imagination, swift brain and scholarly mind, which could absorb and recollect any amount of knowledge, though it grew hopelessly confused (and this was most unlike the Knights) when it was compelled to descend to the dead level of practical business.

At twelve he went to Eton where he spent seven years and fell under the spell of that brilliant scholar and athlete, William Windham of Felbrigg Hall, whose melancholy dark eyes and fatal power to charm, were destined to create such emotional havoc along his path through life. And from Eton, his father sent him to the sterner discipline and higher levels of thought and conduct that obtained at Edinburgh, instead of to what has been described by a contemporary as 'one of those Schools of Vice, the Universities'. The Scottish capital was famous just then as a centre for such learned men as the philosopher Adam Smith and the historian David Hume, who had brought Jean-Jacques Rousseau there only a year or two earlier. The problems of humanity were uppermost in the minds of the intellectuals. At the table of his tutor, the learned Dr. Drysdale who was a friend of Adam Smith's, young Johnes must often have participated in these discussions. Transition was in the air. The first faint tremors threatening the social structure were being set in motion by these philosophers and philanthropists, who explored the realities of life as it is lived and exposed evils which a prosperous Whig society found it more agreeable for their own peace and contentment to ignore. It was still the old Edinburgh 'of the insanitary warren of deep wynds and lofty tenement flats, where the greatest men in Scotland and their families consented to be cabined in darkness and dirt'. In this rugged atmosphere of altruistic preoccupations, while he attended lectures on logic and moral philosophy, young Johnes's mind first consciously bent itself towards that humanism which to some extent at least was to determine the course of his life.

Straight from the frugality and lofty ethics of the windswept north, he was sent off abroad in the charge of Robert Liston. This young Scotsman had already earned for himself golden opinions as a guardian and guide of youth, and the anxious father could trust him to preserve his high-spirited son from the numerous pitfalls that bristled about that well-beaten track across Europe. Mr. Johnes must have taken infinite pains and pulled a great many influential strings to get hold of such an exemplary cicerone for his son, for although Liston was still in his twenties his many great merits were already well known.

He, too, had been a student at Edinburgh, where his attainments and character had been rated so high that before he was twenty he was selected for the post of private tutor to the sons of

Sir Gilbert Elliot of Stobs. He was allowed two years 'to perfect himself in classics, law and dancing', this last accomplishment being then considered indispensable, even as a preparation for Holy Orders. At the end of two years he set off for Paris with his two little pupils—Gilbert, aged twelve, who afterwards became the first Earl of Minto, and Hugh, two years younger, who was destined for the diplomatic service. There they remained for several years, pursuing their studies and associating with the youthful scions of French and English aristocracy. The Elliot boys were devoted to their dark, distinguished-looking young tutor, while their influential relations had nothing but praise for him. Liston had only lately returned from Paris when Mr. Johnes engaged him to escort his son to Europe. No choice could have been happier, for it was the beginning of a firm and lifelong friendship.

Armed with a sheaf of introductions to crowned heads and others, which Mr. Johnes's good friends, Lord Oxford and Lord Bateman, had provided, they disappeared across the Channel and were away for two years, the last six months being spent in Paris. Here, thanks again to Lord Oxford, Johnes was received by such arbiters of taste and fashion as Madame du Deffand and Baron Grimm. Perhaps Liston left him there to finish his education alone, for it has been hinted that he sowed a very extensive crop of wild oats and overspent himself shockingly, though that was the last thing to worry him. What was there to bother about? Encompassed as he had always been by the large, solid fortunes and great territorial possessions of the Knights, a seemingly endless supply of resources, money was the last thing he ever gave a thought to except as the means of satisfying his wants. In Paris that summer he was in the first flush of his youth and those astonishingly sanguine and exuberant spirits which no amount of reverses could subdue for long. It is therefore not surprising if the sparkle and brilliance of the beautiful, brittle Parisian scene, with its elegance, its culture, its exquisite taste (refreshingly different from the stifling material preoccupations that dominated the inhabitants of Croft Castle) did precipitate him into all manner of gay and expensive adventures. But however delightful these may have been, however entangling, they could not continue for ever. The two years allotted to him were drawing to their close. On the 30th November 1769 Mr. Johnes wrote from Croft to his brother: 'My son left Paris last week and I suppose we shall see him here next week or the following.'

The eagerly awaited return was destined to disappoint the vigilant father. What happened plainly shows that the position the Cardiganshire Custos enjoyed in his home was not nearly as authoritative as it was elsewhere. His son duly arrived—a personable-looking young man, ruddy and fair-complexioned, short of stature and strongly built, his features uniting the salient characteristics of both sides of the family. He had the well-shaped head and large clever nose of the Knights, and the Johnes's broad cheeks and heavy jowl, with all their implications of extravagance, love of good fare and the domestic comforts, but not a trace of the calculation that tempered his father's nature. And he could be extremely obstinate. The two years abroad had established him on his own feet and whetted his appetite for the adventures and amusements which life in town and country offered a young man of fortune. The bare idea of the salutary military discipline which would be so good for his character was repugnant. He could not endure the thought of authority or control. He wanted to be left to go his own way, where and as he pleased. His friends were all of the same mind, and no one was compelling *them* to follow an unwelcome profession. He and they were all ardent young connoisseurs of life, as it was represented in the coffee-houses where the literati congregated, and in the drawing-rooms of the great ladies. His mother and grandmother emphatically championed his arguments against an army career with all its obvious perils, vigorously opposing everything the Custos said. The two rich women were the powerful ones in that household, holding all the best cards. Out of the mists of time, very distinctly the little scene evolves—the old lady in her monstrous cap, arrayed in the sable robes of widowhood, standing no nonsense from her expostulating, crest-fallen son-in-law; her daughter, long-nosed and steely-eyed, her silken skirts crackling and rattling with fervour, chiming in and encouraging her son to pursue that idle life of pleasure to which his great expectations entitled him. The Custos had to make the best of it, but a strong undercurrent of injury stamped what he wrote at the end of that December to his brother: 'My son is just returned from London where he went to dispose of his commission in the army, as his mother and grandmother were ready to dye with the thoughts of his continuing in the service.'

For several years the lively young man entirely disappears from sight down those flowery and unprofitable paths. But when in 1773 the seat for Cardigan Borough became vacant, Mr. Johnes saw his opportunity to call a halt to his son's gay progress. Unlimited leisure had begun to pall and many of young Johnes's friends were already concerning themselves with politics. Among them were the two Whig squires whose tastes were similar to his own, Richard Payne Knight and Uvedale Price. It was very much the thing for rich young men to represent their county or borough in Parliament, and at this time, besides, Johnes was swayed by his admiration for Lord North, whom he knew personally. Thus he was quite prepared to fall in with his father's wishes.

He knew little of the boroughs he was proposing to represent and it is probable that this was his first introduction to the land of his forefathers. The Custos immediately started writing round to his friends there and adjured the idle Captain to bestir himself on their candidate's behalf. But he never doubted their success. Mr. Johnes's influence in the country was extremely strong and at Cardigan he owned a large estate known as The Priory.

On their way thither he certainly stopped at Dolecothy and

introduced his son to his uncle and aunt and their family. It was a very simple household, the complete antithesis of anything young Johnes had seen hitherto. What a stir and excitement his arrival must have created, for in the eyes of the inhabitants of Dolecothy the affluence and importance of Croft Castle assumed a fabulous brilliance. And so must its young heir have done when he arrived dressed in the latest fashion, all his equipment of the most expensive, bringing into that rustic home a heady tang of the great world, of fashionable London and the capitals of Europe, of courts and carnivals and imposing names. Many a time his proud parent had jested and bragged about his exploits and the fine company he kept, while he sat quaffing deep draughts of port wine at his brother's dinner-table. And now here he was in the flesh, embodying everything they esteemed and coveted; greeting his aunt and uncle with a heartiness that had not a trace of superciliousness or condescension, and making friends with their little brood. John, the delicate only boy, was rising seven, with three small sisters younger than himself, while Jane was nine years older than her brother and in her sixteenth year. She was of an age to be far more thrilled by her cousin than any of them, as she sat entranced watching him and listening to his rapid, amusing talk; to delight in wearing his ribbons and perhaps she sewed a knot of them on to his coat before he rode off again to the scene of the contest.

As it turned out, the election was not such plain sailing as they had expected, for Johnes was defeated by a large majority and his English opponent, Sir Robert Smyth of Upton in Essex, was returned as member. It was a heavy blow, but one that the doughty Custos would not allow to pass unchallenged, for there was ample evidence to prove that Smyth owed his victory to bribery and corruption. A petition to this effect was brought before the House of Commons in December that year, but it was not until twelve months later that Mr. Johnes was at last able to announce the successful end of the business to the Captain.

'Dear Brother,' he wrote, 'I can now with pleasure inform you that the business is all over, the Contest after ten days attendance finished this afternoon when they cannot go one step further—their number of 1488 has reduced to 600 and such a number of names upon the Stamp Book only correspond with the names upon the Poll. Our poll amounting to 980 was thoroughly established so that we have had a most complete victory and my Son now sits for the Borough of Cardigan.'

CHAPTER IV

The Captain's Daughter

Early in the year of her cousin's successful petition, at Dolecothy, Jane Johnes was finishing with lessons. That February she had her sixteenth birthday, which turned her into a grown-up young lady, ready to help with the management of her father's house.

Although still scarcely more than a child, she already showed signs of a dominating and determined character. It was just as well, for there was no one else to take the lead at home or to keep the small household going. Her mother was constantly ailing, while by this time the Captain had settled down to a state of permanent tipsiness and bad health. Jane entered upon her new status with all due seriousness, keeping a careful account of her expenditure and doings in a 'New and Polite Pocket Memorandum Book'. It has survived till this day and proves that she was a practical girl, well versed in all the household arts. Besides attending to her brothers and sisters, she cooked and sewed; bottled fruit and bottled wine; and melted down large quantities of grease to make pounds of wax candles. She winnowed wheat and barley almost daily in the barn, and sent it to the mill to be malted. When it returned she brewed large supplies of the good strong ale that had such a deplorable effect upon her father. She had ducks and chickens and geese to look after besides, whose layings and sittings she kept careful note of, as well as sheep of her own—this spring she sold her lambs for four guineas. And then there was the flower-border to dig up and sow—in fact, there was no end to all the things she had to do, and her new independence was clearly very agreeable to her.

Not only had she a capable head on her slender young shoulders, but also an exceptionally pretty one. A shower of fair curls fell round a heart-shaped face that might have been painted by Greuze, with its short, delicate nose, pouting lips and pointed chin. It certainly seemed a little unjust that anything as young and as captivating as Jane should be condemned to that melancholy house on the brink of the Cothi, and an isolated valley that was scarcely more than a cleft between the hills. All round the house the trees shivered and sighed and the mountains lowered, their rough sides gashed with the caves that the ancient Britons had dug in their search for gold. The prospect was not a cheerful one for an emotional, highly strung girl who loved pretty things and whose heart hankered for amusements and a sight of the gay world. Her character had many facets, and at present the hard-working, practical Jane was uppermost, owing to the straitened circumstances and responsibilities at home. Close behind these excellent qualities, though as yet unexpressed, was a light-hearted extravagance and a rich enjoyment of all the good things of this world. In her daydreams, her thoughts roamed instinctively towards Croft Castle which she had never yet seen, though the grand, opulent life there had been impressed upon her ever since she could remember. It stood for everything that was to be most envied and admired; infinitely remote from humble Dolecothy. As she splashed about the muddy farmyard after her poultry, with the sombre hills shutting her tightly in the hollow at their feet, she shed many a sigh for that wider, freer life; its spaciousness, and the beautiful gowns and jewels worn by the ladies in those bright realms. Jane loved pretty clothes. She was always sewing and making herself new things, though she had little opportunity for showing them off.

As there were so few neighbours of his own standing, the Captain's guests were drawn from every stratum of society. Better to-do farmers, drovers and others of the sort were often entertained by him, as well as the local gentry. There were young cousins, too, who came from round about, but none of them were particularly interesting to Jane. All the same, when company was expected to dinner she took great pains with her dress and appearance, disguising her lovely hair with pomatum and powder—items that figured regularly in her accounts, costing twopence and fourpence halfpenny respectively. Unrewarding as it must have been to go to such pains for the beery old yokels the Captain gathered round him, it was good practice for better things some day. There were various agreeable possibilities in the offing. The Custos had a particularly soft corner for this pretty niece of his and often talked of her coming to stay at Croft, and she had expectations, too, of being invited to Coldbrook Park by her cousin, Betsy Hanbury Williams. But while she bottled and brewed, with her little sisters and the chickens and hens swarming round her feet, it must often have looked as though nothing very exciting was ever going to happen. Impressionable sixteen was far from being proof against the lassitude and gloom of the valley. On many days she could find nothing better to record than 'Spirits very low'.

By April, however, things began to move rather faster. The Captain, who had gone to Carmarthen to attend Assizes, having celebrated the occasion in his customary manner, was overcome by such a fearful attack of gout that his wife and Jane were hastily sent for. He was staying with his wife's relations, and there Jane remained for several weeks after her parents went home. Although it was not particularly amusing, she had plenty of leisure to refurbish her wardrobe. And now she worked with the happy certainty that her exertions were not being wasted, for at last she was going to pay a visit to her cousins at Coldbrook.

The Custos's elder daughter had been happily married for

several years to her amiable if somewhat feather-brained husband. In 1775 she was twenty-six, less than a year younger than her brother Thomas to whom she was devoted. They were alike in many respects, having the same spontaneous prodigality in their approach to life; a warm-hearted, generous appreciation of things and people which involved each in one extravagance after another. And they both preferred characters that were simple and unaffected. This explains why the childless Betsy, overflowing with loving-kindness, was the first member of the family to rescue her pretty cousin from her dreary home and introduce her to the amusements that were available in a lively country neighbourhood.

Coldbrook was a charming old place, standing among woodlands under the green Monmouthshire hills, and nothing in it had been altered since Sir Charles's day. The vast kitchens were equipped to cater for the large parties he used to bring down from London, while the pictures on the walls, which had been much to the old rake's liking, were sometimes a source of embarrassment to the squeamish. Pleasantly secluded though it was among its woods and paddocks, Abergavenny and Monmouth, with their race-courses and assembly rooms, were both within easy distance. The young couple had plenty of money and were bent on enjoying life. Several times every week they went dancing at the different assemblies and attended the plays that strolling players brought to the towns. Both husband and wife were delighted with their little cousin and made a great fuss of her. On the days they spent at home, kind Elizabeth Hanbury Williams, helped by her maid, took Jane's clothes in hand and did her best to transform her into a fashionable young lady. It was an expensive business and entailed the purchase of all manner of things such as pink 'ribbond' and pink 'gause', a pair of green shoes for five shillings, fifteen yards of lace for a 'Treble Pr. of Ruffles', lace for caps, lace for lappets, and 'Pink Persian for the lining of my worked Petticoat'. Money had a way of melting in Jane's fingers, even in those early days. And this is what happened now, as may be seen by the letter which some time during this visit she wrote to her mother.

'Dear Mama,

'I should be greatly obliged if you would send me some checked muslin for two Aprons, I being obliged to wear Aprons with all my gowns. Send also my false hair and I should take it as a favour if you would change the false tails with me, yours looking better. I wish you would send the Brocade sack for Mrs. Williams to see as Brocaded silks are all the tone now. Indeed my money is grown very short I having bought several things since I came here. . . . I wish Papa would send me a little Cash. . . . I have bought two aprons out of my own Pocket and am working one. I have not above a Guinea and a half to spare.'

There was a constant coming and going of relations and friends that summer. Perhaps because her mother had discouraged her friendship with them, Mrs. Hanbury Williams assiduously invited all her Welsh cousins to visit her. They came and danced and feasted and never a day passed without some festivity, or else devising some new finery for Jane. She remained there all through the summer, long happy days that had nothing in common with anything she had experienced hitherto. Yet here she was, sharing in the rich, pleasure-seeking life of her prosperous cousins, as though she were born to that happy, affluent world. She was devoted to her dear Mrs. H. Williams as she called her, who was all goodness and kindness. From the sophisticated young married lady, Jane must inevitably have picked up a great many interesting facts about life in general and the family at Croft in particular. Betsy would certainly have talked a great deal about her elder brother, who already was invested with an aura of splendour for Jane. She garnered in her fluttering little heart all kinds of tantalizing confidences about that lively young gentleman who spent his time skimming the cream off life in London, Paris and Rome, and wherever else his volatile fancy led him.

And then, one Sunday evening towards the end of July, he arrived at Coldbrook and slept the night there. 'Mr. Thomas Johnes came here to supper,' Jane wrote in her book. And on the following day there is the entry: 'Mr. Thomas Johnes, Mrs. Williams, Miss and self went to Hereford to send Mr. Thomas Johnes on his way. Mr. Thomas Johnes went on for Croft and we for Coldbrook.'

In five cramped lines of her looped, irregular handwriting, Jane contrived to write his name three times. One cannot believe it was entirely accidental. But whatever she may have felt about him he passed across her path with the transience of a shadow, riding off into Herefordshire and not being seen at Coldbrook again that summer.

It was late in September when she returned to Dolecothy. The leaves were already falling from the trees and autumnal mists floated up from the river to veil the woods and hills. After the spacious life at Coldbrook, the junketings and cheerful companionship, the close little valley was like a grave with its silence and separation. For three whole weeks after her return all she wrote in her book was a pettish 'Nothing particular'. Nothing else, day after day. For such simple occurrences as 'putting the Goose to sit' or 'cutting a Chees for the People' which formerly had filled a day, were now not worth remembering.

She went back to Coldbrook again the following summer. Anne and Samuel Johnes were staying there as well—he was at All Souls College, Oxford, where he was reading for the Church. Anne and Samuel were of a different nature from the elder two; more prudent, staid and cautious. But this summer they were all very young and light-hearted, and as pleased with Jane as she was with them. There were plays and assemblies in plenty to amuse them and all the same agreeable fuss about dress. Jane had scarcely arrived than she had to sit down and alter all her clothes 'they having been made so ill'. Nevertheless, some of the things she brought with her were the envy of everyone present, the silks that had come from France on the little vessels that slipped under cover of darkness up the sandy creeks along the Cardiganshire coast. The prestige these gave her was gratifying, and it was pleasant, too, to be able to oblige her cousins by writing to tell her mother that 'Mrs. H. Williams and Miss Johnes would be obliged if you would try and get 30 yards of laylock poplin the same sort as my pink. Mrs. Williams would be very glad if you would get two boxes of Wax candles and a bottle of Laver.'

Although the Custos had frequently begged his brother to allow 'Miss Jane' to pay them a long visit at Croft, she did not go there until the late autumn of 1777, when she was eighteen and a half. She had been at home for a long time before that without a change, and with no society to amuse her apart from the rather mixed and bibulous gatherings at Dolecothy. To go straight from these to the Castle where the greatest state was maintained by her fashionable and awe-inspiring aunt was something of an ordeal. As she travelled along in the chaise her trunk with all her finery strapped securely on behind, her excitement at seeing at last that fabulous place must certainly have been fraught with a good deal of trepidation. All her life it would be her habit to fret and worry herself about what lay in store, and on this long journey—the farthest she had been from home in her life—she had plenty of time for anxious speculation.

She knew already from Betsy that life at Croft Castle was not the free-and-easy affair that it was at Coldbrook. Mrs. Johnes's social standards were high; the entertainments she presided over were impressive affairs, for the company was always very fine. Jane's heart sank, wondering how she would acquit herself in those cold and critical eyes. She wished with all her might that the Hanbury Williams might be there too. She had seen nothing of them for more than a year, and a change had taken place in their routine since her last visit to Coldbrook. Country society not altogether satisfying Mr. Williams, they had bought a house at Bath, where much of their time now was spent, joining in all the fashionable diversions and losing a great deal of money at the card tables.

But as it turned out she had tormented herself in vain, and the weeks that followed left nothing to be desired. On her arrival she found the Hanbury Williams there to give her confidence and Mr. Thomas Johnes to shake it with delicious tremors. This debonair bachelor of twenty-nine was as kind and affectionate as his sister. He was certainly quite as eager that Jane should be happy, for he never felt comfortable himself unless everyone round him was pleased. In fact, she was probably doubly welcome, pleasantly alleviating the heaviness in the atmosphere of his home, which moreover was just beginning to be tainted by a faint odour of disfavour. The young man's tastes and ideas in scarcely any respect coincided with what his parents expected of him, and his spendthrift habits were already a source of anxiety to his careful mother. No serious purpose had so far succeeded in curbing his liberty or checking the irresponsibility of his idle and exceptionally enjoyable life. It was packed with absorbing friendships and interesting personalities, an infinite variety of pleasures and a stimulating array of things to do and to see, to satisfy his inquiring mind. Then there were always fresh treasures in the way of rare books, pictures and other objects to be sought for and, of course, acquired. When he had nothing else to occupy him, he could read for hours together or pursue some new line of research that had attracted his errant fancy. He never stayed long in one place; when not at Croft or in London, he was visiting his friends in the country or travelling abroad. In short, he was frittering away his time and money with very little to show for either—at least nothing that afforded much satisfaction to his parents.

This, however, did not concern Jane. In her eyes both her cousins were perfection, and it was a relief to find that her aunt was not at all formidable after all. Before she had been there many weeks, she wrote an account of her doings to her mother, which tells us all about that winter visit that we shall ever know.

'Croft Castle,

'Sunday night, 12 *o'clock, 9th of Nov.* 1777.

'My dear Mama's long wished for letter I received last post. . . . I am surprised that Papa thinks of letting me stay here all the winter, but indeed I ought not to wish to leave this place as they are all remarkably fond of me. I really believe there does not exist a better woman than Mrs. Johnes. I really have a sincere regard for her. Mr. and Mrs. H. Williams leave this place to-morrow. I shall miss them much. Mrs. H. Williams is the same good-natured person as ever and as fond of me. Indeed I am under great concern seeing her look so bad. She is thinner than ever, really a walking shadow and in my opinion has lost all her Beauty and that agreeable diffidence she used to possess. Nasty Bath has entirely taken it. If she does not alter her way of life she will not long continue an inhabitant of this world. Next summer she is to go to Spa for the benefit of her health. She goes to Coldbrook from here and about the middle of this month she goes to Bath. . . . Mr. Johnes senior and junior goes to London next Monday, it will be horrid stupid upon Miss Johnes, Mrs. and myself after all the company that has been here ever since I came. I have not had a minute's leisure for anything but dressing, paying and receiving visits. Lord and Miss Clive, Sir Robert Gurney, Miss Gurney and Miss Ducane all have been here twice since I came. It is thought that Miss Clive has a penchant for Mr. Johnes junior but it will not do as the young gent does not seem to approve of her. Last week Mr. Harley[1] and Mrs. Harley with their five daughters came here and stayed a two nights. The young ladies are very pretty they were over dressed for the country. Lord and Lady Bateman have been here three or four times, and we have been at Shobdon and at Mr. Harley's. We have also been at Mr. Archdeacon Harley,[2] who married Miss

[1] Alderman Thomas Harley, a rich merchant. He was third son of the third Earl of Oxford, and Lord Mayor of London in 1767. He employed Holland to build his seat, Berrington Court.

[2] Afterwards Bishop of Hereford and father of the 5th Earl of Oxford.

Vaughan the great Breconshire heiress. Lord and Lady Oxford have dined here once. We paid a morning visit to Haywood their seat. I will not attempt giving you an account of all the Plebeians that have been here. Suffice it to say that I have not spent one day without dining fifteen. To make amends for it we shall not see a soul except a few antediluvian neighbours from hence till Xmas as all the genteel company are gone to London. Mrs. and Miss Johnes go in March. I believe they are not to take a house till then. I really did not expect to see so elegant a table. The French cook that they have got sends nothing but made dishes, the house is a very handsome one, a larger I never saw and there is here a elegant suit of rooms, five in the same, it is surprising to see a suit of rooms in an old country house.

'I am very low spirited to-night. Indeed I believe I shall spend most part of it in crying, the thought of parting with Mr. and Mrs. H. Williams affects me much. I should be a most ungrateful girl was I not to be sorry. I am sure I shall never forget her kindness to me, never was there a more amiable woman. Would to God that she would take care of her health.

'Mrs. Johnes is still in high raptures of Wales. She praises everything she had at Dolecothy. . . . Mr. Johnes is very uneasy about the American affairs there came an express down to Mr. Harley on Thursday with Good News which put the old Gent into such spirits that he forgot himself so far and drank so much port wine as rendered him quite tipsy. The last papers contradicted the account that came down by the express—one from Lord George Jermain to his brother Lord Bateman and the other to Mr. Harley but Mr. Johnes insists upon the good news being true. . . .

'On Thursday last Miss Johnes and myself and the four gentlemen went to Leominster Assembly which you will say was very brilliant when I tell you that no less than three lords were there. . . . All the Harleys were there and a great number of right honorables.

'I have wrote a vile scrawl I must beg you and Papa will excuse it as I have not time to write this over. I must beg the favor of you to send me a black cloak and the false tail also some muslin for Aprons. . . . My duty to dear Papa who I hope likes the purse I knitted.

'I am, dr. Mama, your ever dutiful daughter
'Jane Johnes.'

Jane wrote exactly as her galloping thoughts led her, the words dropping helter-skelter on to the paper, taking one as one reads them right back into that dark bedchamber, with the fire smouldering on the open hearth and the tall curtained four-poster disappearing among the shadows of the ceiling. One can see her little figure, wrapped in a pink bed gown, sitting at the table, candles on either hand flickering in the draught that blows through the curtains, sending shifting patterns across the paper, her bent head with its ashen curls tumbling in disarray over her face and shoulders; one can feel the throbbing heart-beats that impel those hurrying fingers. She was completely carried away by all the fine doings, though there was more to it than that. She was, as she declared, in great emotional distress, ready to fling herself down on her bed and spend the night in tears, because 'the thought of parting with Mr. and Mrs. H. Williams affects me much'.

This was, of course, a very excellent reason to give her mamma, since she had to tell someone about it, but was it entirely truthful? It is far more likely that 'Mr. Johnes junior' was at the bottom of it, for 'Jenny' as he called her attracted him exceedingly. He never cared for fashionable young ladies with their tiresome vapours and mincing, affected airs; it was always the forthright, the simple and spontaneous that he looked for in his friends. And Jenny was all that, and more—an alluring, responsive little creature, ready and quick to learn, besides being full of good sense and practical business. As for her, what a number of new and enticing avenues their association must have opened up, and what a feather in her cap it was, too, to be so particularly noticed by this rich and fashionable young man of the world, who mixed with the first flight of London society! It is therefore not unreasonable to suspect that during those idle weeks at Croft, while it amused him to tease and make much of his golden-haired cousin, he had unwittingly made havoc of her emotional heart. And as she sat in her bedroom, writing into the small hours of the morning, a fearful sense of blankness fell like a blight over the immediate future, for he was going away and would not be back until Christmas.

But when Christmas at last arrived and with it the gentlemen, it found Jane herself on the brink of departure. To the great concern of her uncle, who had intended that she should stay with them till the summer, her mother had ordered her to set out for Dolecothy the following week. 'This is a shocking time to travel,' he wrote in great perturbation to the Captain, 'but as it is her orders we must submit and thank you for having spared her so long.'

So Jane went back home and when she was well on her way another letter arrived at Croft saying that after all she might remain there for as long as they cared to keep her. But it had come too late. The chaise was dragging her back through the mud and the rain to that deep, dull cleft between the hills, and there we lose sight of her completely for several years.

CHAPTER V

The Road Winds Upwards

On 20th February 1779, the Custos sat at his desk at Croft writing one of his regular letters to his brother. All he had said so far, covering a couple of closely written sheets, concerned business matters in the country which the Captain must attend to for him. Now, having arrived at a full stop he hesitated. He felt exceedingly tempted to announce a great piece of news, for he could think of little else just then. Still he could not decide whether it was wise to mention it yet or not, though he knew what a stir such an interesting and important event in his eldest son's life was bound to create in the family.

Lately Mr. Johnes had begun to feel his age; he had had a serious illness earlier in the winter which had left him in a very reduced state, laying him open to every disquieting thought that assailed him. And now it may well have plagued him to think what a source of disappointment his son had been this long while, and how rarely he had ever had occasion to impart good tidings concerning him. The political career he had once had high hopes of had amounted to very little; his son was not really interested in politics and resolutely declined to apply for any place or office in his stubborn resolve to be free of all ties and commitments. He continued to represent Cardigan Borough and held a commission in the militia—that was all. What made it all seem worse was the fact that he was generally considered to be clever above the average, and capable of excelling in anything he put his mind to. Many distinguished men enjoyed his society, as for example his very particular friend, Lord Chancellor Thurlow. But he was totally lacking in ambition or any wish to improve himself. The majority of his friends and pursuits were very different from those of his father's younger days. The scene had changed bewilderingly since then and with it the minds of the young men. Now it was nothing but intellectualism and nature—an almost passionate preoccupation with views and scenery. There was his son's great friend and cousin, Dick Knight, who had scarcely come of age than he started designing himself the great mock-medieval castle which he had just finished building at Downton. Now he was throwing good money away decorating and furnishing it in the most extravagant style. At Foxley, young Price was doing much the same sort of thing, making ornamental walks and rides all over the place. They, like his son, revelled in the society of writers and painters and wasted a great deal of money buying their works. Art and nature were the only things they seemed to think about; they took nothing else seriously, not even their politics. There were, of course, exceptions such as William Windham, who had for many years been one of young Johnes's closest intimates. Now he had suddenly abandoned his life of idle pleasure and thrown himself heart and soul into the political arena—a stormy place which had already swept them apart. The Custos, with a sigh, heartily wished that his son had had the good sense to profit by Windham's excellent example.

Nothing profitable, nothing constructive, appealed to him. He took very little interest in the Herefordshire estates, and those in Cardiganshire he had scarcely even seen. Now he was proposing to settle himself in Monmouthshire, not very far from Coldbrook. And this opened up another source of worry, for

John Hanbury Williams was also a regrettable example of good parts running to seed and a fine fortune being dissipated, in his case at the gaming-tables.

The shocking irresponsibility of the younger generation sent a gusty sigh rustling through the air as the Custos braced himself, taking courage in the hope that, now that at last his son had made up his mind to marry and settle down, he might become more inclined to shoulder the obligations of his position. As for the marriage, it was certainly not the great match they had once expected for him. She was only a provincial miss of no particular family, but it would do, he told himself, as he plunged his quill into the inkpot and with masterly uncommunicativeness proceeded to break the great news: 'My son I believe will be married. Matters are now before the lawyers. She has an excellent character in every aspect and she has likewise a very good fortune.'

The name which he refrained from divulging was Maria Burgh. She was a Monmouthshire heiress, the only surviving child of the late Reverend Henry Burgh, whose father had been steward to the Duke of Beaufort, a post that had proved profitable, for Mr. Burgh died a rich man. The year before she became engaged to Johnes, Maria had lost her only brother, when he was barely twenty, and had thus become possessed of the family fortune and the manor and estate of Park Lettice.

On the 26th August that year, the marriage took place at St. Mary's Church in Monmouth. The bridegroom was now styled Colonel Johnes, for on the strength of his marriage his father had had him appointed to the command of the Carmarthenshire Militia. This proved to be almost the last exertion he made on his son's behalf, for in May of the following year, of what cause we know not, at the age of fifty-nine the Cardiganshire Custos died.

For the very first time in her life, Mrs. Johnes of Croft Castle, or the Dowager as she was now styled to distinguish her from

Mrs. Maria, was feeling the pinch of poverty. Of only very comparative poverty certainly, but to one who had hitherto been totally unacquainted with it, it seemed sufficiently hard. Now that her son had inherited his father's property, besides already having his grandmother's fortune, her resources were considerably diminished. The old iron-master's grand-daughter, who was nothing if not a hard-headed, relentless woman of business, immediately set about dealing with the situation in a practical manner, allowing no quarter to her husband's debtors.

'I assure you', she wrote that year to her sister-in-law at Dolecothy, 'that it will always give me real satisfaction to oblige you both in any thing that lies in my power but keeping the Money on the same terms as it is now wch. I must beg to be excused as I always laid it down as a Rule wch. I always intend to observe that the fewest money dealings there are between Relations the better, as that has been productive of more quarrels than any one thing besides, and there is now such demand for it from the general scarcity that the Captain may pick and chuse his security at the same Interest. . . .

'Mr. Adams[1] has behaved so exceedingly ill to my late Dear Friend that he has forced me to proceed in a very disagreeable manner against him as I saw no reason to present him with £14 or £1500 to gratify his foolish vanity when his own Family want it for I think Charity begins at home. I never heard of so much distress in my life as now subsists among all Ranks of People wch. is not to be wondered at for the extravagant way of living that everyone runs into occasions nothing but Ruin and I hear of nothing but People being quite undone.

'I want to let this estate if I could hear of a Substantial Person to take it. I have had only one offer and he was so unreasonable as to expect an abatement of £100 a year and a Barn built, wch. I would not think of doing.'

A stern indictment of her son's behaviour underlay what she wrote. Marriage had not made him any more economical. In-

[1] John Adams of Whitland, nephew and heir of Sir Herbert Lloyd.

fected with the fashionable mania for bricks and mortar, he was planning to rebuild on a magnificent scale his wife's old-fashioned manor-house. He had resigned his seat for Cardigan and had offered himself for his father's old constituency of Radnor. This was bound to be a costly business for his opponent was a Nabob named Wilkins who had recently acquired a fine castle on the Wye. These Nabobs were being a nuisance everywhere, raising the price of parliamentary seats by their determination at all costs to get elected, thereby ensuring their social position in the country. The Dowager was uneasily aware that when it came to the question of spending, try as he might the Indian merchant would never be able to outdo her reckless son. This proved to be the case; at an enormous cost, Johnes was duly elected.

Indeed, for the first time it was beginning to look as if he was taking himself seriously in hand, and would follow in his father's footsteps as a useful and influential figure on the English side of the border. He was entrenching himself firmly into Monmouthshire and had bought a large estate there which, with his wife's, made him one of the principal landowners. There his destiny lay. At Park Lettice he would build the graceful and elegant house of his dreams, different in every way from the dark, inconvenient old castle. Looking after his estates and bringing up his family would be his chief occupations. He intensely desired children, though as yet there was no sign of his hopes being fulfilled. A family to look after and educate would settle him down into a steadier and more reliable character. This conviction may well have been the reason of his marriage to Maria, rather than a headlong love affair. His father's death, following so quickly on his marriage, appeared to fix his determination even more securely.

The Custos died in May 1780, and later that summer Johnes, for the first time in his life, visited his more remote Cardiganshire properties. It is most unlikely that his wife went with him, for she had been in bad health since very soon after their marriage, and the hardships such a journey entailed were severe. Not many years previously the Suffolk agriculturist, Arthur Young, had described Welsh mountain roads as 'mere rocky lanes, full of hugeous stones as big as one's horse', and Cardiganshire was by far the worst conditioned county in the Principality. And so, as there is nothing to suggest differently, we may suppose that he followed his father's old route, stopping at Dolecothy before he entered the county, perhaps leaving his Maria there in the charge of his aunt and cousins, for she was on very affectionate terms with them. It was a sad household that year, for the Captain was slowly dying, paralysed as the result of a stroke.

In a mood of nonchalant good-humour, Johnes rode on from there alone—a sanguine, cheerful-looking fellow, the trend of whose life had somehow never quite come up to perhaps even his own expectations. There was nothing to warn him that day that he had set out on a journey from which there would be no return: that the road he was following was destined to bring about far-reaching changes in his life and character and that within a short while of leaving Dolecothy he would experience the first exciting impulses of ambition and a sense of purpose. It was singular, to say the least of it, that the great change should be wrought by a sight of that mountain estate which his family for generations had held in contempt.

He knew very little about the Welsh properties and probably intended to sell them, for to keep they could only be a source of trouble. He can have had little desire to go to and fro as his father had done and he had never heard much good of them. Barren and bleak, that country was said to be inhabited by a slothful, gutless peasantry whom such minor catastrophes as floods and frost often drove to desperate remedies. There was a well-known tale of a charitable lady who one day met a poor labourer wending his way towards the river Teifi with a bulging blanket slung over his shoulders filled with a wriggling burden. This on inquiry proved to be several of his own small children whom he was about to cast into the river, preferring to drown them and have done with it than to watch them slowly dying of starvation.

At Croft Castle such a story as this had seemed too remote and unreal to affect him, but he had not penetrated very far into Cardiganshire before he began to think differently. His father's generation had accepted as a matter of course the appalling conditions in which many of the poor existed. The younger men were of a more benevolent turn of mind, a characteristic that was particularly strongly developed in Johnes. Now faced with these terrible sights, he was overwhelmed with compassion and an ardent wish to remedy them. It was almost unbearable to feel that vast tracts of the poor land through which he travelled, belonged to him, were his responsibility.

There must have been many halts on the journey at different farms and villages to meet his tenants. What a contrast they presented to the stout yeomen of Herefordshire! A more ill-conditioned crowd he had never beheld than these black-haired, sallow-skinned, lantern-jawed Cardis with their broods of emaciated, half-naked brats swarming in the mire like mites in a mouldy cheese. He listened to tales and beheld sights that wrung him through and through. His own well-clad, well-nourished person became yet another source of shame, as he intercepted the scowling looks darted at him by these scarecrow figures. It was a hail of flints that ended by cracking his comfortable shell of easy-going unconcern beyond all hope of repair.

The starved, ill-cultivated fields and the dreadful dwellings harrowed him too—at the best a two-roomed cottage with a loft accommodated a farmer and his entire family. Often these miserable places were totally devoid of air and light and roofed with a rotting thatch of oaten straw. As for the labourers, they had mud hovels which in some cases were barely high enough for them to crawl inside. The filthy stench that rose from them was sufficient to explain the fevers and other illnesses which perpetually tormented their unhappy occupants. The crops in the fields were often too sparse and stunted to be mown and had to be plucked up by little bands of women and children whose listless movements and pallid faces testified to the hunger and discouragement which pervaded this forlorn country. The sides of the hills were defaced with the rotting stumps of trees felled years before, perhaps to pay the gambling losses of some absentee squire. Tree-cutting had been carried on with a total lack of discrimination; selling timber was profitable enough, but replanting was expensive and therefore seldom undertaken. Since the tenant farmers were forbidden by law to plant trees for sale, they had no interest in the woods, and as all full-grown trees belonged to the landlord, they generally contrived to cut them down and use them for their own purpose before they attained full height. Thus there was little to shade the traveller, and as Johnes rode through the Teifi valley to Tregaron, and thence into the mountains on his way to Hafod, his heart was heavy in his breast. This was indeed the Devil's Grandmother's Jointure with a vengeance!

Yet in spite of everything he was becoming ever more aware that the country had a natural beauty that was nothing short of remarkable. As he penetrated farther into the mountains a wild exhilaration seized his volatile spirits and sent them soaring among the clouds, for never in all his travels abroad had he seen greater natural grandeur, a more splendid savageness, or such romantic beauties as now met his gaze at every turn. His lively imagination, deeply imbued as it was with the fashionable taste for the wild and picturesque, thrilled at the sight of those great rocky formations whose sides were stained with heather like spilled wine; the vast sweeps of moorland glowing with rich tints of emerald and sienna; the racing streams leaping from boulder to boulder in their flashing descent; the terrible, awe-inspiring solemnity of yawning chasms into which the unwary traveller might slip and be dashed to a thousand pieces. But, above all, the air! It was the clearest, sweetest air he had ever breathed, redolent with all the essences of the earth.

He followed a narrow road that climbed and twisted along the edges of a vast, unbroken stretch of mountain and moorland which at that time was almost completely unknown to English travellers. There was no wilder spot in the whole of Great Britain. It formed most of the east side of Cardiganshire, extending into Carmarthen, Brecon, Radnor and Montgomery—over forty miles in length and fifteen or twenty wide. Bogs, crags and torrents made much of it impassable, though here and there a track managed to struggle across it. No region was ever more isolated or more beautiful, though at times with an ominous, rather dreadful, quality. Now and again some shaggy, uncouth figure would furtively conceal himself as Johnes rode by, staring after him from his hole or bush. The habitations here were even worse than those in the lowlands. But all that could be remedied. Trees ought to be planted, acres and acres of them, all over the hills and sheltering the comfortable dwellings Johnes would like to see in place of these wretched hovels. It was painfully evident that this beautiful country had been scandalously neglected. Taken in hand by the right person, there seemed no reason why it should not flourish as well as any other part. But, first, trees must be planted. . . .

All the old stories of the egregious Paynter who had loved this place, and the timid parson who had fled from it in terror, came vividly to his mind the closer he drew to Hafod. Prevailing conditions were appalling, even for Cardiganshire. He recollected other things. Polygamy, which in the lower part of the county the Methodist Revival had done much to abolish, was still practised in these mountains and the chapel in the village of Yspytty Ystwyth served not only for the exhortations of itinerant preachers, but also in winter for wrestling matches which lasted all night long before an audience of old men and young women. Yspytty was a dreary mining village only a mile or two from Hafod, and the swarm of half-naked miners, men and women, who stood among the slag heaps staring at him as he went by, had more the appearance of animals than human beings. And so on, till he reached a point where the river Ystwyth crossed the road, descending along the bed of a deep gorge lined with trees, into the distant valley. But there were trees everywhere now—the magnificent oaks and beeches which the Herberts of old had planted, giving shade and a civilized beauty to the entrance of his domain.

So he turned in and followed the track which led through the green, damp-smelling gloom into a long, narrow valley through which the river flowed and where somewhere the old house stood among such scenes as he could never have imagined. Each new delight he saw surpassed everything, beggaring his powers of description.

Six years before, an English traveller called Henry Penruddocke Wyndham had passed by Hafod, making 'a serpentine course over the doubtful paths of a long morass, while the mountains around us appeared more horrible than any we had seen before. They were of a greater height and larger extent; while their tops ended in so many various and irregular shapes, and formed so undulating an horizon, that a warm imagination might almost conceive that the mountains were impelled and driven on by a supernatural storm, in immense waves and broken swells.' It was this very quality and effect of wild drama which moved Johnes to raptures, which were repeated again and again as the scene unfolded, disclosing ever more rocky masses of extraordinary shape and outline, more precipices, chasms and cascades, enclosing the valley like a jewel, and effectively isolating it from the outer world.

The old house was still inhabited. Paynter had been dead five years, and probably a farmer or a keeper was occupying it when Johnes, in a maze of enchantment, rode up to its door. Although nothing if not luxurious in his habits and requirements, even this ramshackle lodging could not reduce his enthusiasm. He had completely surrendered himself to the strange power this valley possessed of capturing the imagination and enchaining the senses of those susceptible to its influence. His impressionable nature and ingrained love of romantic scenery made him an easy victim. Never in his life had he been as deeply stirred; he would gladly have lingered there indefinitely. As for the inhabitants, they were alarmed and dismayed by the rapturous exclamations and benevolent inquiries of this most extraordinary gentleman. Such a landlord was quite outside their experience. A hectoring ruffian like Paynter or Herbert Lloyd was easier to understand than an enthusiastic and friendly young man who gave no signs of being either a drunkard or a bully like most of the gentry. Instead of assessing his rent-roll and extorting free labour from the peasants, he spent the days peacefully climbing about the hills discovering waterfalls and pretty views, a pursuit that would have kept him happily occupied for months.

He was no longer his own master, though. He had to remember that his wife was waiting for him to come and take her home, to that very different countryside where their lives would be spent. But though he rode away from Hafod after a day or two, unlike his forebears he was determined neither to forget nor to abandon it, and the unfortunate beings who scratched their living out of the rocky soil and slept at night in caves, or in malodorous huts among their beasts. He could not have forgotten it, even had he wanted to. It had done something to him which was going to make it impossible for him to forget it ever again for the rest of his life.

It is uncertain what his intentions were regarding Hafod at this time. In 1781, he was making new plantations there—possibly one of the few plans that fructified during those two years of anxiety and sorrow. The frail life of his delicate Maria was ebbing slowly, painfully away, while he carried her from place to place vainly seeking something that might cure her. In November 1781, they were staying at Bristol Hot-Wells when the news reached him of his uncle's death at Dolecothy.

'Do not ever hesitate in making any use of me,' he wrote immediately to Jane, 'for I now shall look upon myself in a more respectable light, having such a family to attend to.'

The words came straight from his heart. His longing for a family was as strong as ever. From the first months of his marriage he had been compelled to suffer the cruel experience of watching his young wife fading before his eyes while the future they had planned shrivelled in premature decay around them. So now his thoughts turned towards that lonely house by the river, a spot that meant much to him because of those who lived their simple lives there, close to nature. The idea of it appealed to him astonishingly, and of them all it was pretty Jenny who filled his thoughts most constantly.

This was destined to be a winter of endings; his marriage, too, was drawing to its close. In one last vain attempt to cheat the inevitable they moved after Christmas to Bath. And there, on 1st April 1782, Maria died. Nothing remains of her; no picture, lock of hair or scrap of handwriting to give us any inkling what she was like. We only know that she had a good character and that not many weeks before her death she sent to the ruined church at Hafod a set of silver Communion Plate inscribed with her name. This is all that is left of Maria Johnes.

By 1782 the imposing family picture which Croft Castle had framed for many long years had completely disintegrated. Every member of it was either dead or had left the country. The heir was a widower travelling in Europe to recover from his sorrows; its mistress, the redoubtable Dowager, had removed to London where, with her younger son and daughter, she occupied one of the fine new houses in Stratford Place. The cherished dreams of the Custos had come to naught; strangers sat in his place in the old castle which had been so dear to his heart.

By December of that year Johnes was home from his travels. Back in London, he was in excellent health and spirits, as his mother was very happy to see. She would have liked him to stay with her there for a time and his impatience to be off to Wales at such a bad season of the year very much surprised her. Nothing could dissuade him, however, and so as he was set on it she took the opportunity of sending in his care a 'very handsome Muff' as a present for Miss Jane.

Although, with his usual resilience, to all outward appearances he had recovered, inwardly he was in a state of turmoil, for his wife's death had completely overthrown his future. Park Lettice now belonged to her mother. The estate he had bought in Monmouthshire no longer interested him. Typically, he wanted to slam a door on all that phase of his life; to exclude every memory of his brief, ill-starred marriage. He was more adrift than he had ever been, not knowing what to do with himself. He felt quite incapable of making any decision. It was imperative that he should find something to do, for one thing was certain, and that was that he could never return to the purposeless, solitary drifting of his younger days. . . .

All this troubled him as he drove down to Wales, and the nearer he drew to that wild, westerly country the more conscious he became of a comfortable sense of home-coming. It was remarkable how it pulled him back to it; he found himself constantly dreaming and thinking about it. Of Hafod particularly; he could not forget those mountains. They haunted him, beckoning him all the time to come to them. What a setting they provided for a fine house, the artist in him busy with schemes while he played with the notion of going to live up there for good. In that direction he could perceive boundless opportunities for a life of usefulness, doing all the good he could to improve those wretched natives, the very thought of whom made him go hot with shame. His people . . . his responsibility . . . and, strangely enough, this was a responsibility he felt ready to embrace with open arms. Those lofty solitudes might easily be transformed into a perfect paradise. . . .

It was nearly Christmas by the time he arrived at Dolecothy with the muff for Jane, and, if he had recovered his spirits before, they were further improved at finding himself again in this little circle that he liked so well, seeing Jenny's pretty face glowing with happiness at having him there, in its frame of powdered curls. She was nearly twenty-four now and prettier than ever, though there had been little in her life to give her happiness, one melancholy event after another conspiring to keep her at home in that damp valley under the rugged hills. Theoretically, the simple life appealed irresistibly to Johnes, though he was far too much of a sybarite to be capable of leading it himself. But the idea of Jenny in Arcadia, baking and brewing, haymaking and threshing, besides looking after her mother and three little sisters, deeply impressed him. It stirred up something primeval in his blood, a strain that linked them together with the country that had bred them. The strong affinity between them made it possible for him to talk to her as he could to no one else. And so that Christmas, with the holly-berries red on the trees and the little vale transformed to fairyland with glistening frost and icicles like swords suspended from the eaves, and all that nameless excitement and mystery a spell of cold weather brings, they talked and walked together. Every day his affection for her ripened, his admiration increased; slight and small as she was, and highly strung, she had a strength of will that astonished him, while her warm response stirred his enthusiasm for Hafod to a blaze. There must have been tears in her eyes as she listened to his accounts of the poor people there, for her emotional heart was as kind and charitable as his own. And if her tears were not altogether caused by the thought of their sufferings, who can blame her? How sad and lonely life at Dolecothy was for an ardent, vital girl, and what wonderful possibilities her cousin unfolded and spread before her hungry gaze. She had no manner of doubt where his duty lay, and with Jenny beside him it did not seem very difficult after all to make up his mind.

Once back in London again, things did not look quite as simple. He dared not even hint at what he was thinking about, in Stratford Place, for they would all be up in arms at once. The Dowager's cold nature and hard common sense made a barbed fence between them that he shied away from; he would go to any lengths sooner than incur her obloquy. Nor was there much encouragement to be had from his friends when he rapturously described his mountains to them. They were aghast at his wildcat scheme of burying himself in the wilds, dedicating his life and fortune to reforming a pack of barbarians. Even to suggest abandoning his valuable Herefordshire properties and Croft Castle for an isolated wilderness that no one had ever even heard of seemed the summit of insanity, as they did not hesitate to tell him.

The project was, of course, in some respects very much in keeping with the trend of the period—that arrogant individualism which was at once the glory and the curse of the privileged circle of rich, enterprising young men to which Johnes belonged. It was the root from which sprang an astonishing growth of eccentricities that found expression not only in fantastic structures of bricks and mortar but also in spectacular attempts at altering the whole face of a countryside, often to no other end than to create a fine view. Most of his friends with places in the country occupied themselves with improving and embellishing them, though that was altogether different from what he was contemplating doing. If he wanted an occupation, he had much better apply himself seriously to politics, or take up some other form of public service. Under this barrage of sound advice, he was once more all at sea. An inveterate dreamer of dreams, he was always a little ashamed of the inherent weakness that prevented him from soaring to the heights in some profession. Now he resolved to bridle his vacillating nature and do as his friends counselled. When we hear of him next it is already April. He had rented a house in Berkeley Square where his old friend Robert Liston was staying with him.

Liston was now a rising diplomatist, through the good offices of his friend and former pupil Hugh Elliot, who, when he had entered the foreign service, had made Liston his private secretary. They had been together in Munich, Ratisbon and Berlin. Earlier this year, Liston had been secretary of embassy at Madrid where Lord Mountstuart was ambassador, and now he had been recalled to London where he was waiting for an important announcement to be made. This serious, ambitious, hard-working man did all he could to steel his friend's purpose, urging him to follow his own example, for Johnes's aptitude for mastering foreign languages admirably fitted him for diplomacy. inevitably in Johnes's sanguine mind, all kinds of glowing pictures sprang to life. He foresaw future dignities like those his friend was now awaiting with grave suavity, besides all the excitement and interest of posts abroad, the hum and bustle of affairs, the splendid entertainments. . . .

Liston's excellent advice was prevailing when suddenly, to their dismay, another guest arrived at Berkeley Square in the blubbering, protesting person of young John Johnes, Jane's only brother, who had run away from Charterhouse where he had arrived for the first time only a few days earlier. This spoilt darling of his mother and sisters had never been farther from home than Carmarthen in his life. The rough-and-tumble of an English public school had scared him out of his wits. Not knowing where else to go to, he presented himself at his cousin's house demanding to be sent straight home to Wales.

Johnes took him in, and while he fruitlessly attempted to persuade him to be a good boy and go back to school he wrote distractedly to Jenny, begging her to keep the matter to herself, for he dreaded the effect it might have on his aunt. After several stormy days, the naughty boy had his own way and went off on the Welsh coach, leaving his host in a state of nervous prostration. 'It has wore me away,' he wrote to Jenny, 'and could I have avoided it this dagger should have remained in my own breast. . . . However John's behaviour may have alienated my affections from him, be assured they are stronger for you than ever and you and your sisters may and ever shall command my every service.'

How many other daggers had he not plunged in poor Jenny's breast throughout the years! And now at far-away Dolecothy, as she read and reread these words, the still air of the valley was lush with spring. Out of the living earth it came leaping forth in tender buds and blades, while cascades of young leaves rippled their lovely green across the trees. Daffodils and primroses were blowing in the garden, where the nesting birds sang and the cries of new-born creatures sounded from the fields. Wherever she went, there it was proclaiming its joyous message of fulfilment, to quicken her wrought-up emotions and intensify the terrible feeling of loneliness and frustration. What was she to make of his affectionate protestations, with him in London, fast in the toils of that wretched Mr. Liston whom she knew was bent on carrying him off to some horrid foreign land. Now that he was out of Wales and far from her own good influence, it was improbable that he would long withstand the arguments of his friends. There was his family to be counted with besides; his mother with all her money had a great hold on him. They would stop at nothing to keep him away from Hafod. The future seemed utterly hopeless; not a ray of light glimmered in the darkness of her days as, with tortured heart, she pursued her tedious round. She was virtually a prisoner, bound hand and foot by her duty to her mother and sisters, washing and cooking and slaving for them while the years slipped by, till very soon all that was left of her youth would be lost in loveless middle age. The bright dreams which only a few months ago had seemed likely to come true had turned into a trail of torturing thorns. Why could they not leave him in peace to do as he liked! He longed to go to Hafod, to make it beautiful and spend his life caring for the poor people there. Nevertheless, and with a breaking heart, she realized how remote the possibility had become.

On 20th May it was published from St. James's that Robert Liston had been appointed Minister Plenipotentiary at Madrid, and it was settled that Johnes should accompany him as his secretary of embassy. Weeks of good advice had succeeded, to the relief of his family and friends. They set out together early in June and at first Johnes was in the highest spirits, full of cheerful expectations. But as they drove across the sun-scorched plains of France he became more and more subdued, his spirit wilting at the prospect of his new and weighty tasks. All the old terror of being tied, of being deprived of his freedom, began to play havoc with his resolve. He had been his own master for too long for it to be possible for him to submit to authority. . . . As the sun beat down on the ambassadorial travelling carriage his eyes ached damnably from the dust and the glare and he found himself yearning with ever-greater longing for the cool, sweet air of the mountains, their softly glowing hues, the space and freedom there and all the congenial occupations that might fill the rest of his life. Tender thoughts of Jenny mingled with these longings, for without her loving companionship and support they would lose half their savour.

What Liston had to say on the subject can only be surmised, but whatever he may have felt at the time it did not seriously affect their friendship. When they arrived at Madrid, Johnes relinquished his appointment without taking it up, and, thoroughly restless and unsettled in spirit, and perhaps somewhat ashamed of himself, he set out for Paris. There he remained for a few weeks and there he made up his mind. Let them all do and say what they chose, he no longer cared! He would yield to no one, surrender his convictions to none! With a glorious feeling of freedom, and an unbending purpose, he departed for England, with Dolecothy and Miss Jane as his first port of call.

CHAPTER VI

The Wilderness Shall Flourish

To a Cardiganshire even more derelict than it was in his father's time, Johnes returned as its champion that autumn of 1783. All the more important places stood empty. Sir Herbert Lloyd's nephew had spent his estate and emptied Peterwell; and from Crosswood the family had migrated to Devonshire. The son of the Custos's old antagonist now reigned as fourth viscount, but although he was Lord Lieutenant he seldom came to the county, and then never for more than a few days. Other reasons applied to other derelict houses; scarcely a family of standing remained save those who were either too poor or too unenterprising to move away. Thus the astonishing return of the heir of Croft Castle to the old, half-ruined house up at Hafod, dumbfounded them all.

His decision was reinforced by the whole weight of his obstinacy which would increase as time went on. The abuse he met with on all sides only made him more obdurate. He was determined to fool them all before he had done. In a not far distant future his exploits in the beautiful land he was determined to bring before the public would be acclaimed far and wide. He was consumed with the spirit of pioneering; there was a wild exhilaration at finding himself standing alone upon his mountain-top, championing it against the world. He held the keys of a treasure-house second to none; in a short while even the over-rated meadows of Herefordshire would not surpass in fruitfulness those of Hafod.

He was more enraptured with the place than ever. Its magnificent natural scenery provided wonderful material to work on; none of his friends had anything to compare with it. The strong air and virgin spaces fed body and spirit alike with healthy contentment; he had never felt stronger or on better terms with himself. There was utmost relief in knowing that he had come home at last to where he belonged; that for the future all he had should be dedicated to it. Already he had set in train the vast operations that would transmute the wilderness into Paradise. Every able-bodied man in the vicinity had been pressed into his army of labourers who were building a rough stone wall round the eight square miles of moor and mountain which he had marked out for his demesne. Nothing seemed able to daunt him as he rode up and down the hills planning their metamorphosis. Imbued with brimming optimism, he felt himself more than a match for every obstacle, and his remarkable faculty for only seeing what he wished to see facilitated everything. It never occurred to him that his high expectations might be unreasonable; they were simply the inevitable rewards of his exertions.

None of the local wiseacres, of course, agreed with him but as he airily waved aside their discouraging prognostications he reflected that they, too, encrusted with archaic notions and prejudices, should benefit from what Hafod could teach them. As for these kinsmen and old squires who had known and respected his father, they soon found it was useless to say anything to the cocksure son: not only did he not listen, but he belonged to a different world whose deluded inhabitants believed they could conquer whatever they chose with their powerful weapons of gold. Let him try, said the old men balefully; the old rocks up at Hafod, with their thin skin of anaemic soil, would empty his pockets and break his teeth fast enough.

The wildest reports of his doings flew round the county. He gave them plenty to talk about, for the rumours were by no means restricted to Hafod. What was taking him down to Dolecothy every so often, asked the gossips with winks and knowing looks. It was true that the Captain's widow lay dying, but they could wager that it was more than a dutiful nephew's anxiety which accounted for Colonel Johnes's frequent journeys thither and the protracted stays he was said to be making there all through that autumn and winter. It was not very difficult to guess, in spite of the mystery which shrouded everything that went on there, that pretty Miss Jane had a good deal to say to it. He looked far more like a bridegroom than an anxious nephew as he spanked along the road in his curricle, his lively, commanding features glowing with an inner satisfaction, under the wide brim of his high-crowned beaver. Such a picture of energy and riches had seldom been seen on those lonely roads, though people did not particularly care about the disturbance his newfangled ideas threatened to create. Always supposing, of course, that anything came of them, for the chances were that before very long he would wash his hands of Hafod as a bad job. They had not got his measure by a long chalk.

Not a thought of the kind entered his head during those tedious drives to Dolecothy. His spirits had never been higher or his mind more inflexible, with defiance as the spur. He had broken away from his old life for good and all; his bridges and boats were smouldering wrecks in the wide gulf that separated him from it and his indignant mother in Stratford Place. However bitter the winds were that came roaring from the hills and whistling up the valleys to whip him raw through the thick cloth coat buttoned up to his chin, or merciless the drenching rains, they could not detract one tittle from his enthusiasm. Even the melancholy gleam of the water-logged fields with their burthen of withered rushes, incited his zeal. It was all fuel to his reforming flame.

Nothing was lacking in this enchanted epoch. He had found

not only his true home but also his true love. Therefore, however unprepossessing it may have looked to others, for him the wintry landscape shone with the glory encompassing everything. The tousled branches and brambles spangled with rain, glittered with a thousand jewels. The sombre grandeur of the hills looming against the heavy skies pleasantly excited his romantic imagination, just as the gaunt cattle in the fields gave an added picturesqueness to this remarkable country. Whichever way he looked he was bound to see something that thrilled his bursting spirits as with the eager impatience of a lover he urged his horse forward. Though again and again he must have railed against the cruel fate that separated him from his dearest Jenny, whose love and trust upheld him, the light of her pretty eyes irradiating his world. She was and would be for ever his dear companion in this great adventure. Without her to weld him indissolubly to the land that had bred them, he would still have been hopelessly lost. As it was, however, he was very comfortably settled, without a doubt or uncertainty in his mind to cast distracting shadows across his path.

For at some period during this autumn irresolution had been banished for good and all. He had married Jenny secretly, though where and when the ceremony took place will probably never be known. An ambiguous affair altogether, for the bride continued to be known as 'Miss Jane', living at home at Dolecothy looking after her poor mamma. No wonder tongues were wagging as the sturdy bridegroom was seen hurrying from one end of the county to the other, his face shining with health and happiness. In spite of all the mystery enveloping it, the neighbours knew far more about it than we ever shall, for every difficulty has conspired to keep the facts obscure. Even the pages from the register belonging to the church near Dolecothy where all the family's weddings and christenings took place, are missing for the years 1783–4. They may have been torn out later on purpose, or they may not. The indisputable fact remains that the child of Thomas and Jane Johnes was born on 30th June 1784, although nothing else is known. Jenny was still addressed as Miss Jane, and a tradition lingers still, in the village of Llanfair Clydogau, that her little daughter was born in the old manor-house there which the Custos had deserted. This secluded spot may conceivably have served as a convenient retreat for what can only be regarded as a very awkwardly managed business. The infant, who was named Maria Anne, though destined to be known by the far more romantic appellation of Mariamne, was ten months old before her formidable grandmother in London was informed of her existence. For it was not until April 1785, when 'Miss Jane' was staying at Hafod, that Johnes wrote to tell his young brother-in-law that in future he should address his sister as 'Mrs. Johnes', for his mother had been informed of their marriage two days ago.

This certainly did not help to make the relationship between Jane and the Dowager a happy one, though in any case that worldly lady would not have welcomed the Captain's penniless daughter as a wife for her son. There is little doubt that it was fear of his mother that caused him to hide it. As for Mrs. Jane, the 'sincere regard' which she had once felt for Mrs. Johnes had by this time evaporated completely, giving place to an obdurate hostility which increased in fervour with every year that passed.

By 1785, in any case, the married pair were happily and openly living together at Hafod with their child, and Jane's brother and sisters paying long visits, for it was to be a home to all of them. The place looked like a vast, untidy hive with legions of labourers crawling about, digging, hewing, planting; making roads and building bridges; the dull boom of explosions reverberating round the hills as miners blasted away inconvenient rocks. There was nothing to stop Johnes. He had all the money he needed, for he had sold his Monmouthshire estate, though later on he complained that in his haste to dispose of it he had dropped about £30,000. He was eager to get the money, for the work at Hafod had to be pushed on as rapidly as possible. His intention was to bring the place to such a flourishing pitch that when the renegade squires saw how profitable and pleasant their despised patrimonies might be made, they would come flocking home eager to emulate him.

Many of his motives were altruistic, bred by that strong desire for the public welfare which he and his wife had so much at heart. He held it to be a landlord's duty to spend at least part of the income he drew from his estates in improving them and giving work to the people. He estimated that the absentees belonging to the northern part of the county alone, between them drew about £25,000 annually in rents, not one penny of which ever benefited the lands that yielded it. This he believed was the main cause of the prevailing wretchedness. In the new house that he was proposing to build, everything should be assembled that made for beauty and contentment; humanism, industry and the arts should combine to form a perfect design for living. The renown of Hafod would not be limited to Wales; he intended to attract the rich and enterprising from all over England who should see for themselves what wonderful advantages this unknown country offered. Some would certainly wish to buy land in order to build a picturesque villa as an object for their summer excursions. The natives would profit vastly from the influx of visitors and become very different from the poor savages they were at present.

A Welsh Tour had become very fashionable, but owing to the difficulties of getting there, Cardiganshire had hitherto been excluded from the itinerary. This was a mistake, for, as Johnes maintained, nowhere could picturesque beauties be seen to greater advantage. Those who loved mountains invariably craved for the sea as well, and Cardiganshire had a superb coast and splendidly bracing sea air. The little sea-port of Aberystwyth, which was only sixteen miles from Hafod, and its nearest town, was beginning to be known as a watering-place. At present, however, it was chiefly resorted to by tradespeople from Birmingham and other towns near the Welsh border. Johnes aimed at bringing a more distinguished clientèle who, once having tasted its delights, would return again year after year.

The difficulties of reaching it were considerable even for those days. There was not a post-chaise to be hired in the whole county or for forty-three miles north of Aberystwyth. The roads were appalling and there were scarcely any bridges. The discomforts of the journey have been vividly described by a young woman with a lively pen named Catherine Hutton, who travelled there from Birmingham in 1787. She complained that the road was often so narrow that their carriage entirely filled it and sometimes it ran along the side of a mountain without even a bank to preserve them from the precipice. Now and again the track faded out across open sheep pastures or carried them along the stony channel of a brook. Her party halted at an inn not very far from Hafod, and whilst the provisions they had brought with them were being prepared for their dinner the intrepid Miss Hutton explored the house. It consisted of one room downstairs and the upper part also 'consisted of one room only, to which I mounted by a ladder and which I entered by a small aperture left in the floor. This aperture conveyed all the light and air permitted to enter the apartment; for windows and chimney it had none. It had, however, three beds, one for the master and mistress of the house, one for their servant, and one for the accommodation of any traveller who might be so unfortunate as to be obliged to sleep there.' The beds were divided from each other by 'neat mats', which reached from floor to ceiling. She was not very much attracted by Aberystwyth, which she described as a 'poor, petty place'. Johnes, on the contrary, thought it quite delightful and frequently spent a few days there for the bathing and sea breezes. His friends would be as pleased with it as he was.

It was not until June 1786 that the foundation stone of the new house was laid by Mrs. Jane Johnes, as an inscription placed thereon recorded. The architect was Thomas Baldwin, the city architect of Bath. The house he designed perfectly accorded with the idea of a mountain paradise—an elegant Gothic fantasy, all pointed windows and pinnacles, like a miniature fairy palace. It was placed at the head of the valley, sheltered by mounting woods, while in front of it lawns swept gently downwards towards the river. Everything was done that Johnes's extravagant imagination could devise to increase its splendour. French looms were employed in weaving Gobelin tapestries for the drawing-room; blocks of rare marble were brought over from Italy to be carved into exquisite chimney pieces and classical statues by his friend, the famous sculptor Banks. Although Johnes already possessed immense collections of works of art of every description, he went on buying recklessly, without a thought of the cost, all and everything to make Hafod more perfect.

As the house gradually rose and took shape, acres of young trees were being drawn across the mountain-sides; while miles of ornamental walks intersected the demesne. The natural waterfalls and grottoes in which it abounded were opened up into their full glory, and elegant bridges were thrown across the rivers and ravines. Johnes took an active part in it all, wading waist-deep up the river to find the perfect position for a seat or a grot. Gardens had long ago been laid out; and, since paradise was the motif, there was a real little Garden of Eden hidden among the woods at the end of a shady path above the river, entered by a stone gateway carved with the figures of Adam and Eve. This was Jane's flower-garden; two acres of undulating lawns embroidered with flower-borders and sweet-smelling shrubs. It was designed to create the effect of a pattern of jewels flung down in the green glade, at the very feet of a steep, jagged mass of rock which soared above it for several hundreds of feet. There was never such a beautiful or unexpected situation for a garden, although their friends were only too ready to point out that it got scarcely any sun. Nearly everyone was anxious to find fault with all their embryo wonders. But they were so perfectly happy themselves, certain of the infallibility of their plans, that they could laugh derision away. In another year or two their visitors would be dumbfounded by what they would see there—the brilliant display of flowers and fruit in the gardens, crops of wheat flourishing among the rocks, and herds of sleek cattle knee-deep in the juicy grass of the meadows by the river.

It was not only the discouragement of the gentry that had to be countered; the peasants met their friendly advances with deepest suspicion and unconcealed dislike. A magnanimously disposed ruling class actuated by entirely disinterested motives was altogether too great a phenomenon to be believed in. They had no wish at all to be improved or interfered with. The idea of being turned out of the huts and holes which their fathers before them had inhabited filled them with terror, even though they were offered the superior shelter of brand-new cottages. Though they scowled and grumbled, they were glad enough all the same to eat the good dinners and wear the warm garments that were being freely distributed, and which sooner or later it was hoped would bring them to a better way of thinking.

Thus steadily, year by year, money flowed like a golden tide across the barren wastes, until they assumed quite another form and character. The magical properties of gold had triumphed once again, though the mountains proved as voracious as wolves, swallowing up everything and howling out for more. But Johnes, with his boundless faith in them as sources of certain wealth, was not dismayed. Being obstinately convinced of the inexhaustibility of his fortune, there was nothing to make him pause or think again, in spite of the warnings and reproaches that were constantly being hurled at him from Stratford Place.

Both were far too happy in their marriage for anything to affect them. Jane's life had burst into flower with an abundance such as she could scarcely have dreamed of. Everything the world had to offer was poured into her lap. Their palace in the mountains was growing more wonderful each day, and she had boundless opportunities for sharing her good fortune with others. She had not a wish or a whim that her husband did not

Plaster bust of Jane Johnes by Thomas Banks

Dolecothi, showing the wings added by John Nash in 1795
(Subsequently altered and now entirely demolished)

Hafod (by J P Neale, c. 1820)

gratify; there was nothing she might not see and enjoy. By no means all the year was spent in the seclusion of Hafod. Johnes had his regiment to attend to occasionally and parliamentary duties that took them to London. Jane travelled in grandeur in a coach and four; she had all the fine dresses, the jewels, fans and costly trinkets that her heart could covet. She was taken to visit her husband's friends in their Palladian mansions and romantic castles buried in deep parks. In London she attended routs and ridottos, and certainly Johnes lost no time before he presented her to his friend, the awe-inspiring, majestic-looking Lord Chancellor Thurlow, known in the Law Courts as 'Tiger' Thurlow because of the savage way he would pounce upon and maul to death some luckless counsel or solicitor. Charming to look at and adaptable though she was, it must have been an intimidating experience, for Thurlow was formidable from every aspect. Black and swarthy as a Spaniard, his sparkling eyes could flash with annihilating fury, 'a look of Jove when he grasped the thunder', that was made even more terrible by his famous eyebrows which bristled above them like overgrown bushes. Although he habitually expressed himself with coarse energy, lavishly interlarded with vulgar pleasantries, we have Sheridan's testimony that 'however rough he might be with men, he was the politest person in the world to ladies'. Fifteen years older than Johnes, he remained his staunch friend to the end, and it would seem as though he approved of his choice, for he paid them several visits at Hafod during the years that followed.

Then there were the celebrated Sunday evening parties at the house of another of Johnes's friends, Sir Joseph Banks, the distinguished President of the Royal Society, who in his younger days had accompanied Captain Cook on his voyage to the South Seas. There all the world of fashion, literature and science congregated and visitors from all over the world appeared. Sometimes on their way to town they stayed at Coldbrook or at Bath with the Hanbury Williamses, and again at Bath Jane might mingle with the rank and fashion who gathered there, to dip in the waters by day and to play cards and dance in the Assembly Rooms at night, by the light of wax-tapers reflected in flower-wreathed glasses.

During the winter of 1786–7 she was painted by Romney in a large family group which included, besides Johnes and his sister Anne, two of his friends. In his choice of the artist he may have been influenced by Thurlow, who had pronounced this weighty judgment: 'Reynolds and Romney divide the town, I am of the Romney faction.'

In point of fact Johnes had commissioned the picture some years earlier, at the time of his first marriage, and it had actually been begun, though presumably Maria's ill health prevented its completion. For years the unfinished canvas had been stacked up among all the others that filled Romney's studio in Cavendish Square, keeping company with the frail and pretty ladies whose lovers had discarded them after a sitting or two and had no further desire to be reminded of them. Now, after seven years, the Johnes group was rescued from this limbo and dusted; poor Maria was painted out and the glowing Jane put in her place, in the fashionable disguise of a gipsy. When the picture was exhibited at the Royal Academy, this was archly alluded to by a gossiping writer in *The World*, who reported that 'Mr. and Mrs. Johnes, another lady, Major Lewis and Mr. Cook, are in a family piece. Mrs. Johnes is representing a gipsy, narrative and prophetic, telling all she knew. With Mrs. Johnes all is well. But inferior artists and worse judges of life and manners than Romney must be careful not to mimic the idea too far. There are some families in the kingdom where such a picture of the lady telling all she knew would be a libel, though a likeness.'

Banks was, of course, invited to immortalize Jane in marble, for Johnes was one of his most generous patrons and had a warm affection for the man as well as a great admiration for the artist. His name is now largely forgotten, but in his day he enjoyed a high reputation. The simplicity and goodness of his character, his frugal way of life and his complete absorption in perfecting his craft, strongly appealed to Johnes, and Banks spent many summers at Hafod. He made a portrait bust of Jane's charming head with her rich curls drooping on to her shoulders, and besides this she and the little Mariamne served as models for a classical piece. This came in for high praise from the *Morning Post* when it was exhibited at the Academy in 1789 on no less than three different occasions, and twice Jane's merits were publicly hailed. Thus on 28th August that year, had she been in London, she might have read as she sipped her morning chocolate:

'Banks advances very forward in his beautiful sculpture. The Thetis, we understand, is intended as a likeness of Mrs. Johnes, the Lady of the Member for Radnorshire. What degree of similitude there is we know not, but if the artist has not flattered, she is highly beautiful and elegant.'

And again on 26th November of the same year:

'The Thetis dipping Achilles in the Styx is in great forwardness, and will be one of the works in which Britain should pride itself, tho' looking with reverence towards the delicious remains of antiquity. Thetis, as we have previously observed, is a portrait of Mrs. Johnes . . . a lady whose worth and accomplishments entitle her even to the celebration of such an artist as Banks.'

A bewildering diversity of experiences and changes separated her from her girlhood at Dolecothy; now, when she thought of that horrid place, standing 'quite in a pool' as she complained, she shuddered and urged her brother to pull it down as soon as he came of age. The mists that swam up from the Cothi and crept among the trees conveniently obliterated all she no longer cared to be reminded of—the full sum of which we shall never gauge. She had found in her new life of luxury and extravagance her natural element, and only too willingly forgot the contrivances and economies she had been forced to practise in the days when she had barely ten guineas of her own to spend in a year.

In all the brilliant whirl of married life she never forgot her sisters, Mary Anne, Eliza and Charlotte, nor did her husband neglect his promise to attend to them in every way. He adopted the lot of them, and Hafod was as much their home as Dolecothy. Jane must undoubtedly have been the pick of the bunch, for all of the others are scarcely more than names; shadowy little figures hovering in the background, looking after Mariamne and coming in to dinner. Jane, the successful and possessive eldest sister, continued to manage their lives, and if they were not always as grateful as they should have been, it is not to be wondered at. What is Paradise to some to others is often something quite different. Charlotte certainly was never happy there, and constantly complained of the cold. When she came of age she took the bit between her teeth and went to India. It was a bold step for a girl to take in those days, but Charlotte took it and 'went to live with strangers', presumably as governess or something of the kind. After four years of tropical sunshine she came back again and nothing else seems to have happened to her. In spite of all the opportunities Hafod afforded them of meeting bachelors of every degree among the constant streams of visitors, Mary Anne was the only one who married, and she looked no further afield for her bridegroom than a Carmarthenshire squarson whose little property adjoined Dolecothy.

Jane's favourite unquestionably was her brother. John Johnes was delicate, weak-willed and regrettably like the Captain. When he was old enough, much against his wishes, he was put in the army, a choice of profession that was far from judicious, for his brother-officers were a hard-drinking lot whose example he was not slow in following. Jane wrote to him constantly, priming her letters with good advice and working herself up into great states of alarm when as often as not he did not trouble to reply. Not long after he came of age, without consulting anyone, he sold his commission and retired to Dolecothy where he spent his life in much the same way as his father had done before him, with the result that he died before he was fifty of gout in his head.

The Wilderness Shall Flourish

At last, in the late spring of 1788, the new house at Hafod was finished. The builders departed, the furniture was brought in, and Jane sat down at the escritoire in her magnificent drawing-room, among the Gobelin tapestries, to announce the great tidings.

'from the New House
'Hafod May ye 7th. 1788.

'My dear Brother,

'You shall have the pleasure of having the first letter I ever wrote from this house last Monday we came here. We are at present in glorious confusion and you are safe this part from having a sermon. I am happy you took the last as it was really meant I return you a great many thanks for your letter. . . . You are very saucy about my flower garden. I assure you 'tis in high beauty. The kitching garden is going on very fast three fruit houses flourish and the trees in full blow. I think we shall have some fruit this year. Min is very well and will be a prodigious scholar again you come here, she drinks your health every day.'

Min was the little name they gave to Mariamne, now a fair, delicate and precociously intelligent child of nearly four, worshipped by both her parents, all the more ardently perhaps because they knew that she was likely to remain their only one.

CHAPTER VII

The Happy Valley

Their dream came true: the fame of Hafod spread throughout the kingdom. The bold experiment had captured the public interest; everywhere it was acclaimed that out of the arid heart of 'a stormy sea of bleak, denuded hills' a paradise unique in its generation had sprung in response to the golden touch of the great magician, Johnes. As for himself, his engrossing vocation had turned him into a very different man from the vacillating dilettante of former years. His mountains had imbued him with their own rugged and unyielding characteristics. His energy and enthusiasm charged the thriving scene, although it had not perceptibly infected the natives who worked as slowly and indifferently as ever. Owing to this, it was necessary to employ double the number of labourers that would have been necessary in any other country, which, of course, added considerably to the expense. In other ways however they had improved wonderfully. Good food and decent accommodation had put new heart into them and friendly smiles had taken the place of the old scowls. Each midday a gong boomed from a hill-top summoning the men to their dinner; there was a school on the estate for the girls and small boys, and free medical attention and medicaments were available for everyone. Nothing that could improve the lot of the poor people was neglected, for the great purpose was to abolish the tyranny and ignorance that still prevailed among the landowners, by pointing the way by practical example to a more civilized and enlightened way of life.

The same beneficent spirit was to be found all over Hafod. The demesne was open to everyone; so were the principal rooms in the house, with their pictures and other treasures, while the books and manuscripts in the library were available to all who brought an introduction. Johnes liked to call it the Happy Valley, after the ideal abode in *Rasselas*, and a very happy place it was for all of them. Their own extraordinary felicity shed its beams on all around. The blood of the old Herberts, strong in their veins, bound these married cousins ever closer to their mountains; it had swept them back to the source of their origins and now impelled them to identify themselves with it increasingly as year succeeded year. But if it was the clamouring of his Celtic forebears that brought him to Hafod, it was the intuitive feeling for beauty and design that he derived from the English Knights which made it possible for Johnes to handle it with such skill.

The estate resembled nothing more than a vast, skilfully planted garden; a green garden, intersected with raked and weeded paths, ornamented at convenient points where a foaming torrent or a view made it desirable to pause, with picturesque seats and temples. On the lower slopes and along the valley by the river there was abundant grazing now for a large herd of cows; formerly there had scarcely been sustenance for two. Arable lands in ochreous and viridescent strips and patches were suspended among the rocks at angles that suggested an artist's rather than a farmer's hand.

Johnes had to a large extent the qualities and failings of an artist. Therein lay Hafod's strong appeal for him, for it afforded him boundless opportunities for self-expression. With Nature as his medium, he had an unusual and arduous ground for his endeavours; a haunted, haunting spot which he treated perfectly.

His effects were enhanced by Hafod's own peculiar aura that had, perhaps, been imparted to it in far-off times by ancient rites of magic performed in the silence of its solitudes. A strange enchantment had been diffused that lingered over it, bemusing the senses and giving an added value to its beauties. Johnes, though unconsciously, was profoundly under its influence as he created a whole range of different scenes with an ingenuity that successfully disguised where art and nature mingled. His ideas, of course, closely followed the taste of his day. Not only was he well versed in its principles, but he also had the advantage of being guided and encouraged by the two great authorities on the picturesque treatment of landscape—Richard Payne Knight and Uvedale Price, both of whom came frequently to Hafod.

Payne Knight was by far the most interesting and distinguished member of the big Knight clan, and one of Johnes's closest friends and supporters. They had many of the same tastes and characteristics, as well as a certain family resemblance. In Payne Knight the long, clever nose and protruding blue eyes were combined with a small, receding chin—suggesting an irritable, emotionally unstable temperament. A good deal taller than his Welsh cousin, he presented an altogether more elegant and imposing figure, and one that the foolish did well to avoid, for he suffered them not at all. His talents and energies had been assiduously cultivated from an early age, in the forcing-house of a delicate childhood spent at home, with books as his principal companions. He was an insatiable reader and at Downton would sometimes read for ten hours at a stretch when the weather was too bad for him to indulge in his other great passion of chasing the fox. His powers of enjoyment, both sensual and intellectual, were astonishingly acute, and there was not a subject under the sun that he could not talk about with authority, although not always accurately. Like Johnes, he could not stand being contradicted, but though their tastes differed in some respects this did not succeed in parting them. Payne Knight certainly could not have enthused over the immense marble statues that were everywhere at Hafod, for on the whole he disliked them and had succeeded in persuading himself that the greatest artists of antiquity 'rarely condescended to touch marble'. His own passion was for the exquisite early Egyptian and Etrurian bronzes, which satisfied his taste for the minute and delicate. He was a most persevering collector and in London tirelessly searched the shops belonging to the brokers and dealers for coins, medals and gems which he sought as assiduously as he did for beautiful bronzes. He already ranked as one of the leading connoisseurs and the accredited expert upon everything relating to classical antiquities.

His house in London was the centre of a brilliant circle as well as being a museum for his collections. Horace Walpole, whose own star was on the wane, acidly dubbed him 'the Knight of the Brazen Milk pot', though with far greater justice he might have been termed 'the Knight of the Ideal Landscape', for he extended his jurisdiction into the very core of the English countryside. His love of nature was as strong and as highly developed as his love of art, and in this field his companion-at-arms was his friend and neighbour Uvedale Price. Price was the intimate friend of Gainsborough and Reynolds and an energetic improver of his own estate. Like Knight, he regarded nature with the eyes of a painter, seeing the landscape as a series of pictures which it was his purpose to perfect by dint of judicious readjustment and careful addition. Both he and Knight were enthusiastic exponents of the picturesque, aiming at creating 'natural' effects. In order that this should be achieved, all nature's roughnesses and irregularities, such as the blasted oak and savage rock, had to be preserved and given their proper place 'with secret skill and *counterfeit* neglect', thereby enhancing the 'verdant Landscape'. There were no lengths Payne Knight would not go to produce the perfect scene, at Downton even building a farm-house to resemble a Gothic church, much to the pious indignation of at least one tourist who was appalled by this blasphemous travesty of a 'sacred edifice'.

These two rich and erudite Herefordshire gentlemen travelled about England together, visiting their acquaintances and advising them how to improve their estates according to the doctrines which each of them set out in print and published in 1794: Knight in the form of a long didactic poem entitled *The Landscape*. Price in a series of *Essays on the Picturesque*. As guests they occasionally offended their hosts by the critical and disapproving looks which with the arrogance of self-appointed arbiters, they did nothing to mitigate. Thus when they visited Lord Lansdowne at Bowood, the old statesman, who in his younger days had fought gloriously at Minden and held the rank of General in the Army, appeared to be somewhat affronted by their bold criticism of his pleasure grounds. He was no doubt exceedingly satisfied with them, for they had been laid out for him by Capability Brown, the great improver of parks and gardens in the preceding generation. If Lord Lansdowne had but known it, Knight and Price were tireless in denouncing the circular clumps of trees with which Brown had loved to dot the landscape and his serpentine lakes. It did not escape them, at Bowood, that his lordship fixed them with cold surprise, for afterwards Knight remarked complacently to Price: 'He does not know that we are great doctors.'

At Hafod the doctors could say what they chose without offending, for they were as pleased with the mountains as Johnes himself. Indeed, these perfectly conformed to what good taste required of mountains, being savage but not so high as to 'shame the high-spreading oak, or lofty tower'. The praise of two such experts inevitably had favourable repercussions on public opinion. There were never two more appreciative and stimulating guests, though the poor little Miss Johneses were frightened to death by the clever Mr. Knight and scarcely dared open their mouths. Uvedale Price was of a more genial and jolly disposition, romping with little Min and appositely christening young John Johnes 'Uncle Bot'. He and his captivating wife, Lady Caroline, whom Reynolds had painted with the wide, wild eyes of a wood-nymph, were so much pleased with Cardiganshire and its coast that they bought a plot of land on the sea-front at Aberystwyth and engaged a little-known architect whom they found at Hafod to build them an elegant Gothic villa.

For Johnes had not long been installed in his new house before he was busily engaged on additions and alterations. This time he employed an architect-builder from Carmarthen to help him. John Nash, the future favourite of George IV and the architect of Regent Street and Buckingham Palace, had arrived penniless in Carmarthen a few years previously, where in partnership with one Saxon he had built up a good business for himself. How he contrived to do so is not known, but he had scarcely begun than he was lucky enough to attract the attention of an immensely rich Carmarthenshire gentleman, Mr. Vaughan of Golden Grove. Vaughan immediately ordered Nash to design him a bath, and was so much delighted with the plan the architect submitted that he rewarded him with a rouleau of guineas: 'the first money he received as a professional man' Nash, many years later, confided to Faringdon the diarist. From that instant he had prospered and was soon in a flourishing way, building everything from county gaols to classical mansions for the local squires. The Carmarthenshire gentry were considerably more prosperous than their poor brothers in Cardiganshire.

At Hafod Nash may have been responsible for the two long wings in a kind of ecclesiastical Gothic which are shown in the picture which Turner painted in 1798. For Uvedale Price he erected 'a singular building for his summer residence . . . in the gothic style, and castellated form, consisting of three octagon towers, with a balcony towards the sea'. John Johnes also employed him to make an addition to Dolecothy, but although this was eventually carried out according to Nash's design, another builder probably did the work, for Nash left Wales in 1796 and never went back. At first Johnes was delighted with the bullet-headed, pugnacious, amusing little craftsman, though later on he seems to have changed his opinion. Uvedale Price's villa at Aberystwyth must have encouraged him to believe that many others would follow Price's example. But, alas, none did. They came, they saw, they praised, and then they rode away again, one after another. . . .

Visitors arrived perpetually from all parts of the country. From Herefordshire came many of his former neighbours, part of the grand company that years ago had mightily impressed his little country cousin who now received them as their hostess with a charming dignity. Among them were many members of the Harley family. Martha and Fanny, the two rich sisters of that Earl of Oxford whose beautiful wife was so notoriously unfaithful that his children were known as the Harleian Miscellanae, were among Jane's greatest friends and stayed regularly at Hafod. Others came trundling down from London in coaches and chaises, and panting pedestrians of every degree arrived at the door. Scholarly parsons intending to publish the diary of their Welsh excursion; artists who made drawings of the waterfalls and glades; agriculturalists whom Johnes declared were astounded by his cornfields; and rustic sages humbly anxious to gain access to his library. One and all were instantly caught by its spell, and at the lowest estimate it must have been the greatest relief to reach such a haven of luxury after the hardships they had suffered on their way. The lavish hospitality extended to them cast an even rosier glow upon the scene. Even those who knew the place already always found something fresh to see and praise —another plantation or walk, or the last consignment of purchases just arrived by sea from London. Johnes was always devising novel adornments to charm the eye. A flock of peacocks had been loosed in the woods to pit their Oriental brilliance against the cooler hues of the countryside. And strange, beautiful-looking sheep of royal origin, merino sheep given by the King of Spain to His Majesty at Windsor, browsed upon the slopes. These had been sent to Johnes by his friend, Colonel Robert Fulke Greville, who was one of the King's equerries, in obedience to his royal master's desire 'to extend throughout the kingdom a general benefit'.

Charles and Robert Greville, the younger sons of the first Earl of Warwick, were great friends of Johnes, Charles, cold and self-possessed, with delicately chiselled features and a great air of breeding, was an enthusiastic collector of *objets de vertu.* Through his friend, Paul Sandby, the water-colour painter, he introduced into this country the process of aquatint engraving, but he made a far more important contribution to the art, as well as to the history of England, when in 1782 he introduced his mistress, Emma Hart, to his friend Romney, and four years later, with unsurpassed callousness and a cold eye on financial benefits, handed her over to the care of his uncle, Sir William Hamilton, the British Ambassador at Naples.

Both brothers were passionately interested in pictures and delighted in the society of artists. When Colonel Robert Greville made a tour through North Wales in 1792, he took two of them with him as his companions. Greville is frequently mentioned by Fanny Burney under the name of Colonel Wellbred: 'there cannot be a more amiable man—a man of manners, person, address, appearance and conversation—more pleasing—more delightful. . . . He is tall, his figure very elegant, and his face very handsome; he is sensible, well-bred, modest and intelligent.'

This paragon travelled through Wales in a phaeton with scarlet wheels, drawn by a pair of good-looking greys. With him were Julius Caesar Ibbetson and an excellent topographical draughtsman named John Smith who had been a great favourite of Lord Warwick's and had accompanied him to Italy. For this reason he was generally known as Warwick Smith. Ibbetson, that highly gifted painter of picturesque land and seascapes with sailors and rustic figures, had until lately been the victim of endless frustration and fearful calamities both in his domestic and professional life. Poverty and ill health had dogged him from his eighteenth year when, penniless and without friends, he had left Hull and his work as a ship-painter, to seek his fortune in London. Only quite recently, thanks to a Captain Baillie who had recognized his talent and introduced him to Lord Warwick and other art-loving noblemen, his prospects had taken an upward bend. He was such excellent company, so obliging and with an endless fund of interesting and amusing information, that they were only too pleased to have him to stay at their houses for weeks at a time. High-life had gone to Ibbetson's head like the wine he was apt to indulge in too freely, though this did not detract from his value as a companion.

The Welsh tour was a great event. The Colonel took charge of the reins and drove leisurely through Snowdonia, stopping at various places on the way when his friends immediately got busy with pencil and brush. At Conway they listened to the music of the celebrated blind harpist John Smith, and Ibbetson made a picture of him that was exhibited at the Academy the following year. When at last they arrived at Hafod they made a long stay there and did not waste their time. Warwick Smith made a whole series of drawings of its beauties which later were published in London, and Ibbetson found many romantic scenes along the coast to paint. Johnes became very much attached to him and 'gave him a general invitation to his table when in London'. From Hafod they headed southwards, for Stackpole Court in Pembrokeshire, which was often the next objective for Johnes's guests. Its owner, Colonel Campbell, belonged to the same circle and shared many of Johnes's tastes, besides representing in Parliament his old constituency of Cardigan Borough.

During the previous summer, another interesting visitor had paid Hafod his first visit. This was Samuel Rogers the banker-poet, then in his twenty-ninth year and making his first excursion to Wales. Through his grandmother, Sarah Knight, one of the old iron-master's many daughters, he was related to Johnes, while Payne Knight was a very particular friend of his. It is a pity that the pages of the diary he kept, covering the time that he spent in Aberystwyth and at Hafod, are missing, for his account would have been especially interesting. It would certainly have had little in common with the eulogies of the parsons and schoolmasters who were bowled over by the easy opulence of the mountain Elysium and flattered by the geniality and agreeable conversation of its founder into swallowing all his theories and fantasies. Rogers, that arch-gossip, with a malicious eye for the foibles of others, would not have been deceived. Being a relation he knew a good deal that others did not. Johnes was already regarded as something of a black sheep by the prudent Knights, and Rogers must have been all agog to see the cause of these family schisms, upon which the carefully husbanded fortunes of the iron-master and the Liverpool merchant were being flung away. As that angular, pallid figure flitted from room to room at Hafod that summer, and in and out of the flickering shadows of the walks and groves, his attention was probably chiefly engaged in assessing the likely expenditure. Romantic beauties were not entirely lost on him, but he could view them coolly, his emotional faculties as schooled and muted as the poetry that he wrote with such laborious and emasculating pruning and polishing.

It was not only distinguished friends and intelligent travellers who met with a warm welcome at Hafod. All the Cardiganshire neighbours were bidden there, too, and we can be quite certain that they did full justice to the rich hospitality. But what they saw there entirely failed in bringing about revolutionary changes either in their ideas or mode of life. Johnes's extravagant theories and designs were as foreign to their way of thinking, as impossibly highly coloured, as the iridescent, trailing plumes that his peacocks scattered about his lawns and drives.

As we have seen already, all the more important houses in the county were empty. The remaining squires were men of simple needs and habits, whose little mansions were sometimes scarcely better than larger and more commodious farm-houses. A good dining-room was the main apartment and perhaps a small parlour was the only other living-room. 'I shall only need a dining-room,' one of these worthies is reputed to have instructed the architect who was to build him a house; and really nothing much else was required when most of the day was spent in the open air and the principal pleasures indoors were supplied by the kitchen, the brew-house and the bed. There was very little display or luxury in those old Cardiganshire homes and their owners wanted nothing better. They were very well satisfied with the existing order of things, enjoyed their authoritative positions as landed gentry, and being as a rule quite devoid of interest in books and learning, saw neither sense nor reason in educating peasant brats who were much better kept in that state of ignorance and subjection to which their Maker had called them.

In short, the landowners were as much opposed to innovations and reforms as the poor. All the high-falutin schemes that were being carried out at Hafod made them groan at such useless extravagance, and as soon as they were out of earshot they threw up their hands in horror. In spite of his mile-long pedigree, Johnes was certainly no Welshman. He knew nothing whatever about the land and its capacities, in spite of his wonderful talk and ideas. A queer sort of country gentleman he was altogether, unlike any they had ever come across. They had never seen such an odd fellow, who appeared to be quite contented to remain indoors in wet weather for days on end poking over his books; who refused to have the foxhounds brought to Hafod lest they disturbed the hares which it amused him to see hopping about the paths; whose house looked more like a museum than a country gentleman's home; who drank wines from France and the Rhineland in preference to good strong ale and kept a lot of foreigners about the place—a Frenchman to cook for him and an Italian tutor to educate his little daughter. And the chatelaine of Hafod gave them plenty to talk about, too, for most of them remembered her in the old days at Dolecothy, running about the yard in her clogs looking after the fowls and brewing the heady malt liquor which flowed at her father's table. Nor had they forgotten all that clandestine business about the marriage. . . . Well, in any case, she was now very much the grand lady, sitting in her magnificent drawing-room laying down the law to them all

Hafod (by H Gastineau, c. 1830)

An artist's impression of Hafod by J M W Turner, 1798

Richard Payne Knight of Downton Castle, Herefordshire

about what should be done to make Cardiganshire and everybody in it better. It had its humorous side, but it could also be damned annoying. Although curiosity took them there, the neighbours were neither approving not particularly well-disposed towards Johnes. This intrusion of peacocks and paradise into their rough old mountains was more than they could stomach. Their prophecies of downfall and disaster rivalled in intensity the mutterings of the Dowager in Stratford Place.

Jane was well aware of what was being said, but she shrugged her shoulders with a superior smile and blamed the selfish lives their neighbours led and the cruel way they neglected their poor. She was far too contented with her lot, had too great a faith in the infallibility of all her dear Mr. Johnes thought and did, for any jibes to touch her, even though things at Hafod were beginning to be not nearly as easy as outward appearances suggested. There were dreadful times when Johnes scarcely knew where to turn for even a few pounds in cash, when the rents were paid out in wages the instant they were collected and not a penny was left to pacify the demands of the tradesmen. More than once she had had to throw herself upon the mercy of her brother, who already had lent them a few hundreds. In the end, of course, their agents always succeeded in finding the money; a sale or a mortgage was arranged and the trouble blew over. Her husband's resources were enormous as he often reminded her to calm her; when 'the old witch', as Jane called her mother-in-law, died, his income would be splendid.

Fortified in times of anxiety by this expectation, the enchanted months and years sped by, filled with long, happy days of activity, planning improvements for Hafod and benefits for their colony of natives. When company was staying they made excursions to the sea and all the beauty spots round about, chief among them being the famous cataract on the Hafod estate, four miles away, known as the Devil's Bridge. When the summer nights were fine, the grounds and the valley would be wonderfully illuminated, fireworks called Bengal Lights giving a weird, unearthly loveliness to the waterfalls. And the party from the house would wander forth into the starry, sweet-scented gloaming—a delightful period picture of gentlemen in tie-wigs and braided blue coats and ladies with lace thrown over their piled-up curls, and billowing silken skirts. Among the shadows of the woodland walks, slashed with slanting moonbeams, they would disappear from sight on their way to visit the famous echo, lingering among the rocks to listen while their voices repeated themselves again and again as with winged speed they flew across the hills.

This halcyon epoch was violently interrupted by France's declaration of war against England in February 1793. Its immediate repercussion upon Hafod was the embodiment of the Carmarthenshire Militia, with Colonel Johnes at its head. Hafod was closed for nearly eighteen months while he was away with his regiment; the country was in a fever of panic, expecting at any moment to be invaded. With detachments of his men he marched all over the West country, to Bristol and even as far south as Plymouth, to guard the coast.

Fired with zeal to serve his country in her hour of peril, he threw himself into his military responsibilities with all his accustomed ardour and enthusiasm. Characteristically, he made the welfare of his troops his own personal care. If the British Army was shockingly organized and equipped for war, it followed that the lot of the militia was immeasurably worse, and unable to obtain assistance from the War Office, Johnes finally clothed and fitted out his men at his own expense. He was extremely proud of his regiment and very popular, and at such a dangerous time it was a relief to feel that he was usefully employed in a profession that had much to recommend it. Besides the human element, always of paramount importance to him, it gave him plenty to think about and constant changes of scene.

For his wife, however, there were no such relieving features, and we find her the following winter living in a hired house in

Swansea, where the regiment had its headquarters, feeling thoroughly fretful and low-spirited. The Colonel had just left for London, where he had gone to attend Parliament, little Min was ailing, and Jane herself was overwhelmed with fears about the unsettled state of the country and the dreadful war. She wished with all her heart, as she wrote that day to her brother, that 'Mr. Johnes had nothing to do with Parliament and was out of the Militia we then could retire to our Mountains where by endeavouring to do all the good in our power, I trust we should be safe. As Mr. Johnes is now situated should any revolution happen in this country we should soon fall victims to a cause whether right or wrong Heaven only can decide.'

Early the following June they returned to Hafod, ostensibly on a fortnight's leave that somehow managed to extend itself until the end of the year. As Johnes declared, no lover could have returned more eagerly to his beloved than did he to Hafod, to find it looking more beautiful than ever under an Italian sun and an Italian sky. More urgently than ever did they long 'to remain among these dear Mountains, and endeavour to make our poor neighbours happier, and if possible, better—at present they stand in need of both physical and moral assistance.' Jane at once embarked upon her former occupation of Lady Bountiful and a large consignment of medicines was at her behest put on board the London sloop bound for Aberystwyth. Johnes's wildest expectations were at once aroused by the discovery of 'a very fine Chalibeat Spring' near the Devil's Bridge; 'a future Tonbridge may rise among my barren mountains', he exclaimed with a triumph doomed to be of short duration, for like most of the airy castles he loved to build his flourishing Spa disappeared very quickly again into its own element.

A more tangible and almost materialized dream was the addition of a large octagonal library, designed by himself, to house his ever-increasing collection of books, which had been under construction for some long while. An offspring whose Moorish antecedents were to be plainly discerned in its features, bellying out from the main structure of the house, crowned with a splendid dome and cupola and decorated with pierced stonework. Its Oriental appearance was maintained within in the splendour of its decorations and the costly marbles forming the columns that supported its gallery. It was loudly praised as 'the triumph of the place' and a present-day writer[1] has even suggested that it may have contributed to the germ that finally flowered into Kubla Khan.

That August the poet Coleridge, accompanied by John Hucks, was making a walking tour among the Welsh mountains. They slept a night at the Devil's Bridge, and while they were there they cannot have failed to hear wonderful accounts of Hafod. Next day, as they crossed the mountains on their way to Tregaron ('a miserable hole, in the which we were constrained to sleep, and to break the windows in our bedroom to let in the fresh air'), they must have passed close by it. Their most direct route lay through its grounds, a road open to all. It is not to be marvelled at if that wonder of airy grace, standing among its lawns and bosky groves above the river, with the outlandish-looking circular building with its dome and Moorish decorations incongruously attached to it, seen through the shimmering, dew-spangled light of early morning, stamped itself indelibly upon the poet's sensitive imagination. Coleridge was at all times peculiarly vulnerable to visual impressions. There it was, spread out to charm his eyes, the pleasure-dome, the caverns, the sacred river. . . .

And here were gardens bright with sinuous rills,
Where blossomed many an incense-bearing tree;
And here were forests ancient as the hills,
Enfolding sunny spots of greenery.
But oh! that deep romantic cavern which slanted
Down the green hill athwart a cedarn cover!
As e'er beneath a waning moon was haunted
By woman wailing for her demon lover.

[1] Mr. Geoffrey Grigson in an article published in the *Cornhill.*

The wild enchantment was there, whose echoes had rung through the centuries. Twelve years before Coleridge passed that way they had captured the fervid imagination of another enthusiastic lover of nature and the arts—George Cumberland. He was a cousin of the dramatist, Richard Cumberland, whose 'hollow character' he detested with all his heart: the prosperous playwright appears to have resolutely discouraged the attentions of his poor relations. Lack of means and expensive inclinations had cast a blight upon George's youth, but in 1782, in his twenty-ninth year, he had been released from his uncongenial employment as a clerk in an insurance office. The unexpected inheritance of a modest competence made it possible for him thenceforward to lead a life of leisure and indulge his natural inclinations. Full of artistic appreciation and half-developed talents (as a lad he had been a student at the Royal Academy), his life was brimming with pleasant prospects of foreign travel, painting, collecting prints and pictures, in that long-ago summer when he and his lifelong friend, Charles Long, walked together over the Welsh mountains.

It was not chance that brought them to Hafod. Long, a wealthy and ambitious young gentleman who held a good post in the Treasury, was a friend of Johnes's and had no doubt heard him raving about its beauties. Even in its desolate state they were enraptured with it, and on Cumberland, at any rate, in the twelve years which had elapsed since then, the impression it made never faded. During this long interval Long had steadily risen into eminence as a painstaking and persevering Tory politician and a liberal patron of the arts, while poor Cumberland's happy expectations now lay far behind him, with little but worries ahead. His days of carefree roving had been finished and done with for several years by the winter of 1793–4, when he met Johnes for the first time at Payne Knight's house in Whitehall. He had married, and his family was increasing as rapidly as his little income was dwindling.

'There are two spots in this Island that dwell in my mind,' he wrote that summer to his brother, the farming vicar of a rural Gloucestershire parish. 'One is Crab Nitor, the other Havod. Mr. Johnes has again most cordially pressed me by letter to come and see his improvements. . . . (He) is the Member for Radnorshire, a good pleasant fellow as Long tells me who does not value himself or his Cash, and from what I saw of him in town last winter I think I could pass a pleasant week with him. . . . If I go there it will be to ease a longing that haunts me, so much do I prize those mountains.'

Breaking his journey at Downton Castle on the way, Cumberland arrived on horseback at Hafod in the early autumn. He was a short, snub-nosed man whose orbicular countenance beamed with the good-natured affection he felt for his friends and the pleasure he took in everything he saw; he had an engaging spontaneity that the carking cares of domesticity had not been able to quench. He and Johnes got on splendidly together and it was the beginning of a lasting friendship. Cumberland's warm, ungrudging appreciation, his ingenious notions and flair for evolving new and unorthodox methods, made him a most entertaining and obliging companion. Nothing pleased him more than rendering small services, while his artistic taste and knowledge were by no means to be despised. He was intimate with a number of well-known artists, among them Johnes's favourite sculptor Banks, and William Blake rated his talent for drawing very high. 'Pray let me intreat you to persevere in your designing,' he wrote to Cumberland on one occasion, 'it is the one source of Pleasure all your other Pleasures depend upon It. It is the Tree your pleasures are the Fruit. . . . Go on if not for your own sake yet for ours who love and admire your works, but above all for the Sake of the Arts. Do not throw aside for any long time the honour intended you by Nature to revive the Greek workmanship.'

Cumberland unfortunately was an incurable amateur and did not heed his friend's injunctions. Like the butterfly he was, he darted hither and thither, sunning himself wherever his fancy led him. Hafod, in spite of its autumnal glory, stirred his pen into activity and not his brush. He was moved to write a long and minute description of it, for as he remarked in his opening sentence: 'Hafod is a place in itself so pre-eminently beautiful that it highly merits a particular description.' Painstakingly he proceeded to conduct his readers over every inch of the four fine ornamental walks that led from the house and wound and climbed for many a mile. An exhausting experience, leaving the senses completely stunned by such a plethora of rocks, trees, and waterfalls. But when it was written it met with great praise. When Cumberland read it aloud to Johnes one evening in London the following winter, he was highly gratified by it, while a party of eminent critics, to whom a similar treat was accorded, pronounced it a very elegant performance. It was published under the modest title of *An Attempt to Describe Hafod* and was generally approved of, though it did not sell quite as briskly as its impecunious author could have wished. This handsome public tribute to his mountain paradise pleased Johnes exceedingly.

Cumberland's little volume did seem to set a crown upon the achievements of exactly twelve years. It was still, so to speak, high summer; no ill wind had so far succeeded in spoiling the bloom. Even the French wars had not been able to interfere with it for long, for although Johnes continued to command the militia which remained under arms, in the years that followed he somehow contrived to do so almost entirely from his desk in the octagon library at Hafod.

CHAPTER VIII

Mariamne, 'Dearer Than The Light'

Without his child, these triumphs would have lacked much of the bubble and sparkle that, through the force of Johnes's high spirits, dazzled his friends. His buoyant nature, easily carried away by every wind that blew, had found shelter and security in his domestic life. Jane always supplied the loving understanding and support upon which he depended, while Mariamne not only provided a reason for all he did, but the encouraging knowledge that Hafod would continue to flourish long after her parents were dead.

His every hope and expectation were bound up in his little girl, the only child left to them. A son had been born long ago, the same summer as Jane had laid the first stone of the new house, and, living long enough to be baptized Evan, had died. Thus to this ewe lamb, as Johnes would fondly call her, both parents clung with a tenacity which in the mother's case was quickened by anxiety. Mariamne had always been delicate, succumbing to one ailment after another, though she recovered almost as quickly as she collapsed. Her father adopted a more philosophical attitude towards her childish maladies which, of course, she would outgrow. Jane was always too ready to torment herself with imaginary terrors and Miss Min was the finest little girl anyone could wish to see. Not a shadow would he permit to mar the brightness of their future, of which his little heiress was the brightest star.

His high opinion of her was not exaggerated. This promising child seemed to have been endowed with all the talents. She assimilated knowledge as easily as the air she breathed. She was fluent already in French and Italian; she could draw charmingly, play on the harpsichord, and sing like a bird. A generous supply of the fine intelligence and artistic qualities of the Knights had descended to her through her father, whom in other respects she favoured, though she had an individuality very much of her own. She had a sense of purpose and an earnestness that had never distinguished his own happy-go-lucky youth, and in her full blue eyes might be discerned a depth and penetration more usually found in those of some wise old woman than in a child's. But she could also be headstrong and boisterous, brimming with vitality and sparkling with an intuitive understanding like a flame that sometimes seemed as though it burned almost too fiercely for her fragile little body to bear it.

Her father from her sixth year had supervised the lessons taught her by her Italian master, Mr. Trossarelli. He was determined that every good quality of heart and mind should be perfected in her, and the readiness with which she responded to his training made their relationship even more ideal. So strong a current of understanding flowed between them that it swept his love upwards to the peaks of adoration. No child ever had a happier home or loved it better. She was a child of the mountains, the offspring of that irresistible call of their blood that had welded him and Jane to one another and to Hafod. But Mariamne seemed to belong to the place in a way that often perplexed them. It was the delight of this little golden-haired dryad to wander alone in the gardens and woods for hours at a time; a habit her elders could not understand any more than she could explain the strange and wonderful feeling she had of not being alone at all, but one with all the throbbing, secret life that

Nature manifested all around her. Even her beloved father was quite unaware of it. Thus the dryad was sometimes prey to that abysmal loneliness which is the heritage of every sensitive, intelligent child.

On 30th June 1795 she had her eleventh birthday, and the occasion found them all safely installed at Hafod. It was a particularly happy summer, for not only was it fine and warm, but the memory of their year's banishment was still fresh in their minds, making their pleasure at being home again all the keener. The continuation of the war gave a feeling of precariousness that made them cling to Hafod with even stronger devotion. The idea that they might have to go away again seemed terrible to Mariamne. She was thankful that her clever papa had devised an excellent scheme which made it possible for him to stay with them all through the summer. The place was now the scene of most unusual sights and activities, of martial sounds and trampling feet, that may have reminded some of the old people of those stormy times when the Scots Greys had invaded their solitudes. For up on the hill behind the house two companies of the Carmarthenshire Militia were camping. Stalwart figures in scarlet decorated the landscape, the sharp reports of muskets snapped across the air and the ascending smoke of camp-fires festooned the trees. Now and again the ensign in charge, with waving plume and rattling sabre, sent chickens and children scuttling into the hedges as he came galloping along the roads, and trumpet calls thrilled the silence of pale dawns and starry dusks. Hafod, in short, was more than ever a centre of public usefulness, a thought that afforded great satisfaction to the Colonel.

This year, as usual, the birthday was kept as a high festival for the whole estate. The house was thrown open to every man, woman and child belonging to it and a day of merry-making and feasting culminated towards the evening in a dance. The Cardiganshire country-folk of that era had not that fear of gawdy colours which later on assailed their descendants, plunging them into the melancholy shades of perpetual mourning. On

Mariamne's birthday it was a gaily-dressed throng that descended in little groups from the mountains and came toiling up from the valleys, to the fairy-tale palace that might have dropped down from the clouds. The men wore the traditional sky-blue worsted coats and breeches such as their forefathers had worn for centuries past, while the women had snowy mob-caps under their high hats, and bunchy skirts of linsey wolsey which they had woven themselves (often from wool gathered off thorns and gorse-bushes) in vivid stripes and checks of red, blue and white, which swung blithely above their buckled shoes.

On this great day they might wander where they liked through the picture-hung rooms with all their wonderful contents, which to those unaccustomed eyes bewilderingly enhanced the impression of fairyland. Tables of verde antico, alabaster and porphyry were loaded with costly trifles. Ornate French glasses reflected the light that streamed through the delicate window-traceries and glinted and glanced off polished surfaces and the burnished, heavily embossed implements in the sculptured fire-places. There were antique busts of poets and philosophers, and contemporary ones by Nollekens and Rossi of Johnes's friends. These last were by far the most interesting to his guests that day who had seen the originals in the flesh when they came to Hafod. Between the windows in the dining-room they could see the majestic features of Lord Thurlow, whose brilliant talk, plentifully flavoured with oaths, often resounded through this room (even the great Dr. Johnson respected the Lord Chancellor's conversational ability, for he said on one occasion to Boswell: 'I would prepare myself for no man in England but Lord Thurlow. When I am to meet him I should wish to know a day before.'). Making a pair to him, was a bust of Francis, Duke of Bedford, the charming 'Loo' adored by the ladies of Devonshire House, whose wild extravagance was off-set by the remarkable strength of his mind and character. Orphaned at three, a duke at six, his upbringing and education were so much neglected that when he came of age he could barely speak English correctly, but within a few years he had completely remedied these shortcomings and now occupied a prominent place in Whig politics and public affairs. Hanging at one end of the room was the great Romney group, and near it was a portrait of another familiar figure—R. Payne Knight. Nor were curiosities lacking to be gaped at, for in a place of honour in the entrance hall might be seen a fragment of the base of Pompey's column at Alexandria, and a petrifaction found in the old bed of the Nile, which a local warrior had brought home from Egypt and presented to Johnes. Though perhaps on the birthday they were pushed into a less conspicuous position, to make room for the tables that overflowed from the dining-room, ready spread for the feast which to most of the visitors was far the most interesting and eagerly anticipated feature of the day.

What a jubilee it was, an occasion such as had never been dreamed of in the old, bad days that were still near enough to be keenly remembered by most of the company. This was exactly the sort of gathering that Johnes and his wife enjoyed above all entertaining at Hafod. There was nothing more rewarding than to see their home framing such amicable scenes of good-fellowship, or to hear the hills, which once had echoed nothing more joyous than croaking ravens and bleating mountain sheep, ringing with the shouts and laughter of boys and girls indulging in the boisterous sports of the countryside and all the clack and clatter of a jolly crowd. The sun shone, flags flew, a band played, and old eyes grew misty as they watched the little heiress tripping about. Her diminutive figure was often lost in the mob that surrounded her, though this did not frighten the sturdy child or prevent her from laughing merrily at their sallies and answering back. Never very far behind Mariamne came her smiling, elegant mother clinging to the arm of her husband. Having grown vastly stouter with advancing years, Johnes's somewhat taurine appearance was further accentuated by a thick shock of grizzling hair arranged with picturesque disorder, and a deep jowl overflowing his neck-cloth. But his jolly red face diffused such cordiality and welcome that all he encountered were imbued with the same cheerful spirit.

They must certainly have given the impression, that day, of being one huge, harmonious family. This was the feeling that Johnes was doing his utmost to inculcate into them, and lately he had formed a friendly society of all his employees with himself at the head. And now, as with pride he observed the unabashed friendliness with which his little daughter faced the crowds swarming round her, the people pushing and jostling each other in their determination to shake her by the hand and wish her well upon this days of days, the future of his happy valley seemed assured. There was no questioning her popularity . . . she had won all their hearts. His own love for her glowed warmer than ever as he watched his little Min, who was shaping exactly as he had hoped. A warm-hearted, jolly-looking country child who could ride her pony and help her mother in the still-room, and was already more proficient in the arts and accomplishments than many a fine young miss in London town!

And so, with the happy conviction that year after year this feast would be held, while everything for everyone present would continue to get better and better, the day drew on in paeans of song and feasting. When at length darkness descended and the company danced in the lighted hall and outside on the lawns, the night was filled with merriment and music, interspersed with the sizzle and explosion of squibs and rockets which sprayed the trees and mountains with golden rain and fell in showers of blazing jewels from the sky.

It was that other side of Marianne's character that was the mystery. Where she got it from none of them could think—that absorbed interest she took in even the humblest, dingiest weed and insect. Patiently she sought them in every nook and cranny out of doors, bringing them in with infinite care, and pressing and drying them. She went to endless pains to classify them as well as she could, for she had nothing to guide her but the books which her father gave her. He was proud of her taste for natural history, even if he was bewildered by it, and did everything in his power to help. It was not much he could do, for he knew nothing about it. 'I only shine in Botany but like the Moon by borrowed light, or rather to please her, who is dearer to me than The Light,' he had lately written to a new friend of his, a brilliant and distinguished naturalist of whom we shall hear more. The passion was so deeply rooted in Mariamne that, in spite of having no one to teach or help her, and perplexing and hard to understand as the books often were, she doggedly pursued her lonely study.

The life that quivered and flowed in every stem and leaf and winged and crawling creature, was part of her own life, fulfilling that primal need and inherent longing which were only appeased when she was searching the dim caverns among the trees, hunting the banks and shaggy grottoes, for new ferns and flowers to carry back indoors with triumph. It was daunting to know that in its essence her triumph was bound to be a lonely one. It was sad never to have had a companion or anyone who could really sympathize. Many botanically-minded gentlemen stayed at Hafod, but their interest in her seldom went farther than according her an occasional smile or a condescending pat on the head. Sometimes the feeling of isolation that it gave her was quite overwhelming. However, during this wonderful summer of 1795, a possibility had dawned which by the beginning of August was almost a certainty. A friend and counsellor was at long last near at hand, one of the most distinguished botanists in England. No less a person, in fact, than the eminent Dr. Smith, founder and president of the Linnaean Society, whose acquaintance her father had made the previous year.

Nothing could be more exciting; it seemed too good, almost, really to happen. The poor child was in paroxysms of alarm lest something should occur to prevent him from coming after all. She sent him urgent messages that she would never, never forgive him if he did not come soon, and he *must* make haste, for all the finest flowers were in bloom, and there were numberless curious insects for him to see in this fine weather. Standing by her father's chair one morning, while Johnes was attempting, through the disturbance she was making, to write to Dr. Smith, she jumped up and down with excitement, shaking the table, and sending everything upon it rattling and spinning all over the place so that he could scarcely order his thoughts or control his pen. Not that he minded this at all. Her bright eyes and flushed cheeks did him good to see, and to tell the truth he was just as anxious as she was that his friend should come as soon as possible to see what his clever little daughter had been doing.

He felt confident that Smith was the very man to appreciate her. He was the type who would go to endless pains to help her, for as a sensitive, delicate child himself he, too, had loved flowers and spent many hours studying them. He was always happy to give a helping hand to the aspiring young, for he believed that 'the fairest flower in the garden of creation is a young mind, offering and unfolding itself to the influence of divine wisdom, as the heliotrope turns its sweet blossoms to the sun.' With this sentiment, so far at least as Mariamne was concerned, Johnes was in hearty agreement.

'You will see she is quick at taking hints when you come—more I will not say, except that upon my word of Honour, it is all her own thought and execution,' he had written already, and now, taking advantage of a lull in the storm of impatience, he added:

'She wishes for you with an earnestness that only her Bawling can equal. I really cannot write more for her tongue is more voluble than her fingers *now* are on the Harpsichord. We are in very great beauty—and if we can fight off the scarcity till Harvest, shall do well, as there is a fine appearance of plenty. I have had the pleasure of saving this country a second time from a famine.'

James Edward Smith, now in his thirty-fifth year, had already established himself as the leading authority on natural science among the younger men. Fortune had favoured him, for he was born the son of a prosperous father and himself endowed with a high degree of intellectuality and understanding, combined with a pleasing personality that made him much liked wherever he went. He was a native of Norwich, where his father carried on a thriving trade as a wool-merchant. It was not until he was eighteen that he seriously took up the study of botany. By one of those curious coincidences which seem to link together the destinies of certain individuals, it was on 10th January 1778 that he first made a start. Upon that same day the great naturalist Carl von Linné, generally known as Linnaeus, died at Upsala in Sweden.

At Edinburgh, where he went to study medicine which was to be his career, he also studied botany under one of the earliest teachers of the Linnaean method. When he came to London in 1783 as pupil to a fashionable doctor, he brought with him an introduction to Sir Joseph Banks. It was in the atmosphere of genial erudition, which made Sir Joseph's house in Soho Square the favourite meeting place of the intelligentsia, among the cabinets and glass cases containing his famous collections, that young Smith's happiest hours were spent. And he was breakfasting with Sir Joseph one unforgettable morning in the December of the same year when a letter arrived from the Professor of Medicine at Upsala, writing on behalf of Linnaeus's widow, to offer the President of the Royal Society the whole of Linnaeus's collections of books, manuscripts and natural history for the sum of a thousand guineas. Sir Joseph handed the letter to Smith, saying that as he intended to decline the offer he strongly advised him to make the purchase instead 'as a thing suitable to his taste, which would do him honour'.

A thousand guineas was far beyond the means of a young medical student, and in haste James Smith wrote off to his father, imploring him to advance the money: 'I am so ambitious as to wish to possess this treasure, with a view to settle as a physician in London, and read lectures on natural history.' It took him a great many months before he was able to persuade the cautious wool-merchant to put forward the necessary sum, but at last the bargain was concluded and transport to this country arranged. And it was said that when the King of Sweden, who had been abroad when the sale was arranged, heard that these scientific treasures were being lost to his country, he was filled with indignation and sent a man-of-war in vain pursuit of the English vessel that was carrying them away.

With this acquisition and his own genius James Smith's position was firmly established, and now, ten years later, his name was one of great importance. The Linnaean Society had been founded in London, of which he was the president. Duchesses and ladies of fashion, men eminent in all the professions and peers of the realm, all came flocking to the lectures he gave on botany and zoology at his house in Great Marlborough Street. In 1792, Queen Charlotte had honoured him with a command to arrange her herbarium and instruct herself and the princesses in the elements of botany.

Albeit one of the most simple-hearted and unassuming among men, Smith not unnaturally was exceedingly flattered by these royal attentions—he had travelled a long way from the sparse and puritanical home of his nonconformist father. 'I am come to town for two days from Windsor,' he wrote to a friend that November. 'I return this day. I am delighted with my pupils: we all sit together at a round table. I lecture from my notes, which the Queen takes home from Frogmore to Windsor to make extracts from. . . . A conversation of half-an-hour or more follows the lecture. Nothing can be more polite and pleasing.'

Alas, as he wrote these words he little suspected how soon and how summarily these agreeable interludes with the royal ladies would be put an end to. A few years earlier he had visited the Continent, his main object being to obtain his medical degree at Leyden. When that had been accomplished, he had travelled about Europe visiting many distinguished people, one of whom was the widow of Jean-Jacques Rousseau. In 1793, he published a three-volume account of his tour which Her Majesty lost no time in reading, with the completely unforeseen result that Dr. Smith was informed that his attendance at Windsor was no longer required. With crowns toppling in all directions and the unsettled state of the country generally, the Queen had been seriously alarmed by several passages praising Rousseau's doctrines, besides taking great exception to an unfortunate reference to the unhappy Queen of France as another Messalina. Queen Charlotte had discovered that the apparently mild and courteous botanist was nothing more or less than a bad and dangerous character.

Mortifying and distressing though it was, there was nothing Smith could do about it except to see that the offending passages were removed from subsequent editions, and to get what comfort he could from the reflection that though his 'Tour' had lost him the Queen it had gained him many delightful new friends. Among them was Colonel Johnes, whom he was now about to visit.

He was staying in Norwich that summer and the journey from there to Hafod took a great many days. Though travelling was always something of a trial to him, for he had never entirely thrown off his early delicacy, he set out in the best possible spirits of eager expectation, for he had heard many glowing accounts of the mountain paradise from friends who had seen it. When at last, one Monday evening, the Ludlow coach deposited him in Aberystwyth the little town seemed astir with life and fashion. It was now the favourite resort of all kinds of well-known people, from ladies requiring ozone to the accomplished acquaintances of Uvedale Price, whose Gothic villa was an arresting feature of the bleak sea-front. No sooner had Smith arrived than he ran into friends, Sir George and Lady Caley, and in their company spent a pleasant evening. Horses from Hafod were waiting for him and in the morning he set off thither, enjoying, as he said, 'a charming ride over the hills'.

'And here I rest, as, after much turmoil,
A blessed soul doth in Elysium,'

he wrote to a friend two days later. It perfectly expressed his feelings. His highest expectations were more than fulfilled by the 'sumptuous house' and the rocks and cascades—'all of the wildest kind'. Yet once again the spirits were at work, snaring and enchaining another victim who till the end of his days would never hear Hafod mentioned without a catch at his heart. It was not only the beauty of the place, but the grandeur of the concepts that inspired it, the way Johnes and his wife put them into common practice, that aroused his enthusiasm. Here was the ideal kingdom of his dreams, with everything in it that made for goodness and contentment. But by far the most extraordinary being there was the child.

Mariamne Johnes amazed him. She surpassed everything he had believed a child could be. She was not *like* an ordinary child, he declared, as he extolled her merits in letter after letter to other learned botanists. She was quite outstanding in the maturity of her mind, her genius for music, and above all for the wonderful turn she had taken for botany and entomology. 'She has made out every plant within her reach, that is in Flora Londinensis, or English Botany, and has the latter almost by heart. She longs to botanize in a chalk country. She is almost equally fond of insects, and her whole delight is to walk with me about the woods, searching for mosses and insects, patiently attending to everything I say, and telling me all her observations, doubts, queries etc. This is the more extraordinary, as she has had no companion till now . . . it is a most remarkable instance of early ardour.' If she continued as she had begun, he was convinced that a great future awaited her in the realms of natural science. He was touched and stirred beyond measure by this little girl whose nature strained towards all those things which he, too, held to be most dear and sacred.

The radiant fortnight that he spent there was all too quickly over. There was so much to see and do, such a variety of expeditions and amusements were planned for him, that there was never a moment to spare. If he was not being carried off to explore the Devil's Bridge or to ride with his host to see a fine view or the latest plantation, he was running downstairs to the music-room where Marianne was waiting to give him a tune on the harpsichord. Then there were all the interesting contents of the house to be looked at, and the rare and valuable books in the octagon library. He was really shocked by such extravagance when Johnes put into his hand a slender volume consisting of twenty-six drawings of shells which had come from the famous collection of M. Paris de Meyzieux, saying that it had cost £130. And this little book was not an exception, for many others had been equally expensive. 'Mr. Johnes', said Smith, and for once one detects an unmistakable whiff of disapproval, 'spares no expense for anything he has a mind for.' There were copies and manuscripts of old French Chronicles which were beyond price and the curious Quixote Library which was famous and consisted of an entire collection of all the books mentioned by Cervantes as having formed the library of Don Quixote.

Smith's strong humanitarian sympathies, which had prompted his unlucky praise of Rousseau, strongly approved of the active benevolence that he saw going on all round. The Johneses, he declared, were the 'Guardian Angels of the country', and one day Jane told him that for this very reason the neighbouring gentry did not like them: 'for they wanted to keep all the old tyrannic notions, and never think of other people's starving, if they do but eat themselves.' He was much struck by Johnes's recent gesture of importing a ship-load of wheat from Bristol 'to sell at cent per cent loss'. And all the while he was yielding more and more to the spell of the strange and lovely scenery; the hanging woods, the milky cliffs, the glittering streams and secret flower-gardens, that were impregnating his sensitive imagination with a wonder that would never leave it. Hafod, he declared, was in every sense a paradise, while its owners were 'all goodness, sense, taste and munificence'.

There was only one disappointment, and that was the botany. Nothing alpine was to be found there or anything at all of interest. It was a very minor disappointment, for on his botanizing expeditions the lack of rare flora was amply made up for by Mariamne's company. Their long walks together were far and away the most memorable events of this first and happiest visit. One likes to picture the pair of them as they set out together, morning after morning, from the house that seems positively to dance in the sunshine of those long-lost summer days; the tall, slightly stooping, soberly dressed doctor, with his long, clever face and kindly brown gaze bent on the little girl in her straw bonnet and high-waisted frock, tripping confidently along at his side. He cannot help smiling as he listens to her chatter, for her observations are both shrewd and amusing—or 'funny' which is his word for her. And so they descend the sloping lawns towards the river and cross the wooden bridge, pausing for an instant on the far bank to decide which path to follow. Then off they go, climbing the shaggy hillside, and as they go higher and farther among the mountain heights, their voices gradually fade, their laughter dies away.

There is no longer time for idle chatter. All their attention is engaged in searching the banks and trees for their elusive little inhabitants, straining their eyes in all directions to find floral or entomological wonders. Every now and again they come to a standstill while the doctor discourses gravely on some tiny object in the palm of his hand, which she examines intently through his glass, before he begins to explain. Mariamne listens solemnly, palpitating with the importance of the moment, drinking in all he has to say. And so they wander on, and presently to please him she begins to sing, in clear, touching strains, some Italian air by Handel, her silvery notes echoing in the silence of the hills. The romantic mood he was in this autumn intensified the rapture with which he listened; he felt quite carried away by this little singer through whom flowed all the choicest gifts from Heaven. With himself, too, his love of music was almost equal to his love of natural science. Never had voice sounded sweeter than Mariamne's now, thrilling among the clear blue heights.

His secret thoughts were much occupied with all kinds of sentimental yearnings and dreams of a graceful, brown-eyed girl with the euphonious name of Pleasance Reeve, whom he was hoping to marry. Nothing could have been more exalting, therefore, than listening to the child's spontaneous melodies in the midst of the noblest scenery he could wish for. And before very long she would change her songs to the old ballads of her native land, for these were what they liked best. And soon his deeper notes might be heard mingling with hers, the rarefied air resounding with the majestic music of Morfa Rhyddlan, which was their favourite one of all.

Wild on old Havren's banks the modest violet blooms,
And wide the scented air its fragrant breath perfumes;
Bright shines the glorious sun amid the heavens
When from its cheering orb the clouds are driven;
A form more beauteous still adorns the flood,
Gwendolen's fatal form, Llewellyn's blood!

At the end of the first week in September when he left Hafod and her life subsided with a bump from the heights they had walked together down to the humdrum levels of ordinary existence, Mariamne's great consolation was to write to him. 'I cannot tell you how sorry I was after you and how much I miss you,' she assured him at once, in her big, beautiful copper-plate hand. Great comfort, too, lay in the knowledge that never again could the old loneliness torment her, for he had promised to send her regular letters and to elucidate all her puzzles and queries. He would continue to help and teach her from a distance, and he had given a solemn pledge to come and stay again next year.

Accordingly she threw herself into her researches with greater fervour than ever, literally leaving no stone unturned in her anxiety to find rare specimens for him. Nowhere was safe from her sharp little eyes. Even in her papa's room she discovered one day a most curious beetle dead on the floor, instead of on a sunbank where it ought by rights to have been. All her choicest finds were despatched at once to London and were 'very much at his service' should the doctor find them valuable.

Smith responded nobly. Although he was an extremely busy and much-sought-after man, and on the brink besides of becoming engaged to his charming Miss Pleasance, he still managed to find time to write frequently to Mariamne and to devise all kinds of gifts to stimulate her efforts and give her pleasure. He not only sent her all sorts of specimens, but a little box of insects as well which she hailed with joy. It was 'The most valuable present you can possibly give me,' she cried, straight from her heart, pressing a tiny fern and enclosing it in her letter. Mr. Trossarelli's dexterous brush was also enlisted to paint an exquisitely delicate reproduction of an uncommon lichen that clung too obstinately to its rock to be scraped off and posted. Butterflies arrived for her in cases and Smith even suggested sending a 'living tortoise', but this Mariamne firmly rejected as 'a thing I have not the least desire to have, therefore I must beg you will not give yourself any further trouble about it.'

With all these shared interests, insects and, best of all, letters arriving at Hafod perpetually to sustain her, the child's life seemed to grow richer with every week that passed.

CHAPTER IX

'A Frightful Dream Which I Cannot Unravel'

Although that September Dr. Smith had carried away from Hafod nothing but radiant memories of an ideal community, securely established among glorious surroundings and encompassed by every amenity afforded by an overflowing generosity and benevolence, behind all this seeming prosperity lay quite another state of affairs. The war and all it might inflict, in the way of partings and separations, was not the only disagreeable prospect confronting Johnes. In London it was being rumoured that Hafod had ruined him. With his astonishing capacity for ignoring everything unpleasant, for resolutely pushing it out of his mind and pursuing the course he had marked out for himself in blissful disregard of uncomfortable truths, he refused to be flustered by it. His resources were enormous—a reassuring conviction that sustained him in spite of the warnings and adjurations of his bankers and lawyers and the piles of bills pushed out of sight at the back of his drawers. He had decided to spend the winter at Hafod, for there it was only too easy to forget an ugly world where mothers were heartless, creditors vociferous, and attorneys a pestering nuisance. He was confident that somehow in London they would sooner or later find some means of clearing him, and in the meanwhile he was preparing to apply himself with energies redoubled, to the cultivation of his land.

It was an unfortunate fact, and one that could no longer be overlooked, that up to the present Hafod had yielded nothing in the way of financial returns. The wonderful crops and pastures, flocks and herds, though of great ornamental value to the landscape, had proved far from satisfactory from an economic point of view. From the start large sums of money were continually being poured into the land, and the time had come for drastic steps to be taken to remedy matters. Hafod must be turned into the paying proposition that Johnes had always claimed it would be. He had identified himself with it to such a degree that its failure to come up to what he had anticipated was his own personal failure as well—a thought not to be tolerated. Accordingly he had summoned to his rescue one of the most eminent living authorities on agriculture, Dr. James Anderson.

If Anderson could not find a way to make the mountains flourish, and wring the gold from their grudging flanks, no man in the country could. He had been a practical farmer in his native Scotland from the age of fifteen, and only a few years ago had earned great renown for himself by reclaiming an enormous tract of barren mountain farm-land in Aberdeenshire, which he had brought into excellent cultivation. Johnes had known him for nearly a year and had great confidence in his powers. The next few months, with Anderson as the companion of his walks and rides, promised to be exceedingly interesting and agreeable and their outcome would do a great deal to mend other troublesome matters.

The weather-beaten, wiry little Scotsman arrived towards the end of September, and Johnes was not at all surprised to hear him immediately rate Hafod's agricultural potentialities quite as high as he did. Anderson was a man after his own heart, for he was almost as celebrated in literary circles as he was in agrarian ones. He was a prolific writer of learned articles on every kind of topic as well as editing a scientific journal. His general knowledge was enormous and he was an amusing talker, full of entertaining anecdotes and reminiscences. But even his shrewd eyes (if we can believe what Johnes reported) must have been blinded by the genii of the hills, for he was wild about their possibilities and full of plans for draining, watering, and putting the whole estate on a firm financial basis.

With his customary open-hearted enthusiasm, Johnes gave the doctor *carte blanche* to do as he liked and placed his legions of workmen at his disposal. Together they rode through the russet, dilapidated countryside during that boisterous October, rejoicing in the stormy magnificence all around them and the music of rushing waters in their ears, while they discussed their ambitious plans and schemes. Everything Anderson said renewed all Johnes's fondest hopes, and banished any qualms he may have experienced for good and all. He felt 'more wild about the place' than ever. His good doctor would very soon get it all into good order for him, and after that things would run along quite smoothly. Never had Johnes cared less for the world or felt more independent of it in the isolation and peace of his mountains. Life could not have been more enjoyable than it was just then, with the long days spent in the open farming and planting and planning to make Paradise even more spectacular and successful. In the evenings they sat by the fire in the octagon library, handling rare folios and sipping rare wines, while the ladies bent over their embroidery and the dogs stretched on the hearthrug growled gently in their sleep. Nothing seemed likely to interrupt the continuity of weeks stretching as far ahead as the New Year perhaps, when suddenly an urgent summons for Johnes to go immediately to London crashed down on them like a thunderbolt. It may well have been one of several, but this time it was couched in words of such grave import that even Johnes could not ignore it. Rudely shaken out of his pleasant dreams, with many a heavy sigh, he resigned himself to go back to the outside world and face the bothersome truths that he might no longer ignore. But even now his optimism did not entirely forsake him, for he assured them all before he left that matters would be quickly settled, and he would be back at home again within a fortnight.

'My Dear Dr. Smith,' wrote Mariamne that 2nd November, 'I received your kind favour last post, it gave me great pleasure to hear you are well. It has been terrible stormy weather and very cold. My Dr Papa left us last week for London, I was very sorry after him, but he promised me to come back very soon. I sent your Microscope with him and a small box of insects. I hope they will not be much damaged as I took a great deal of pains in packing them.

'I have not found one Lichen insect or plant since I wrote to you last. Dr. Anderson has been so good as to fix on a very pretty spot for a flower Garden for me which you and I never visited. When it is formed I shall be very impatient for your company, as I promise myself great pleasure in working with you in my little Garden.'

But week after week slipped by and still no sign of his returning. On the 10th December Mariamne was lamenting that 'I almost begin to despair of seeing my Dear Dear Papa again here—if they do not release him soon I believe I must come after him.' For Hafod was an entirely different place now that his surging current of life was switched off. Everything had become uncommonly flat and melancholy. The worries and fears which vanished like smoke when he was about now were heavy in the air. Jane, who had never caught her husband's light-hearted insouciance, with nervous preoccupation awaited the arrival of the bi-weekly postbag, though when it came his letters contained little that could cheer her. She sighed and whispered to Eliza as they sat over their needlework, and these conditions the sensitive child only too readily picked up.

Luckily she had the interest of her new garden to think about and to keep her exercised, for she certainly scrambled up there several times a day. It was some way away from the house; Dr.

Anderson had chosen a most unusual site for it, on the very summit of the high rock that formed the background of Jane's flower-garden that lay hundreds of feet below. Once gained, it disclosed a view of remarkable beauty, extending across range after range of mountains. That it could not have been more exposed, perched high in the air as it was, had not deterred the sturdy Scotsman who planned to enclose it in a rough stone wall. This, with hardy and judiciously planted shrubs, should provide the necessary shelter, while a zigzagging path would minimize the steepness of the ascent.

The arrival of a new head gardener was another interesting event; Mariamne quickly made his acquaintance and wrote her report to her 'Dear Dear Dr. Smith'. 'I am exceedingly obliged to you', she began, 'for your very friendly Letter which I received 30th of Novr I assure you I am highly flattered with your friendship. The new Gardener from Scotland is arrived his name is Mr. Todd, he was a gardener at the Botanical Garden at Edinburgh, he says he knows you by name, but never had the happiness of seeing you—he understands Botany pretty well.'

A week or two earlier she had been 'most obliged' to Smith for informing her of his engagement to marry Miss Reeve, who as his wife would accompany him when he came to Hafod next summer. The eleven-year-old Mariamne greeted the news with joy, for it in no way interfered with her own little idyll. But all these agreeable occurrences could not entirely prevent the winter months from being fraught with sadness, with Mamma looking so anxious, and dear Papa away, and the queer, deserted feeling the house had in spite of all the rest of them being in it.

In London, meanwhile, Johnes was undergoing such an ordeal as he had never believed to be possible. In the grisly light of stark and menacing truths he was gaining an entirely new opinion of human nature. Gone now was that pleasing veneer of civility and good-fellowship, the frank, warm friendliness which had flowed between him and his acquaintances, whose approval and affection had always counted with him for so much. In that charmed circle of rich, gifted, easy-going men his excellent qualities of heart and head had, until now, made him specially welcome. In the eyes of the world his fortune had no doubt been greatly magnified by his extravagant ideas and princely habits. Now the glittering bubble had exploded. What precisely had brought this to pass is not clear, but try as they might the lawyers could stave off the raging spate of debts no longer. No more loans could be raised, no more sales of land could avail him. The tempest roared unchecked and unrestrained—tearing down all the suave façade, and with it every vestige of cordiality and approval. Those whom he had deemed to be his best and closest allies, who had always been happy to oblige him with a hundred or two every now and again, were among the most heartless and rapacious of his persecutors. He was completely unmanned by it all. Hurt and bewildered, he was forced to conclude that where money was concerned friendship counted for naught. Still he could not quite fathom how this dreadful change could have come about —the ice-cold, inimical glances to which he was treated in the clubs and coffee-houses, and the scarifying comments that whipped him as he passed. It seemed terrible that men of quality and feeling could throw away anything as precious as friendship in their greed for filthy lucre. It was an aspect of life he had never until then apprehended, and its ugliness appalled him. Matters were further complicated by the fact that some of his fair-weather friends were connected with trade. There was Mr. Alderman Harley of Berrington Court, for one, who had a wine-merchant's business in the City and had kept the cellars at Hafod plentifully stocked for years. But this pleasant arrangement had proved singularly unprofitable for the Alderman who now, tired of having his bills ignored, referred the matter to the Law Courts.

It was most unfortunate and humiliating, for Herefordshire must have resounded with it. As we have seen, ties of closest friendship had bound the two families together for the last half-century. The Alderman, one of the brothers of the Custos's old friend and patron, Lord Oxford, was an important member of a powerful clan whose opinion carried great weight in London and Herefordshire. Nothing could have been more harmful to Johnes's reputation or better calculated to set his mother even more implacably against him. The proud heiress of Richard Knight had indeed been brought low by her spendthrift son. It made her still more determined to resist his encroachments on her fortune in every way possible. There was not even a pretence of affection between them now. All that Johnes held most dear, his marriage to Jane and his beloved Hafod, she had never ceased to censure. Her existence had long been regarded as an obstacle which he hoped might be removed at an early date. Then he would be free of all financial care; his debts would be paid and a handsome present made besides to his kind and patient friends. This had been his avowed intention, but unfortunately the patience of his friends had run out, while the Dowager continued to enjoy good health.

It was the injustice that afflicted Johnes most. Surely it could not be necessary for his friends to clamour thus for money which they did not really need and for a certainty would receive within a year or two. The old Alderman, for instance, was as rich as Croesus; his daughters had all made great matches, and there was no good reason why he should be so impatient. And it was the same with the others, whose representatives hung round his doorstep, thrusting long, incomprehensible accounts under his nose, while they threatened him with the law, unless he satisfied their claims forthwith. It was quite impossible for him to pay, for no money was to be had anywhere. While in Stratford Place, lapped in riches, the old lady sat triumphant, for had she not been foretelling this catastrophe for many a long year past? This was salt to his sores with a vengeance!

Two there were, at any rate, who remained loyal to him and supported him through this winter of despair. One of them was Lord Thurlow. The old tiger had wounds of his own now to lick and bitter complaints to make against the ingratitude and faithlessness of princes. The King he had faithfully served, even at the cost of his principles, had lately dismissed him from his favour as well as from the Chancellorship, a heavy blow which had caused him to withdraw altogether from public life to the shelter of his pretty villa at Dulwich. Payne Knight was the other great ally, and it was in his house at Whitehall that Johnes stayed during these wretched months. What balm it must have brought his harassed spirit to return to that temple of culture and fine taste after the moral and mental confusion of long days spent in interminable conferences with bankers and lawyers, who were fiddling to arrive at some way of pulling him out of the imbroglio. His reeling senses were perfectly incapable of understanding what they were about. He was as much at sea as some quivering bewildered creature of the forest, brought to bay by a snarling pack. He was like one of the wild, black cattle that roamed his Cardiganshire hills, among all those cut-and-dried men of business. In the stimulating company of Mr. Knight he was able to forget his cares for a while as he looked through his friend's latest folio of drawings and admired his latest purchase. Then Windham, whom Johnes had loved all his youth, might drop in, or one of the Grevilles, or Sheridan or little Rogers, though with bankruptcy just round the corner, Johnes can scarcely have welcomed the attentions of the gossiping, inquisitive poet. Payne Knight's unswerving affection was especially encouraging, for besides being far the most influential of the Dowager's relations, he entered whole-heartedly into the spirit of Hafod and rated its beauty and worth very high.

It was not until after Christmas that Johnes was at last free to go. He set off as fast as he could on the long, four-day journey which he ended by finishing on foot, walking the last twelve miles of it over the mountains through the wind and rain of a stormy New Year's night, so great was his haste to be home. It was pitch dark; the mud was over his boots, the wind blew a gale in his face, and he was drenched to the skin and splashed all over with dirt; but he struggled defiantly onwards, hurrying as though the howling wolves in London were still in hot pursuit. But when at long last he stood in the flickering lamplight of his own front-hall, wild and dishevelled, and Jenny with Min at her heels came flying towards him down the passage in answer to his call, and laughing and crying threw themselves upon him, as he locked these dear creatures tight in his arms, his sufferings disappeared and nothing seemed to matter very much after all . . . nothing mattered at all, so long as these precious beings were safe and well.

The relief of being at home again was immeasurable, with his beloved wife who was always his better-half in the fullest sense of that hackneyed phrase, to sustain and console him. The whole house vibrated with their happiness at having him back and Mariamne skipped jubilantly round with shining eyes, tightly clutching in her palm the little diamond beetle he had brought her. It was, as she said, 'an insect she had long wished for'. And many times during those weeks he climbed up the steep hillside to her garden which, on first beholding it, he had declared to be the most singular and surprising one he had ever seen; 'the pensile garden of Semiramis would be a farce to it.'

The shock to his nerves had been so severe that he could not stop indoors; if he was still for one moment, such poisoned thoughts laid hold of him that he felt completely undone. The crisis in his affairs was by no means over—only temporarily delayed. He had to cut down his expenses to a minimum . . . turn off half his servants . . . not buy another thing, however trifling . . . he could not bring himself to think, even, of the appalling measures his advisers had insisted upon his taking. While admitting that he had in a way perhaps deserved this lesson, he still could not feel that he had much to reproach himself with, he reiterated over and over again as he tramped over every inch of his estate or indulged in long, soothing talks with his clever new gardener.

The blinkers had been torn from his eyes much too roughly

Thomas Johnes by Thomas Stothard

Jane Johnes as Thetis dipping the infant Achilles by Thomas Banks

for the smarting wounds to heal. The way his friends had failed him continued to hurt him more than all the rest of his misfortunes put together. Two months after he left London he was writing feelingly of it to Smith. 'I found that whenever money comes in competition with what is commonly called friendship the last vanishes away like an airy vision leaving the Dross behind. I was more hurt and vext at being undeceived than at what concerned myself, for a few years must make them see clearly how much they have been mistaken.'

In the spring, politics were claiming his entire attention, a rush of activities which kept him in 'a continual bustle', and did much to restore his confidence and composure. A short time before he had resigned his seat for Radnor, in order to present himself as the next candidate for Cardiganshire in the place of Lord Lisburne who was retiring. And now that this had come about, the prospective member entered his coach with Jane, looking very fashionable in her silks and feathers, and drove all over the country, calling on the principal families and soliciting their support. With the shocking roads and unbridged rivers, this was a dangerous business that involved the risk of broken bones, but they carried it through with a flourish. Fearful of perils though she was, Jane was not at all averse to charming the rustic gentry, some of whom she even allowed to be very genteel, pleasant people. Adversity had made Johnes's passion for the country stronger, if possible, than before. He rushed from one mansion and village to another, spreading such a feeling of warm good-fellowship wherever he went, such surging faith in their own powers and the wonderful opportunities which Cardiganshire afforded, that even the dullest of its landlords was kindled to some kind of interest by his glowing promises which were further enhanced by the good dinners to which he entertained them in the principal taverns in the towns. Elections were convivial occasions, and the county was kept in a pleasant stir by its candidates. Mr. Vaughan, Lord Lisburne's son, was at the same time offering himself for the Boroughs, Colonel Campbell having lately been raised to the peerage as Lord Cawdor.

In June, at Cardigan, amidst the wildest enthusiasm, Johnes was elected by a large majority, and Mariamne, writing soon afterwards to Dr. Smith, gave a vivid description of his triumph. 'There was a very numerous assembly of gentlemen there and an immense crowd. They gathered from all quarters. They thought Mr. Vaughan had a great number but Papa had twice as much—he was carried very grand for I had a full view of him. I assure you his chair was very smart for Mama had made some beautiful artificial roses and ornamented a great number of ribbons with foil.' The victory did his wounded spirits all the good in the world, for no one, he declared, had ever received 'more marks of personal attachment'. With high good humour he told his constituents that he would keep his Parliament at Hafod, for there he could be of far greater service to the county than in London. It bound him even closer, while the ache of his scars caused him to shelter even more resolutely behind the mountains. There he would remain, in blissful oblivion of the rest of the world. It was encouraging, too, to think that he had never fought a cheaper election—it had cost him only a very few hundreds. The old, light-hearted fecklessness came bubbling up from the amnesia exhaled by the finest, sweetest air in the world. With easy optimism he looked forward to the future, and Cardiganshire growing better, thanks to his exertions, every year.

This exultation and renewed peace of mind were not destined to last. Never again was his life going to be the same as formerly. The dark threat of insolvency continued to loom too uncomfortably close to be forgotten, while a heavier blow than any his friends could deal him was approaching from another quarter. Some time in July Mariamne fell seriously ill with baffling and alarming symptoms which proved to be the early stages of a spinal disease. None of the local doctors understood her case, and their comfortable assurances that she would quickly recover did little to calm her terrified parents. When Dr. Smith and his bride arrived in August on the visit the child had been passionately awaiting, they found the lively little dryad of a year ago a helpless invalid, scarcely able to stand without being supported.

It was a party of three that arrived in the one-horse chaise, for Smith's favourite sister accompanied them on this visit which made a lasting impression on the young wife's sensitive imagination. Mrs. Smith was as much delighted with the beauty of the place and the kind-heartedness of its owners as her husband had been a year earlier. Although the child's alarming illness must necessarily have robbed their stay of half its delight, the parents, with remarkable fortitude, were determined that their anxiety should interfere as little as possible with their guests' enjoyment. Both the Johneses were thoroughly pleased with the doctor's choice. Pleasance Smith was a notably charming girl, whose lively, dark-eyed countenance reflected an uncommon degree of intelligence and understanding—qualities that endured throughout her astonishingly long life, for she lived to be 104. 'He who could see and hear Lady Smith without being enchanted', wrote an elderly savant many years after this bridal visit to Hafod, 'has a heart not worth a brass farthing.'

Although she never revisited it, the recollection of the fortnight she spent there was still vivid in her mind nearly forty years later when she wrote of it in her Memoir of her husband. ' "All Nature and all Art" conspired to make it enchanting,' while Colonel Johnes was its life and soul. With his colloquial way of talking and endless store of interesting information, she found him exceedingly 'agreeable in conversation . . . rapid, allusive and obscure to those who had more limited knowledge than he possessed'. And she recalled the glory of the early mornings when she stood at her window watching the sun swimming up from behind the mountains, while 'singular cries' of 'Pavo! Pavo! enlivened and animated the otherwise silent solitude, as a flock of peacocks came flying out of the woods and alighting on the roof, unfurled the lustrous blues and flaming greens of their plumage between the battlements.

Nothing was lacking to make it perfect, though there was little happiness or peace of mind for its creators that summer or for many others to come. The birds of ill-omen flaunted their splendour on a house whose lights were dim and flickering, looking as if at any moment they might peter out altogether.

As Mariamne showed no signs of improving, in the autumn the family moved to Bath, for Johnes was determined that there she would be cured. They spent the winter with the Hanbury Williamses, for the childless Betsy was as much devoted to her little niece as though she was her own child. Every famous doctor who came to the town was called in in consultation, but though they one and all declared that she would do very well, Mariamne grew weaker and weaker every day.

'Great God, what a miserable year has 1796 been,' Jane wrote to her brother that December. 'May the New Year bring with it brighter prospects.'

It was true enough. There was nothing to be seen in any direction that could inspire much hope. On all sides the prospect looked black as night, while the news got daily worse; there was nothing but ugly reports of hunger, riots and political unrest. From across the Irish Sea came horrifying tales of murder and rapine, while the fear of a French invasion pressed more heavily than ever as Britain's naval supremacy was threatened by the alliance of the Dutch and Spanish fleets with the French. Probably it was some time during this winter that Johnes made a rousing speech in Parliament, which later on Coleridge cited as a fine example of hyperbole. Resounding phrases and highly coloured epithets rolled forth effortlessly from his fiery imagination, and on this occasion were turned to good account as with deep emotion he endeavoured to stir up lethargic members by describing the appalling catastrophes that would follow a Napoleonic landing: 'Houses plundered, then burnt, sons conscribed, wives and daughters ravished . . . but as for you, you luxurious Aldermen! With YOUR fat will he grease the wheels of his triumphal chariot!'

Fears and disputes were pervading his private life as well. Besides his agonizing anxiety about his adored little daughter, he was embarked on the long and bitter battle against his mother which dragged on, in and out of the Law Courts, for several years. Finally he succeeded in getting full possession of Croft Castle and its estates, apparently on the grounds that it had been settled on him at the time of his marriage to Maria Burgh, his mother only retaining a life interest. His eagerness to get money —anyhow, anywhere—had become an absolute obsession. He was incapable of controlling his extravagance, in spite of warnings and the heavy retrenchments he had been compelled to make at Hafod. All the time he was flinging money away on one thing after another, buying everything he saw or heard of which might prove useful or ornamental. He had every right to do so. If it were not for his mother, he argued, he would be one of the richest men in the country. As she had chosen to set herself against him he would resist her to the last ounce of his strength. From this distance of time and with little evidence it is impossible to judge fairly what appears to have been a somewhat questionable business, about which even Johnes at first was not quite easy in his mind. It estranged him for ever from his family at Stratford Place as well as from many of the Knights. But ravenous though he was for money, it did not help him to make good bargains for himself. When Croft was at last in his hands he only succeeded in disposing of it after many disappointments and delays, and then for a very much smaller sum than he had hoped for.

In February, as Mariamne appeared to be a little better, her parents left her in the care of her aunt, in order to spend a few days at Hafod. But scarcely had they arrived there than Johnes was urgently summoned to London by Payne Knight, who was keeping a friendly eye on his interests. Jane was left alone with the servants in the creaking, half-empty house, with most of the rooms plunged in a shuttered twilight that made the dust-sheeted furniture look ghostlier than ever. The perishing cold and wailing winds of February and the dismal aspect of the mountains, at best cannot have been very agreeable for a nervous, highly strung creature like Jane. To put a last touch to her discomfiture, one morning a messenger arrived post-haste from Aberystwyth with the alarming tidings that the enemy was about to land. Within a few hours French soldiers would be pouring across the hills on their way into England, burning and destroying as they went. A woman of far tougher fibre might well have been intimidated by such news, but Jane Johnes rose to the occasion with great spirit, as will be seen by the letter which she immediately despatched by a messenger to her brother at Dolecothy.

'Hafod Thursday Morning.

'I have this moment heard that the sail of the french are off Aberystwyth and Aberaeron. If you are able let me beg of you to come over and bring what Arms you can powder and shot; they will not sell any at Aberystwyth. I am not quite sure if I am doing right in asking you to come over. I leave it to your better judgment to act as you think best. I feel very odly in this business but I will defend the house as long as I can. I trust to God for the rest and if I fall hope to be happy hereafter.

'You need not bring any People with you. We have enough here if we had Arms.'

What a day of frenzied preparations that must have been, of barring, locking, barricading and disposing her men at suitable points to intercept the enemy, but when evening was drawing in her fears were set at rest by 'a very civil letter' from a distant neighbour, informing her that the alarm was over and the French gone.

She sat down at once to inform her brother, who had not been at home when her earlier communication reached Dolecothy. She had received a letter from him by the post that same day on quite another topic, one which in its way was even more serious, for already it had done much to spoil their relationship and had made him very chary of coming to Hafod. Jane was continually entreating him to try and find money for 'poor Mr. Johnes', either by parting with his own or borrowing other people's. Half-heartedly, John Johnes did as he was bid. He may have been down in Carmarthen that very day, reluctantly persuading some sniggering attorney to arrange another loan for his needy brother-in-law.

Her letter continued: 'I have just received your kind letter, I am truly sorry that you have so much trouble on our account but I trust the time is not very far distant when we shall be a Comfort not a Plague to our friends, for surely the wicked old woman will not last for ever.'

In May 1797 Dr. Smith published in two immense, superbly illustrated volumes, his *Natural History of the rarer Lepidopterous Insects of Georgia*, which in a dedicatory letter he inscribed to 'Miss Johnes of Hafod':

'My dear young friend,

'The tribute of a dedication, at least of an honest dedication, is usually paid to established worth or pre-eminent knowledge; yet, as it is also sometimes permitted to breathe the effusions of affection alone, it may surely be allowed to combine those effusions with hope. When you look over the book, it will remind you of many hours we have passed together, in the practical investigation of similar objects to those which it illustrates, amid some of the noblest scenery of Nature; hours equally delightful to you and to me. To you they unfolded the exquisite perfection and endless variety of the creation; to me they displayed a youthful mind, affected and improved by the contemplation of such objects as the God of Nature intended it should be. May that mind never be less ingenuous, less ardent in the pursuit of truth and virtue, nor less affectionate to all who endeavoured to inform and direct it, than I then beheld it! Such is the sincere and ardent prayer of,

'My dear young friend,
'Your most affectionate,
'And faithful servant,
'J. E. SMITH.

'*London*,
'*May* 29, 1797.'

But her parents' pride in this tribute, her own pleasure at the honour done to her, must have been sadly alloyed by her grievous illness which pursued its fluctuating course all through the summer. By October her condition was so grave that Johnes entreated Smith to come at once to Hafod. He did not hesitate; his devotion to the child swept every other consideration to one side. Ignoring the dissuasions of his friends who greatly feared the ill effects his delicate health might sustain from travelling such a great distance at that inclement season; leaving his many other commitments and his pretty young wife and pleasant home at Hammersmith, he started off immediately for Wales. And several days later, as he informed his 'dear Pleasy', he arrived late one evening at Llandovery, where he had 'much ado to get a bed and supper'.

'I could scarcely have got forward, the chaises were so much engaged, but there was a Mrs. Hughes an elderly widow lady in a chaise of 4 alone, going to Aberystwyth, and she graciously "allowed me to share her magnificence" and was very good company. We came to Llanpeter 20 miles over a country much in the Rhayader style, very wild and fine. Here our roads were to separate, and being anxious to get to Hafod, I did not much relish going round by Aberth. 15 miles out of my way. There are no chaises at Llanpeter. Here I experienced true Welch hospitality. This good lady knowing the business I was upon would fain have given up her chaise to me, saying she wd. go home on horseback, as she could sleep at her sister's 6 miles off and send for her horses thither. It was with difficulty I could avoid accepting this kind offer. But luckily I got a good riding horse, and a welch guide, and so I set off, after a spare dinner, for Hafod, 23 miles. The road lay over the wildest and highest hills . . . but the afternoon being most delightful, and the views very fine, I enjoyed my ride much. Almost the whole country I traversed is Mr. Johnes's and I passed Llanvair, a miserable town with a grand collegiate church partly in ruins,[1] where was the ancient seat of his family. It was dark before I got opposite to Maen Arthur, but I heard the river roar. Just as I got to Hafod it began to rain, and was a very wet night. I was tired, but am no worse for it to-day—I rang the bell, and John came, who was delighted to see me, and in a moment Mr. Johnes came running downstairs, and gave me the most hearty welcome—He led me all the way by the hand upstairs to the dressing-room, where Mrs. Johnes and my dear little patient received me with equal cordiality. Mr. Johnes was all the evening half out of his wits for joy, and both he and Mrs. Johnes are every moment showing me the most friendly attentions. When I first saw Miss Johnes she was so much agitated by joy I could hardly judge of her, but I am happy to tell you she is much better than I expected. She is taller and looks more healthy than last year. The projection of her back is rounder, not sharp—her limbs are greatly better. . . . Indeed I have great hopes of her. . . . The machine has done wonders. Jones the maker is here—but he is a drunkard—he is going soon. There is also a Mr. Tait, an architect, a pleasant man.'

Unfortunately his first impressions were wrong; he remained there till January nursing her through a dangerous illness, and went back there again in May to attend her. Leaving her then, as he hoped, well on the road to recovery, he had not been gone many days before she had a serious relapse and again they despaired of saving her. 'It all appears like a frightful dream which I cannot unravel,' wrote the demented father.

[1] Smith evidently mistook Llanddewi Brefi for Llanfair. It is a few miles further on.

Disaster succeeded disaster. Whilst they were still in the utmost anxiety over Marianne, he was aghast to learn that his regiment, whose affairs he appears to have somewhat lost touch with, had offered itself for service in Ireland, to assist in quelling the rebellion that was raging there. As the regiment was stationed at Liverpool, he knew for a certainty that it would be sent over immediately, and its Colonel was bound in honour to follow it without delay. This blow from a totally unexpected quarter left him stunned, and furious, besides, with his Lieutenant-Colonel who had volunteered without consulting him. The idea of being torn from his poor invalid, who could scarcely bear him to be away from her even for an hour, was bitterly unendurable. He it was who supported her through the painful treatments prescribed by the doctors; who adjusted the fearful steel stays without which she could neither stand nor walk; whose abundant vitality kept her flickering little flame alight. If he left her now he dreaded to think what the consequences might be. If she so much as suspected what might happen, he believed it would kill her. He was left, however, with no choice. His duty to his regiment outweighed all personal considerations. Like a doomed man, he made his secret preparations to leave for Dublin at a moment's notice, but day after day for a fortnight, for one reason or another, he deferred his departure. Whilst he was still hesitating, the news arrived that two-thirds of the regiment had refused to embark, and many of the men had mutinied and were now in irons. This fresh development threw him into greater irresolution than ever, and whilst he was still trying to decide what to do, he heard that the rebellion was rapidly ending and accordingly he might honourably remain where he was. The relief was inexpressible, but the strain of the whole business had been too severe for him to risk a repetition of it at a later date. The only thing to do was to resign his command.

He was not to be allowed to get out of it as easily as he hoped. The King summoned him to London, and in private audience did his utmost to dissuade him, with promises of unlimited leave until Miss Johnes's health was perfectly restored. But Colonel Johnes, who had already indulged in years of leave, stood firm as a rock by his decision to retire, and having convinced his monarch of this, he set off again for his mountains as fast as he could travel.

All these distresses did not prevent the usual flow of summer visitors and sightseers. One who arrived this year was a travel-stained young artist, riding a pony, who was making a sketching tour in Wales and searching for the birthplace of his ideal painter, Richard Wilson. This was J. M. W. Turner, who weeks before had set out for Wales from Bristol where he had been staying with a friend of his father's, a worthy fell-monger, who had given him the pony and lent him a cloak and saddle, neither of which was he destined ever to see again.

Only Turner's beautiful representation of the house remains to tell of his visit, but we can be sure that Johnes, with his deep sympathy and admiration for artists and their works, took a very different view of him to that which, years later, the fell-monger's niece recorded, for she only perceived a careless, slovenly youth of very plain appearance who could talk of nothing but his drawings.

Lesser stars in the artistic firmament came in plenty, but all meaning has gone from their names. There was old Mr. Moore who stopped in the house and 'Did but two sketches' owing to his infirmities, and 'a very fine drawer, Laporte' was in the grounds for some time, making very fine drawings. Then one Friday morning in August a tightly packed carriage drew up at the door, carrying a benign and prosperous-looking gentleman surrounded by a bevy of golden-haired damsels, of all ages between fourteen and four-and-twenty. This was the rich Norwich banker, John Gurney of Earlham Hall, with his seven 'most enchanting' daughters. They were on their way back to Aberystwyth from the Devil's Bridge where, in 'a sort of little inn, where we slept, we had a very happy evening; for we were wet, and were obliged to put on our dressing-gowns and sit over a turf fire, in the public-house; singing and being sung to by the interesting Welch inhabitants.' Thus Elizabeth Gurney in her journal; earlier in the day she had almost fainted with terror as she climbed down the rocks above the waterfall, and had to sit down until she recovered herself. So timid indeed was this delicate, fair-haired girl that even to bathe in the sea at Aberystwyth 'required much exertion of courage'. Yet in years to come, as Mrs. Elizabeth Fry, she would walk calmly through the noisome sinks of Newgate and stand alone among a crowd of half-bestialized women prisoners whom even the prison governor dared not approach without a guard.

Not one word did Elizabeth Gurney give to Hafod in her journal, but their visit was such a rush that scarcely had they breakfasted than they were gone again. Johnes complained he did not have time to speak to half of them, and considered it a most uncomfortable and crowded way of travelling, though the Gurneys did not seem to think so and were ready to be pleased with everything.

In September, Payne Knight, who continued to 'act a very friendly and manly part' in Johnes's affairs, came from Downton bringing with him an immensely obese, somewhat obscene-looking individual, plethoric and crafty-eyed, dirtily dressed in shabby grey clothes and a greasy black hat. There was nothing in his appearance to suggest the regal state that he maintained at Arundel Castle and in London. This was Charles, the 11th Duke of Norfolk, nicknamed the Jockey, who for political reasons had forsaken the Roman Faith of his ancestors and joined the Church of England. In Herefordshire, he was a neighbour of Payne Knight's, for his marriage with Miss Frances Scudamore had brought him Holme Lacey, a fine place of which he now enjoyed undisturbed possession, for his Duchess had gone mad soon after their marriage and been put away. As travelling companion and guest he must have had serious drawbacks. 'That dirty devil the Jockey of Norfolk' Creevey called him, and his aversion to soap and water was said to be such that his servants had to take advantage of his drunken stupors in order to wash him. Gross and gluttonous as he was, drinking his wine out of a huge silver tankard and beef-steaks vanishing 'like magic when placed before him', he still managed to have great knowledge and taste and genuinely appreciated talent and enterprise. He was President of the Society of Arts, and from his hands in years to come Johnes would receive many gold medals for his works at Hafod, some of which in 1798 the Duke had the opportunity of seeing with his own eyes.

There were many who during these two years believed that they were witnessing the final phase of Johnes's reign at Hafod. Friends and counsellors alike were making strenuous efforts to induce him to abandon it, to go and live cheaply abroad for a few years, until his affairs were once more in order. Johnes, however, resolutely opposed every suggestion of the kind. He would economize at Hafod and nowhere else. There he would continue to do all the good he could, for his poor people must on no account be allowed to suffer for his follies. It was decided that they should live there all the year round, leading a simple, economical country life, with only ten servants indoors. He was becoming increasingly interested in farming, and this and tree-planting would provide him with plenty to do out of doors. Dr. Anderson, who was now a frequent visitor, would act as his adviser.

It was an arrangement that suited Jane very well. She had never much cared for London and greatly disliked visiting. She was happier on her own ground, dispensing favours rather than receiving them. While as for farming, in her opinion it was 'one of the best amusements a country gentleman can take to'.

CHAPTER X

No 'Common Sort of Farm'

At the end of the eighteenth century agriculture in Cardiganshire was in a very bad way altogether. With the possible exception of some parts in the south of the county, where the soil was more fertile and there were a few enterprising proprietors and farmers, the methods generally resorted to were as primitive as the implements and tools that were commonly employed. In these respects, the landlords were as unprogressive as their tenants, and were reputed to be more interested in adding to the size of their estates than they were in improving their land. An official of the Board of Agriculture who had been sent down to report upon prevailing conditions, had declared in his melancholy findings that the Welsh plough was 'perhaps the most awkward, unmeaning tool to be found in any civilised country; it is not calculated to cut a furrow, but to tear it open by main force'. The narrow, low-wheeled carts with a heavy beam to which two oxen were yoked behind a pair of horses, were of an equally primitive character. Carts were a comparatively recent innovation and were beginning to take the place of the old-fashioned, ox-drawn sledges which could carry very little. Carts and tools alike were home-made, of any old bits of wood and metal that the farmer could have for the taking, for he had no money to spare for equipment. The archaic objects which he and his labourers fashioned as they huddled round the open hearth in the kitchen at the end of the day's toil, were the same that had been handed down from one generation to another, thus acquiring a reputation of infallibility that made their owners cling to them with fierce and jealous obstinacy.

In every department they made do with what could be got for nothing; seaweed and sand which could be brought in bags on horseback from the coast were spread on the fields in preference to lime, which had to be paid for. Necessity decreed it, for the earnings of a farmer were miserable. There were scarcely any local markets where he might sell the surplus of his produce. The towns were small, with few inhabitants, while all who could afford it in the country districts kept a pig and perhaps a cow to vary the barley bread and potatoes of which their diet otherwise consisted. Those who could not did without. The nearest sale for bacon and salt butter was to be had at Bristol, a weary tramp of several days that was enough to break the heart of the under-nourished, heavily-laden farmer and his sons. And it was to Bristol, too, or else far north to Liverpool, that he had to carry his sacks of oats and barley. As for his cattle, these were generally disposed of to the drovers, who took them right across England to sell at the fairs in Essex and in Kent. With such appalling difficulties confronting him, and reducing his miserable profits, it is not to be wondered at that one after the other relapsed into a state of idleness, seeking the comfort that circumstances denied them in liquor. For there was little to be had in any other quarter. The farms where they existed, were, as we have seen, the most miserable places, built of mud and rubble and generally placed in a hollow under a steep bank which in rainy weather became a watercourse. The murk and stench within were warranted to poison forthwith any little sprouting of energy and ambition. Such a thing as a store-room was unknown, and the two rooms the place usually consisted of were generally a clutter of beds and sacks of roots and corn. As for a dairy, the farmer's wife had to content herself with any small recess that was available, or perhaps a lean-to shed at the back, which served for half a dozen other purposes besides. As a contemporary writer opined, this may well have accounted for the consuming fevers which were prevalent among the peasantry.

Many of the younger people, finding life at home intolerable, were drifting away, the men going for soldiers or sailors, while whole families were emigrating to America. A great wave of emigration was sweeping the county. American agents seeking recruits for the New World, were luring the poor Cardis to forsake their homes and kindred by dangling before them the most dazzling promises of what awaited them across the Atlantic Ocean. If one contemporary writer may be believed, the fate in store for the unhappy emigrants was a 'Lamentably melancholy' one. 'Ignorant of the country to which they were going, and the nature of the employment in which they were to be engaged; to obtain their passage they accepted the agent's own terms, and thus ignorantly became the property of these human harpies. So ignorant were many of them that before they lost sight of land they supposed they must be arrived; and after arriving there were sold as slaves into the back settlements of Vermont and Kentucky: others that were able to pay their passage there, finding the nature of the country, were desirous to return; but, unable to pay for their passage back, were obliged to engage in the most servile employments and submit to the most degrading conditions, to escape death from hunger.'

Another factor that militated against better farming was the smuggling which was very active all along the coast. The opportunities it offered of large rewards, and casks of wine and spirits to drink and to sell, did a great deal to distract the farmer's attention from his own poor acres. Smuggling was an infinitely more exciting and profitable occupation than to embark on all the expense and labour of high agriculture, such as Johnes was advocating and practising up at Hafod. Many a desperate midnight rider passed along that way, galloping over the mountains laden with 'Whisci smygl' and other luxuries, obtained off the coast

Mariamne Johnes aged about nine

Dr James Edward Smith, President of the Linnaean Society

near Aberystwyth, to be 'dropped' at different hiding-places between there and Hereford. It was not unknown for a squire to have a share in one of the vessels that ran into the creeks by night, adding spice to his fun by making the local excise officer his boon companion. And on stormy nights at sea a bright light cunningly placed in a window lured many a rich merchantman to a rocky doom, while the wreckers, the farmers and their men, reaped a richer harvest than any their own land would ever yield them.

With indifference on the one hand and reckless irresponsibility on the other, it had been almost impossible for the unselfish endeavours of a few public-spirited men who did their best to raise the standard of agriculture, to gain ground. A Society for the Encouragement of Agriculture and Industry had been formed in 1784 and had begun with a flourish, stimulating a certain degree of activity by offering premiums for different branches of husbandry and the domestic manufacture of flannels and stockings. The women took the coarse stockings they knitted to the local fairs, where they were bought 'for the use of the inferior military' and several 'genteel families' with praiseworthy public-spiritedness, 'used neither cloth nor flannel but what had been manufactured in their own houses'. All the same, the Agricultural Society had almost petered out by 1796; members had fallen off and no subscriptions had been received for years, except from the faithful few.

Needless to say, prominent among them was Colonel Johnes who had been one of the keenest of the founders. But now, to all intents and purposes, the Society was dead, just as every other useful project sooner or later died of hunger and neglect in that inclement climate.

But Johnes would not heed the skeleton finger pointing towards his new and up-to-date home-farm, where all the latest methods and devices were given a fair trial and large-scale experiments in every branch of agriculture were being carried out. It was established for the benefit of the county. All were welcomed there and were given every opportunity of seeing and judging for themselves. Successes and failures alike were profitable as good and bad examples, while the light, well-drained buildings (put up by his own workmen at very little cost) were excellent models for others to copy. The dark, stinking beast-houses on the farms were a crying scandal; it spoke volumes for the hardiness of the horses and cattle of the country that they managed to survive at all in such infamous quarters and on a starvation diet. The good results of proper accommodation and feeding gleamed all over the sleek, well-nourished occupants of the Hafod byres and stables. The great Suffolk Punches tossing and stamping in their stalls, and the delicate-headed milkers munching contentedly as they nosed about their troughs, were undoubtedly much better nourished and housed than the gaunt, hollow-cheeked farmers who came to stare at them. Every known make of plough and every other implement was imported and tested, the ones turning out best being cheaply copied on the place and given or sold at a nominal price to all whose endeavours made them worthy of encouragement. Johnes would not spare any expense or neglect any expedient in his determination to wrest from the earth its store of hidden treasure.

The unappeasable sense of personal responsibility was as strong as ever. Nothing could quench it. The experiences of the past fifteen years had in no way diminished his faith. The dreams he had cherished long ago of transforming the whole county were back in force, glowing with possibilities. It seemed to him a comparatively simple thing to replace that terrible, unnecessary poverty with prosperity and plenty. In this, above all, he longed to succeed. He could not endure to see the scarecrow figures crawling about in their vile surroundings, among the crops of thistles and molehills flourishing in the fields. They must be rescued, as he had rescued his own people at Hafod, who were at last becoming acclimatized to a more civilized way of living. He had no doubt at all that the farmers merely required being taught a new and better way of farming for them to adopt it eagerly. Once they had fully grasped the paramount importance of hard work and thriftiness, miracles would be accomplished in no time. Look at what the Scottish farmers had achieved in a comparatively few years. Cardiganshire offered far greater opportunities, if only he could induce them to realize it. By every means in his power he would push them on towards the wonderful benefits that were waiting for them just round the corner. No lover was ever more ready to sacrifice his all to prove himself than this elderly enthusiast. He cared desperately for his country's welfare, with an all-consuming, indiscriminating ardour. The last thing he took into account in his plans was the human element. He never paused to consider what might be going on in the primitive minds of these farmers; stubborn and secret to a man as their own hills and as ready to resist every suspected threat of encroachment or interference. Nor did he give a thought to the causes that were largely responsible for the existing conditions. He had never allowed himself to admit difficulties, and he would not do so now. As he conjured up the glorious panorama of what was going to be, his heart throbbed at the prospect of the resplendent gold and green of a land where a stout, ruddy-cheeked peasantry would cheerfully labour. In the background many neat homesteads dotted the landscape. So he dreamed, while the elemental spirits of the earth confused and dazzled him with heady emanations and trails of glittering dust. He was easy to sway. Like a pack of wild colts his thoughts galloped away from the dull level of actuality to the shining realms of illusion which seemed more real than truth.

Not that he wasted his time with idle dreaming. He had plenty to do. There was always something new to be tried out, besides all the routine work of the farm to watch, and, of course, constant visitors to be taken over it. Then he was continually reclaiming waste land, ploughing up vast tracts of it in the mountains. It was a costly business, but the results would more than recompense him. When the peaty soil was well drained and limed, he found it produced excellent crops of potatoes, grain, yams and grass. Now every single mountain farmer had many such acres at his disposal. Why could he not also turn them to good account? The great expense of the reclamation was quickly forgotten in Johnes's enthusiasm at the result. He really did believe that all that was required to emulate his success was hard work and a measure of perseverance. The chief problem was to know how best to bring this home to them.

Believing in the value of good example, he persuaded several indigent though respectable Scottish families to exchange their native hills for those of North Cardiganshire. They would serve as living emblems of that thrift and industry which he tirelessly recommended. As the 'Cardi'—and to a greater degree than ever in the lonely mountains—had a deep-rooted objection to 'foreigners', local opinion was probably not at all impressed for the good by this introduction of 'bonny Scots farmers'. An expert ploughman was also brought down from the North to demonstrate the use of the Rotherham plough, for in spite of Johnes's efforts his tenants still persisted in employing their own 'unmeaning tool'. Undismayed by their recalcitrance and unwillingness to learn, he continued to think out new ways of influencing them. Later on, in 1801, at the time of Addington's ministry, he was extremely anxious to invite a hundred Swiss families from Grisons to come and settle on his estate. He planned to let them 7,500 acres of particularly barren mountain—though, of course, no worse than that to which they were accustomed—at 1s. 6d. an acre for three lives. This the hardy mountaineers should reclaim, founding a colony which in a very short while would be a model of fertile prosperity, bringing great wealth to the whole country. Thus at least did he dream, for it went no further. When he laid the scheme before Addington, the Prime Minister unreservedly refused to co-operate by advancing 'the 100 families £10,000 for the expenses of travelling etc.' as Johnes required him to. Though he afterwards declared that Addington deserved to be cursed for it, he all the same had slight misgivings himself about the fundamental soundness of his proposal.

In order that the principles of good agriculture should be made available to all, he wrote and distributed a treatise, '*A Cardiganshire Landlord's advice to his Tenants,* in which he lucidly propounded the plan of farming best suited to the county, reinforcing his arguments with extracts from the writings of such proved authorities as Dr. Anderson and Arthur Young. He took care, too, to stress the urgent necessity of paying greater regard to cleanliness, particularly in the dairy, that scabrous hole which makes one marvel that a single child survived to grow to manhood; he was the first to introduce to their notice vessels of Swansea pottery for containing the milk, in lieu of the greasy old leaden troughs that were in common use. His advice was made more palatable by the promise of rewards; there was nothing he would not promise, in order to infuse them with even a little vitality and enthusiasm.

'But that nothing may be wanting on my part,' he wrote, 'to promote a better system of cultivation, I intend having your farms inspected; and giving to those who have managed their farms in the best manner such implements of husbandry as may encourage them to proceed, in so praiseworthy a track. . . .

'Upon the proper rotation of crops depends the well-doing of the farmer. This doctrine I am very anxious to imprint in your minds, for in this country the course of crops is most miserably neglected; or rather there is only one continuation of oats until the ground is completely exhausted. There is scarce an idea of meliorating green crop, or a proper fallow, between the crops of grain. As I am determined, by rewards and otherwise, to put an end to this destructive system, I shall very plainly open my mind to you. In all the leases I grant there will be a clause to prevent this destructive practice from being continued, which shall be religiously kept; on the contrary, I shall not forget to reward those who follow a better system.'

At last the light was kindled. Premiums, money prizes and

gold medals, all coming out of Johnes's capacious pocket, stirred up a competitive zeal as nothing else had done. A marked improvement in the appearance of the farms began to be noticeable, most encouraging to his heart. Meanwhile, in his own undertakings he was going from strength to strength. He introduced specimens of every different breed of milch-cow at Hafod in order to compare their merits and to discover which was best suited to the country, on one occasion importing forty heifers from Holland. Then he disproved the theory that different kinds of cheese could not be produced on the same land, for Jane and her sisters made wonderful imitations of Parmesan, Stilton, Cheddar, and many other kinds. Johnes was enormously elated. He had discovered another fine industry which would bring profit and fame to Cardiganshire if only the farmers would bestir themselves and take the trouble to develop it. All the best varieties of cheese might be manufactured in the farms and sent to the big dealers in the cities. What a triumph this would be! But the same trap which had throttled others before him quickly snapped its sharp teeth on his hopes, for, try as he might, he failed to get a market for his cheeses anywhere. Not in the whole of Wales or England. It was a crushing disappointment, for he found himself left with five tons of them on his hands—all made of the richest cream. In the end he had to sell them to his work-people for a few pence a pound.

The chief purpose of his retirement to Hafod must have been seriously undermined by his farming exploits, which were carried on with an extravagance which made even his most respectful admirers blench as they recorded them in their diaries. But then with Johnes it could never have been otherwise. 'I should be miserable without a Farm,' he told his friend, George Cumberland. 'However a common sort of Farm would not do for me.'

In the autumn of 1799 the farming vicar of Driffield, in Gloucestershire, the Reverend Richard Cumberland, made a journey on horseback into Wales and paid a call at Hafod. And in the account that he wrote to his brother George we hear an echo which may well have represented the general local opinion.

'At Blane Cwm, by the elegant bridge,' wrote Mr. Cumberland (this bridge, which had been designed by Baldwin of Bath, had been thrown across the Ystwyth at Johnes's expense), 'I met with an old farmer and treated with him for the purchase of 150 wethers. . . . Finding I was going to Hafod, he observed that Mr. Johnes was a worthy man but was ruining himself with schemes as (says he) he won't listen to what such Gentlemen as you say.

'. . . I was so fortunate as to find the family assembled under the portico without company—Mr. Johnes received me in a very friendly manner . . . and invited me to accept a Bed etc. He then shewed me the House with an addition since you were there of an elegant Dairy, the best I ever saw and before Dinner he walked with me over some of those walks you have so well painted, and part of his farm, of which he is not a little proud. . . . You have by no means exaggerated the beauties of this extraordinary spot which none but a painter and poet could describe at all.

'Mrs. Johnes's sisters appeared at Dinner. Mrs. Johnes suffered so much from a rheumatic complaint in her face that she quitted us soon after which I much regretted as she promised me an agreeable lecture on her Dairy which seems their favourite Hobby . . . they make all sorts of Cheese under Dr. Anderson's direction. Mr. Johnes has just laid the foundation of a new church . . . in the evening he entertained me with some of his Essays on Agriculture which are well written and will be of general utility.'

Much to Johnes's disappointment, Mr. Cumberland insisted on setting off for home at an early hour next day, but not before he had taken another good walk round the estate with his brother's book in mind. It was four years now since its publication, and any little income it had brought its author had long since ceased. Indeed, George's finances were at an extremely low ebb. It was about this time that his straitened means and the expense of his large and hungry family compelled him to leave his villa at Egham where he had lived happily for many years, dabbling with the arts and collecting fine engravings by Bonasoni. Johnes did all he could to persuade him to come and live in Cardiganshire. He even offered to lend him a bathing house which he had built on the coast and never made use of. There Cumberland, with his wife and eight children, could live rent free and enjoy all the wonderful advantages the country could give them. Cumberland should cultivate the soil and pay frequent visits to Hafod, for he and Johnes thoroughly enjoyed one another's society. Cumberland seems to have favoured the plan, but Mrs. Cumberland put her foot down and refused to hear of it. To live in penury in a bathing house on the Welsh coast, hundreds of miles from anywhere, was more than this much-harassed lady could contemplate. The idea was accordingly abandoned, and soon afterwards Cumberland bought a small farm in the Mendips. He hoped through farming to add to his income, but he very soon found himself in a worse plight than ever, perfectly incapable of managing his stock and being robbed on all sides. He appealed to Johnes, who put him in touch with the ever-helpful Dr. Anderson, and in a letter which the latter wrote him a glimpse of Hafod is obtained from another angle.

After strongly recommending that Cumberland should get rid of his farm with as little delay as possible, on the grounds that, besides the many difficulties involved, a gentleman novice was invariably preyed upon by everybody, he added: 'The art with which these little designs are carried forward is such as to elude for a long time the efforts of a dignified mind to comprehend it. . . . Our friends, Mr. and Mrs. Johnes, tho' persons of no inconsiderable talents, have never been able to do it, and at this hour have their domestic comforts wonderfully diminished by it.'

Side by side with farming, planting trees went on apace. Johnes had been making plantations on the estate ever since

1782, but from 1796 onwards his activities in this direction increased to a vast scale and were said to be unequalled by any contemporary landowner in the British Isles, with the sole exception of James, Earl of Fife.

Between October 1795 and April 1801 he planted two million, sixty-five thousand trees, nearly half of them being larch, which flourished vigorously in the most exposed places. Beech did particularly well, too, but every variety of timber tree was represented in his woods and all seemed to thrive. Planting was by far the most fortunate of his enterprises; the losses he incurred were astonishingly few, for trees prospered for him as nothing else did. Year after year, in tens and hundreds of thousands, they were set in every foot of ground unfit for cultivation. No mountain-top, however bleak and inhospitable its aspect, was to be left uncovered by that green cloak of woodland which he dreamed eventually of drawing across his whole vast estate. Here and there, for picturesqueness, some jagged peak might be permitted to transcend the verdant mists of larch trees, or a spur of rock breaking forth from among the hanging woods; otherwise nothing naked would be allowed to offend the eye.

Without these outdoor pursuits to keep him constantly on the move, jogging or tramping all over his demesne and far beyond it, he could scarcely have endured the uncertainties and stresses that were racking them at home, all through the last years of the century. Their poor Min's illness dragged on interminably and at times it looked as if all their happiness, all their hopes and ambitions, were doomed to crash into ruins as the slender thread of her life threatened to break for ever. It was a heart-breaking, nerve-racking time of crises that she managed to struggle through, and remarkable improvements that were never maintained. For two whole years her state was so precarious that Johnes never left Hafod for a single night. The illness of this delicately nurtured girl was conducted against a backcloth of almost Hogarthian squalor. The doctors who were summoned there all appear to have been either confirmed drunkards or else reduced to that level by the lavish hospitality of the house. There was young Dr. Jones from London, who was constantly being sent for to readjust the steel stays; he was 'the greatest Beast' in a house that Johnes ever saw. The local apothecary's diagnosis could never be relied on for the same reason, and even good Dr. Davies from Carmarthen, an old family friend, was stricken with gout soon after his arrival and had to keep to his bed. Indeed, it was a wonder that Mariamne survived at all.

There are only fleeting glimpses of her to be had now and again, and they are sad enough, for she was very different from the active, busy little girl of a few years earlier. We see her walking on crutches, or lying in the portico surrounded by her plants with her pet birds swinging in their cages from the roof. And on one occasion, when she was 'vastly better', she sang for the first time for two years to a houseful of visitors (for visitors continued to come and go as usual). She sang a touching Italian song, *Tanto in Addio*, with such sweetness and feeling that her little audience was moved to tears. 'We were a lot of maudlin Whigs,' said Johnes, and the sight alone of the delicate cripple girl must surely have been enough to melt the coldest heart.

But these recoveries never lasted any length of time. Only a few months after this she was seen at Bristol Hot Wells looking such a picture of 'debility and distortion' that it seemed likely, if she lived at all, that she could never be anything but an object of pity. It was fortunate for Johnes that he could not see her thus. Blinded by his devotion, she was always perfection, always improving in appearance as well as in character. When she was not dying, and he walked in a perfect nightmare of dread, she was always growing stout and vastly better-looking and everything would soon be right again. It was another manifestation of the myopia which made him oblivious of many other painful facts; in this case most mercifully.

He had many other troubles. Constant disputes over money continued to harry him and wound his feelings as old friendships cooled off and supplies threatened to run out altogether. He and

Jane would never again see the brother she had loved with such possessive devotion, for John Johnes had married in 1797 and soon afterwards had pressed for the return of the money Johnes had borrowed. When this was not forthcoming, a quarrel broke out which parted the two families for ever. Johnes had nothing to spare for his debts, for his own need was greater almost than at any other time. Planting on such an extensive scale was a costly business, though, of course, it was the finest investment he could make and gave a wonderful amount of employment to the poor. Somehow he managed to keep going. First Croft was sold, then a year or two later Stanage Park—the old home of his Grandmother Knight. After that, in quick succession, other estates in Cardiganshire and elsewhere, as the capital he received for each was absorbed by present expenses and the backwash of old liabilities. And, since nothing was to be spared him, it was discovered that the steward he had trusted implicitly for twenty years had been systematically defrauding him, while the same applied to a local attorney. But now he was better able to meet such blows with calmness, for harsh experience had steeled him to 'the real face of mankind'.

His works at Hafod did not go unrewarded. They were proclaimed on all sides, bringing the place even more prominently before the public eye. From 1800 onwards he was awarded a number of gold medals for his services to agriculture and afforestation, which naturally did much to encourage him and spur him on to further activities. In 1804, Dr. Anderson, who had left Scotland and retired to end his days in a little house at Isleworth, told Cumberland: 'I have just seen our friend Mr. Johnes, and find him the same and as keen a farmer as ever. He is certainly blessed in possessing as good a disposition and as steady a flow of animal spirits as any human being ever possessed. He talks of Hafod as a paradise, and of his improvements with rapture, as if he had never met with a single disappointment in his life.'

CHAPTER XI

"Another Laurel"

At Hafod the year 1800 came in with every sign and prospect of good fortune. A wonderful change had come over everything. Though out of doors it poured and blew incessantly, and the dilapidated beauties might only be seen from the windows through flashing screens of rain and leaden coils of cloud, the atmosphere in the house was strangely clear and luminous. It was like a fabulous spring in mid-winter. All the long-drawn-out suspense, the shocks and anxieties, had vanished with the old century. Such a miraculous and well-maintained improvement had at last taken place in Mariamne's health that by next autumn a new Italian master would be installed there to complete her education. The boundless joy and relief felt by the whole family filled the house with vernal gaiety.

Johnes was feeling more vigorous than ever and the impending sale of Stanage contributed enormously to his high spirits. Each time he sold an estate he revelled in hallucinatory visions of a future gloriously free from debt and all financial cares. This had the unfortunate result of making him spend even more recklessly. He was now adding a large conservatory to the house and rebuilding the parish church entirely at his own expense, from a design by Wyatt. This new Gothic church would be ornamented with a fine altar-piece by Fuseli. Honours were falling to his share, besides, for while the year was still in its infancy he was appointed to the Lord-Lieutenancy of Cardiganshire. Although he declared that his friends were far more eager about it than he was, it could not fail to gratify him. At the least it signified that all he had done for the county during the past seventeen years had not been overlooked in high places.

Nor was this all. Now that disabling weight of dread was lifted from his mind, he had returned to a literary work he had been desultorily occupied with before Mariamne's illness. The idea of it had originated as long ago as 1794, at that hired house in Swansea where Jane had lived whilst he was with his regiment. At the sale of M. Paris's famous collection in London, he had bought among many other things a particularly fine printed vellum copy of *Froissart's Chronicles*. One winter's evening, as he sat by the fire reading it aloud, interpreting from the old French for Jane's amusement, she was so much delighted with it that she suggested that he should set about making a proper English translation. She would write it for him, she said, if he would give her the profits to 'build an habitation for six poor old men and six old women'.

The suggestion was worth considering. There had been no English translation of *Froissart* since the one which had been published by Lord Berners in 1523–5, at the command of Henry VIII. It is unlikely, however, that Johnes would have gone further with the matter if Jane had not persisted. Jane, the eager and devoted, always supplied the encouragement and impetus which he stood in such dire need of. We may be sure she gave him no peace until he had written off to his friend, Mr. Edwards, the learned bookseller of 11 Pall Mall, laying the proposition before him and asking for his opinion.

James Edwards was one of the most famous bibliographers of that day, the friend and adviser of many literary celebrities for whom his shop provided a regular meeting-place. Many of the treasures which he had a rare genius for discovering in all corners of Europe, found their way to Hafod. Edwards stayed there a number of times, and, in spite of lending him money, he always remained one of Johnes's staunchest allies. Now, in 1794, he not only warmly encouraged his plan of translating the *Chronicles*, but made him a most generous offer for it as well. Lord Thurlow, on reading a few tentative chapters, was equally emphatic that they should be proceeded with. Thus, somewhat unwillingly, Johnes continued. 'Si je n'avois pas peur, je tremblois,' he told a friend afterwards. He had worked at it spasmodically until, in 1796, Min's illness made it impossible for him to stick to any occupation indoors. *Froissart* was thrown on one side, where it lay neglected but not forgotten for four years.

To his astonishment he found that he could not forget it. The splendour of medieval life, like an endless succession of the richly illuminated manuscripts he loved to peruse, responded too closely to chords in his own nature. It had a distinct affinity with not only the traceries and battlements of his own mountain fortress, but its very location as well. He felt curiously at ease in that bygone age of chivalry and brave adventure. It was delicious to be transported out of reality into one of his own airy castles. The priestly chronicler was an agreeable and congenial companion. Far from renouncing the pomps and pleasures of the world, Froissart had openly rejoiced in them. He had a rich enjoyment of every form of pleasure, of music, feasting, assemblies, wine and good living, none of which were at all disagreeable to Johnes. In fact, it was an age exactly after his own heart, full of courage and virtue against a lavish background of romantic, magnificent pageantry. While he sat by his poor child, supervised his farm and rode across the hills, the thought of it seldom left him. It continued to germinate and flourish all through those years until now, when a fine harvest of fruit was only waiting to be plucked and distilled into the spirited prose which flowed naturally from his pen. Jane's offer to do the writing for him had long since been forgotten; so were the aged paupers whom his labours were intended to benefit. The huge dimensions of the work, far from daunting, only whetted, his ardour. Whatever he undertook must be of titanic proportions. The friends who laughingly assured him he was a great deal too indolent ever to carry out such a tremendous undertaking, only egged him on. Opposition immediately awoke the pugnacious boy who had never grown up with the rest of him and was always passionately eager to prove himself right. In any case, there could be no drawing back now, no procrastination or petering out of interest. At the age of fifty-two his intellectual energies and fervent imagination had fused at last and found their fulfilment in translating early French chronicles.

'I shall wake old Froissart from his sleep on the first day of the new Century,' he wrote to James Smith, and was true to his word. In his splendid octagon library, all through those long winter evenings, and far into the night, he worked with all the ardour of renewed love, candles in branching candelabra lighting the stacks of papers and venerable parchments piled up round him. Out in the night, like hosts of inky skeletons, his trees rattled their bones and sighed as the wind wailed its lamentations round the domed roof. But under the dome it was like some cave of Oriental magnificence. The huge fire licking up the chimney cast reflections that glinted and trembled on the pillars of variegated marble, on the books that rose, tier upon tier, from floor to ceiling, on inlaid woods and exquisite intaglios. It threw into high relief that enchanting head of Jane which Banks had sculptured long ago, and the ancient mosaic dug up at Tivoli which was set above the fireplace; it enhanced the richness of Persian rugs and silken draperies. Never was setting better calculated to enflame alike inspiration and pen. Nor was this all, for to carry this scene of splendour one step further, the wine in the flashing glass decanter which stood at hand to refresh the Khan of Hafod while he laboured, was Tokay from Hungary (only his friends must not hear of this or they would think him lost beyond redemption!). His new wine merchant in Amsterdam, who had taken the place vacated by that fair-weather friend, Mr. Alderman Harley, was behaving most handsomely.

No phase of his life had been more satisfactory. His literary activities made a perfect complement to the days spent in the open air. As daylight lengthened, and his zeal mounted ever higher, he would often be at his desk at four in the morning and never later than six. He intended that his should be a richer and more comprehensive version than any hitherto attempted, for he would make additions from many contemporaneous manuscripts which had not hitherto been published. His agents and friends were commissioned to watch the catalogues and sales for anything that might be of use to him. He was in constant correspondence with learned medievalists, who assisted him in elucidating obscurities and deciphering difficult names. Foremost among them was another Scottish Dr. Anderson—Robert Anderson, M.D., the biographer of the *British Poets*. In 1794, the learned Dr. Percy, Bishop of Dromore, who had edited the *Reliques of Ancient English Poetry*, had also promised valuable aid, but now, six years later, his increasing blindness prevented him. In his place Dr. Anderson obtained help from Sir Walter Scott who was 'strong in Border history'. All these new contacts and discoveries added interest and excitement to days that were never dull. Month succeeded month, one year followed another, and still nothing could make him falter from his purpose, while the pile of completed pages grew higher and higher.

The years before 1800 had wrought another important change in his literary destiny. Mr. Edwards had made such a comfortable fortune after fifteen years at 11 Pall Mall that he was on the point of retiring altogether from business, and in consequence was not in a position to do anything further about the *Chronicles*. In December 1801 Johnes published, with J. White of Fleet Street, a translation of Sainte Palaye's *Life of Froissart*, which he had made in the astonishingly short time of a week. It is, therefore, not surprising that his text was full of inaccuracies, in consequence of which he got badly bitten by the critics. This did not disturb him unduly, for he himself thought little of it. It was merely intended as 'a harbinger', he said, 'to sound the world, and indeed to give some little information, for I am sorry to say that 18 out of 20 know no more of my poor old Gossip than the Man in the Moon'. Although he grumbled that White seemed 'to charge us poor authors most exorbitantly', it did not prevent him from selling him the *Chronicles* long before they were completed.

By 1802, he was seriously considering the question as to his best means of getting his work printed, for a book of that nature required his constant supervision. George Cumberland suggested that he should print it himself at Hafod, an expedient which would spare him many unwelcome journeys to London, but Johnes immediately rejected the proposal as being altogether too troublesome as well as exceedingly expensive. All the same, the idea appealed very much to him, and he kept on finding fresh things in its favour. His own printing press would make him even more independent than he was already of the outside world. For a long while he had been busy providing Hafod with everything that could possibly be required for pursuing practically every branch of learning, and enjoying every civilized pleasure and comfort. It was like a well-provisioned fortress where they could shelter contentedly from the storms and stresses of life and the ingratitude of mankind, for years at a time if they chose. With this object in view, he had been buying collections of every kind that would keep his child happily employed in the only spot on earth where she could be certain of enjoying real felicity. All this made the thought of his own private press peculiarly tempting. Besides other considerations, how very much more assiduously he would work if he had 'the printers for ever at his back'. As for the great cost, mere money had never made him hesitate for long, and in October that same year a printer duly arrived with his apparatus, which was set up in a cottage on the estate. The Hafod Press was established.

Within six months this printer proved to be 'a rogue' and was replaced by a Scotsman, James Henderson, who continued to preside over the Hafod Press during the seven years of its existence. He was a careful craftsman, but although the books were well produced, there was nothing to distinguish them from many other volumes that were being published at the time. White was responsible for the distribution and sales. Between 1803–5, the translation of *Froissart* was published in four instalments, each in an edition of 300 copies in quarto volumes and twenty-five magnificent copies in folio. Almost at once, White republished them in an edition of twelve volumes, for they proved to be extremely popular. They were read eagerly and were sold almost as quickly as they appeared, though the hard-worked, unbusinesslike translator had to content himself with nothing more than the glory of his fine achievement. No emoluments were forthcoming; in fact, it was very much the other way, and he spoke bitterly of White whom he declared had used him very ill.

It did not deter him from adding to his laurels by undertaking further translations. Besides the satisfactory feeling they gave of successful accomplishment and the praise and approval of the public, the work was far too absorbing for him to wish to relinquish it. He was aware that he was doing a great service to lovers of history, which, in fact, proved to be the case, for although his translations were not by any means free from errors of all descriptions, subsequent versions for the next hundred years were based on them. And what a relief it was for the much-harried translator to escape from the tedium of lawsuits, debts and spiteful relations into his medieval ivory tower, glittering with arms and escutcheons, banners and helmets, all refulgent with the rainbow lights pouring in through stained-glass windows. How much more congenial it was to mix with that jolly company of knights and soldiers, priests and merchants, in camp and battlefield, at masques and tournaments, than to suffer himself to be tormented by human monsters whose only wish was to gnaw him to the bone.

As he wrote to James Smith: 'I have been so scurvily treated by ingrates of this Century I am happy to retreat some centuries backward for pleasure. . . . Monstrelet takes up the History where Froissart leaves it. . . . I shall go on with [his chronicles] for I have now too much pleasure in the occupation to leave it off.'

These were not the only literary researches that were being carried out at Hafod during the first years of the century. A great addition had been made to the library by the present of a valuable collection of Welsh manuscripts from one of Johnes's cousins on his mother's side—Sir John Sebright of Beachwood, a Herefordshire baronet and well-known character of the time. Sir John was the Member for Hertfordshire, a leading authority on hawking, and as eccentric in his habits as his appearance was uncouth. In his younger days he was always accompanied wherever he went by a performing dog whose antics at dinner amused him a good deal more than they did his hosts. Later, the dog was replaced by Sir John's bevy of daughters, all as plain and ungainly as their sire. This did not prevent him from taking a great interest in their appearance. He took a hand in their education himself, learning the fiddle in order to teach them to dance and giving them lessons in deportment even after they grew up—such a ludicrous performance that no one who saw it ever forgot it. He came to Hafod several times and his magnificent present of 180 volumes of manuscripts which had lain for many years in the library at Beachwood, was welcomed by Johnes with every expression of gratitude and pleasure.

They were part of the collections of Edward Llwyd, who had been an eminent archaeologist and naturalist towards the end of the seventeenth century. Llwyd was said to be the illegitimate son of a Cardiganshire lady by a dissolute Shropshire squire. He matriculated at Oxford in 1682, and two years later was appointed under-keeper of the newly completed Ashmolean Museum, ultimately succeeding as Keeper. He was sent by the University to spend some years in Wales in order to study its antiquities and explore its natural history. Now, nearly ninety years after his death, many of the unpublished fruits of his researches returned to his native shire. In the eyes of all true Welshmen this collection was by far the greatest treasure Hafod possessed. Scholars came flocking to see it from all parts of the country, but it was to the Bard of Glamorgan, Edward Williams, that Johnes entrusted the task of classifying it.

Thus a highly picturesque and interesting-looking man might often be encountered wending his way up through the green gloaming of the steep drive. Iolo Morganwg (Ned of Glamorgan) as he was generally known, was as remarkable as his appearance suggested. Frail-looking and elderly, his long silver locks flowed loosely over the high collar of his bright blue, brass-buttoned coat, while a tall, chimney-pot hat was tilted over his angular, wrinkled face. In one hand he grasped a thick staff, in the other a pencil and book, for it was his habit to read and to annotate as he walked along. A pair of canvas wallets slung over his shoulder carried a change of linen and a few books and papers—all he required on his long excursions up and down the country. His needs were scarcely more at any time. He lived sparsely, disdained possessions, disliked money. Always a vigorous champion of freedom, he was himself gloriously free from material desires and encumbrances. He was as free as the wild mountain air, the woods and streams, whose secrets none knew better than did Iolo.

He was the son of a stone-mason and had been such a delicate child that it had not seemed worth while to his thrifty father to incur the expense of educating him. He taught himself the alphabet watching his father inscribing gravestones, and appeased his hunger for books with the bare half dozen his mother possessed. At twenty-three he migrated to London and spent seven years in its environs working as a journeyman mason and occasionally earning small sums which he spent on books, by contributing little articles on country lore to the *Gentleman's Magazine*.

In London he made a number of literary acquaintances. Not long after his arrival he had an encounter with Dr. Johnson for whose works he cherished an intense veneration. At a bookshop where the great man was in the habit of calling on the first day of each month to inspect the new publications, Iolo ventured to introduce himself as 'a poor Welsh mechanic smitten with the love of learning, and particularly anxious to become proficient in English'. He then handed the Doctor three grammars and respectfully asked him to advise him which was the best one for his purpose.

With an angry scowl, Dr. Johnson seized the books, barely glanced at them, contemptuously looked Iolo up and down, then thrust them back at him with an uncompromising: '*Either of them* will do for *you*, young man.'

'I felt', said the Bard, when many years later he recounted the incident, 'my Welsh blood mount to my forehead, thinking he meant to insult my humble station, and my poverty; so I retorted with some asperity as I took back the grammars: 'Then, Sir, to make sure of having the best I will buy them all', which he proceeded to do, ill as he could afford to, and left the shop far less pleased with Dr. Johnson than with his writings.'

Among the many interesting men whom he met were Talleyrand, Benjamin Franklin, Boswell and the poet Cowper. He published by subscription two volumes of English poems during this time which attracted considerable attention. Southey held him in high esteem and paid him a tribute in *Madoc*:

—Iolo, old Iolo, he who knows,
The virtues of all herbs of mount or vale,
Or greenwood shade, or quiet brooklet's bed;
Whatever lore of science or of song,
Sages and Bards of old have handed down.

On his return to Glamorganshire he kept a village shop, combining the sale of books with groceries, and conspicuously advertising East Indian Sugar as 'Uncontaminated by human gore'. As a passionate opponent of slavery, he later renounced some property in Jamaica which a slave-owning brother of his, who had gone out there and prospered, bequeathed to him. The care of the shop must generally have devolved upon his wife, for Iolo was almost perpetually on the road, exploring every corner of Wales and searching out the local traditions and history.

At Hafod he was always a welcome guest. He had all the qualifications that Johnes admired, combining with his implacable honesty and simplicity an astonishingly diverse knowledge on many subjects. As a guest, his requirements were as unorthodox as the rest of his habits, for instead of retiring to bed he sat in a high-backed chair by the fireside, a small table beside him for his books and writing materials, sleeping, reading and writing in snatches all through the night. A special chair was made for his use when he stayed at Hafod.

With what eager expectancy must the grey-haired, spectacled Bard have journeyed there, through the desolate wilderness of ignorance which darkened the rest of Cardiganshire. Though Hafod's light grew stronger and brighter every year, it failed to kindle that blaze of enlightenment of which Johnes had dreamed. It shone forth alone upon a night as dense as ever. As Iolo approached it across the mountains it was like adventuring into another land, so impossible would it appear that these arid regions should frame a treasure-house of learning. Not only when he arrived would he have the freedom of its wonderful library, but he was certain of encountering at least two kindred spirits in the owner and his daughter. Though agriculture and afforestation took up so much of Johnes's time and thought, they had only enhanced his love of knowledge and every branch of art. Indeed, in every sense arriving at Hafod was always an adventure. There was no knowing whom Iolo might not meet. Perhaps it would be Payne Knight who at the end of last century had stirred up a hornets' nest by publishing a long philosophical poem in which he asserted that many of the doctrines taught by the Christian Churches were false, since there was no God other than Nature. It was a heresy that had scandalized many of the intellectuals and had driven old Lord Orford to such frenzies of pious rage that it may well have expedited his death which occurred only a few months later. It certainly would not have shocked Iolo, for his own views were very similar. Or he might find one of the learned bookmen; someone like James Edwards or Francis Douce—Nollekens's friend and Keeper of Manuscripts at the British Museum; or an artist like Banks or Stothard. More congenial though to Iolo than any of them would be one of the celebrated champions of human liberty who were sometimes to be found at Hafod—such men as Major John Cartwright, the philosopher and humanist, thanks to whose repeated applications, great-coats had finally been issued to private soldiers; and the scholarly nonconformist minister of Gateacre, William Shepherd, an eloquent and tireless upholder of religious and civil freedom. Such opinions as theirs were equally agreeable to Johnes, being much in keeping with his own. He wholeheartedly agreed with Cartwright's assertion that: 'The liberty of man is . . . the immediate gift of God and the seal of it is that free will which he hath made the noblest constituent of man's nature.'

For these men particularly the little mountain paradise, lying in the heart of unspoiled nature, had a particular appeal. And as they explored it in company with its founder, conversing as they went along upon their favourite theme, Johnes may often have recalled how desolate it was in the days of his old father, when that cruel tyrant, Sir Herbert Lloyd, had ridden beside him over those very mountains and the cowering natives had dwelt like beasts in their huts and holes. . . .

But it mattered very little to Iolo whether he found visitors staying or not. Hafod in itself had everything to stimulate his imagination and nourish his eager brain, and one of the most interesting things there was the printing press. He had struck up a great friendship with James Henderson, the tall, fair-faced printer who within a short while of his arrival at Hafod had learnt to speak Welsh fluently. He and Iolo would set off together to call on the local wiseacres, sitting in their kitchens talking and drinking *cwrw bach* (small ale) for hours together. Henderson made his mark in the neighbourhood during the years he stayed there by giving private lessons in Greek and Latin to clever boys from the local school. Thus in yet another direction the Hafod Press contributed towards the cultural reformation which Johnes was doing all he could to promulgate.

CHAPTER XII

The Golden Cage

In the six years that had elapsed since its inception, the pensile garden which Dr. Anderson had designed for Mariamne had prospered surprisingly well. This little pleasance, hidden in a dwarfish thicket on the mountain above the famous rock, had become one of Hafod's most pleasing features. It was well stocked with flowering shrubs and a flourishing array of all kinds of alpine and other plants indigenous to high latitudes, while a pretty moss-house lent a 'hermit-like air to the retirement'. Its romantic situation and the vast extent and variousness of the views that could be seen through a frame of flowers and leaves hanging on the very brink of a dizzy precipice, provoked all sorts of exquisite emotions that were given poignance by the sadness of its air. For a long while a sense of calamity, a creeping chill of frustration, hung forlornly over this little garden. All those who were privileged enough to be allowed to see it (for it was not generally shown) knew it had been intended as the special territory of little Miss Johnes, and that almost before it was completed, before she had ever worked or played there, she had been stricken down by a fell disease. And their guide would tell them how, during her brief recoveries, she would be brought there in her wheeled chair, to watch its progress—a sad little procession of parents and trusted servants carrying her up the steep track where formerly she had raced and scrambled as nimbly as any other young creature of the mountains.

By 1802, however, the air of the garden had entirely altered. Melancholy pervaded it no longer, for the eighteen-year-old Mariamne now came there as she chose, spending many hours happily employed in planting, pruning, watering and caring for it generally. It was her favourite refuge. In that solitary spot there was nothing to interfere with the satisfying sense of oneness which continued to link her closely with all breathing, growing things. As for her father, he was quite sure there never was such a wonderful garden and was always thinking out new treasures for it. And this year was particularly momentous in that two deaths of a widely different character occurred, each of which contributed an ornament to make it, and the way to it, even more interesting.

In the spring, while playing tennis, the Duke of Bedford ruptured himself, and in spite of undergoing a terrible operation, which he bore with unsurpassed fortitude, he died. Johnes, whose affection for him was heightened by admiration, soon after erected a graceful obelisk to his memory which was placed on a natural platform at the top of the rock immediately below the garden. It was in the Duke's capacity as the 'Friend of Agriculture' that he commemorated him. For some years before his death he had farmed on a great scale at Woburn, where he had inaugurated the famous sheep-shearings to which farmers of all degrees were invited to come from all over the Kingdom. Johnes must certainly have attended at least one of these occasions where all his contemporaries assembled, ploughing matches, sheep-dog trials and similar diversions bringing a note of excitement to long days spent in the solemn inspection of flocks and herds and endless acres of arable and grazing. This farmers' heaven lasted for many days, while the hospitality extended to all was on a princely scale. The Duke had rendered many public services, and it was fitting that there should be a memorial to him at Hafod, for its owner on a smaller scale aimed in the same direction. It provided a welcome excuse, besides, to the breathless tourist to pause on his steep ascent to Miss Johnes's garden and read the epitaph written thereon to a great and good man—'the most judicious and munificent promoter of the National Agriculture'.

The other death to be commemorated took place at Hafod itself, and this time the arts combined to honour it. It was a humble, nameless little creature, but none the less dear to Mariamne. It was her pet robin that died. Samuel Rogers happened to be staying in the house at the time and the sight of the young girl's distress lit his creative fire. And thus it came about that for Mariamne he wrote his charming 'Epitaph on a Robin-Redbreast':

Tread lightly here, for here, 'tis said,
When piping notes are hushed around,
A small note wakes from underground,
Where now his tiny bones are laid.

No more in lone and leafless groves,
With ruffled wing and faded breast,
His friendless, homeless spirit roves;
—Gone to the world where birds are blest.

Where never cat glides o'er the green,
Or school-boy's giant form is seen;
But love, and joy, and smiling spring
Inspire their little souls to sing.

We may be sure that Mr. Rogers's kindness, in writing such a beautiful tribute to her poor little bird, quickly dried her tears. She was enchanted with it. The verses must immediately be engraved upon a monument worthy of them, and who could be better fitted to design and execute this than their dear old friend, Mr. Banks. Rogers knew Banks, too. A little dart of pain may well have pierced his heart as Mariamne Johnes, with his verses in her hands, declared that Banks should engrave them for her beneath a pretty vase. Only a very few years before this Rogers had been in love with Banks's daughter, Lavinia, who was now the wife of another. It was said that she had refused Rogers because of an ill-timed flirtation he had indulged in at Brighton, where for a few brief days he had basked in the autumnal charms of Lady Jersey, the Regent's former mistress. And now for Mariamne, his muse and Banks's chisel would be united in the shapely urn which, the following summer the old sculptor himself would bring down to Hafod, and place in position in her pensile garden.

That Mariamne should have been instrumental in quickening Rogers's usually recalcitrant inspiration was not surprising. All the elderly savants who visited there united in praising this talented, fair-haired girl with the profound blue eyes and remarkable understanding. In her essence she was still the same as the child who had delighted to wander alone in the woods and fields, losing herself in the very heart of nature and intuitively learning its secrets. These primal emotions and urges were hidden now by an air of reserve and shyness that had developed later, and perhaps it was only when she sang that their fire was released. She sang and played beautifully, filling the house with music which had become one of its greatest charms. She would sit playing the pianoforte for hours at a time sunk in a dreamy melancholy that cut Jane's heart to the quick, for too well she knew what caused it.

Many bitter reflections must have tormented poor Jane, recollections of her own girlhood rising up to taunt her, as she gazed at her precious little daughter. Jane at eighteen, had been graceful and light-footed. She was eighteen the year she paid her first visit to Croft Castle and had danced all over Herefordshire and lost her heart for good and all. How different at eighteen was Mariamne, though never, never must it be even whispered. But it was there for all the world to see. Her destiny could be likened to that of the nightingale in a golden cage whose eyes are torn out to make it sing more sweetly still. The cruel marks that her illness had made on her could never be obliterated. She was deformed—humpbacked. Her ardent, sensitive spirit was doomed to imprisonment in a distorted body that set her apart, in shameful separateness, from other young girls. For her it was safer not to yield to the natural instincts and impulses of girlhood, to indulge in sweet dreams of love and a handsome lover. Nothing of that kind could be for her, in spite of her father's cheerful assertions that one of these fine days he would be called upon to hand her over to the care of a younger protector. And some of his larch plantations were intended for her marriage dowry. In his eyes she was the most perfect of all human beings. He would not, could not, see that there was anything wrong. Though Johnes singularly lacked subtlety or discernment, Mariamne was plentifully endowed with both, and many a time was reduced to silence by the blank incomprehension of this otherwise kindest of fathers.

There was an example of it that very year. Among the stream of summer visitors was his old friend the ambassador, Sir Robert Liston, who came with his good-looking wife. Liston's career had been one of great distinction. He had been *en poste* without a break since his appointment to Madrid in 1783. Stockholm had followed, then Constantinople, Washington and now The Hague. He pressed Johnes to bring his wife and daughter to stay with them in Holland, a delightful suggestion that was accepted with alacrity. The time had come for Mariamne to see something of the world. His plan was to take her to London for part of the following spring, then across the Channel to France to spend a few weeks in Paris, and thence to the British Embassy at The Hague. It was a scheme calculated to thrill the heart of any young girl, especially one with such an eager, lively mind as Mariamne's. She would be able to go to the Opera in the different capitals, hear the finest music, visit palaces and museums, and see the world's most famous pictures. The pleasures and opportunities afforded by such a tour were endless. Yet while they discussed it that winter she remained strangely quiet and unresponsive. Johnes was at last compelled to observe her curious reluctance. It disappointed and perplexed him. When he pressed her for an explanation she only begged him to defer the journey for another year. But why? he asked, still more puzzled. Finally she admitted that she would like 'to improve herself and grow taller'. Although he willingly complied, and the idea was given up, he still did not perceive the barbed arrow that goaded her. That she should wish to remain at Hafod where she had everything her heart could desire seemed to him perfectly understandable. It would never enter his head that the mountains which exhilarated and soothed him could also be a wall behind which a wounded creature might cower for shelter. For his part, he was only too ready to stay where he was for the next twelve months, for his printing press was being installed just then and he had occupations enough to fill every moment of the day.

As for Mariamne's desire to improve herself, he spared nothing in order to further it. Next summer, when Banks arrived with the vase for her garden, he found all the muses congregated—a royal academician as her drawing-master, an elderly Italian opera singer to perfect her playing and singing. Johnes had invited his old acquaintance Ibbetson to come and live with them for a year to teach her, but Ibbetson, who was living in Westmorland, married to a young wife, refused, and Stothard had been engaged instead to spend part of the summer with them. This he continued to do for a number of years.

Thomas Stothard was then nearly fifty and at the height of his fame, chiefly as an illustrator. Hafod provided exactly the retreat that his quiet, retiring disposition, his acute feeling for beauty, most coveted. It was always his instinct to eschew society and find his pleasures in nature and in books, though always in relation to his art which engrossed him absolutely. Out of doors he was perpetually hunting butterflies and looking for flowers in order to study their beautifully blended colourings, a habit which must immediately have endeared him to his pupil. No choice of master could have been happier, for although at first Johnes found his reserve a little disconcerting, he became in time a great friend of the family, and one of Mariamne's most devoted admirers. He praised her talents and the beauty of her mind—there was evidently a close mutual understanding between these two reserved and sensitive spirits, and to him, as to many others, it was Mariamne who gave to Hafod and their visits there a very particular delight.

Giuseppe Viganoni, the singing master who also would frequently return for many summers to come, was a singer of some repute in his day and a member of Mr. Gould's Operatic Company at Covent Garden. The house rang with music, his voice and Mariamne's uniting in giving most beautiful concerts which enraptured all who stayed there. Life in the mountain paradise that summer reached a high peak of perfection, though a shadow was cast on the whole family by the bad appearance of Banks when he arrived. He was one of Johnes's oldest friends and the place abounded with his works. He had stayed there time and time again, since 1783, but it was all too evident now that this would be the last visit he would ever pay them. He had recently had a stroke which had paralysed his right arm and finished his career, for he would never model again. Thus the memorial to the Robin-redbreast, inscribed with Rogers's verses and representing Mariamne Johnes in bas-relief, mourning over the tiny corpse, was one of his last achievements. Overgrown with moss and ivy, almost lost among encroaching trees and bushes, it was still standing where he placed it one morning that September of 1803, nearly a century and a half later.

Home, always the best place, was never better than during the early years of the century. Nothing seriously disturbed the serenity of the prospect. Even the financial situation had been greatly ameliorated, thanks to the exertions of a resourceful solicitor, Mr. Hugh Smith of Bloomsbury Square, who was unravelling the tangle to good purpose. Johnes, in his impetuous, boyish way, was devoted to this reassuring man. Smith was his 'Good Angel', his 'Trusty Squire' and many other similar things. Ill-natured jokes went round the family to the effect that Johnes could not exist without having this attorney perpetually at his side. Smith was often to be found at Hafod and by means best known to himself certainly succeeded in keeping his patron very comfortably afloat. Not a whisper of economy, not a sign of privation, marred those arcadian years.

It was a time of ripeness. Johnes could sit back and survey the scenes he had fabricated with justifiable pride and satisfaction, before he threw himself once more into whatever enterprise happened to be engaging his energies. Perhaps it was some bad farm, 'an unlicked cub' that he had taken in hand, or waste areas that were being reclaimed, or a new walk or an artificial waterfall. There was always something of the kind going on. If he doubled his present life, he declared, it would still not be long enough to carry out all his plans.

As his middle years gradually declined towards the still sufficiently remote shadows of old age, the roots that fixed him there grew tougher than ever. The longer he stayed at a stretch, the more loath he was to leave it even for a few days. His astonishing current of energy and high spirits were fed by the air and the unseen forces that pervaded his woods and mountains. Their power worked through his very being, drawing him into a stream of activity which as long as he obeyed its incessant clamouring satisfied him as nothing else could. And in a sense it was the same with his wife. Her days were spent contentedly looking after her conservatory, her dairy, the little school and all her many charities. They had settled happily down to the regular routine of late middle age. Happy in one another and in everything around them, they asked for nothing better.

Outwardly, in any case, Mariamne asked for nothing better either. She conformed only too readily to the limitations of this retired existence, thrown back upon herself for her pleasures and

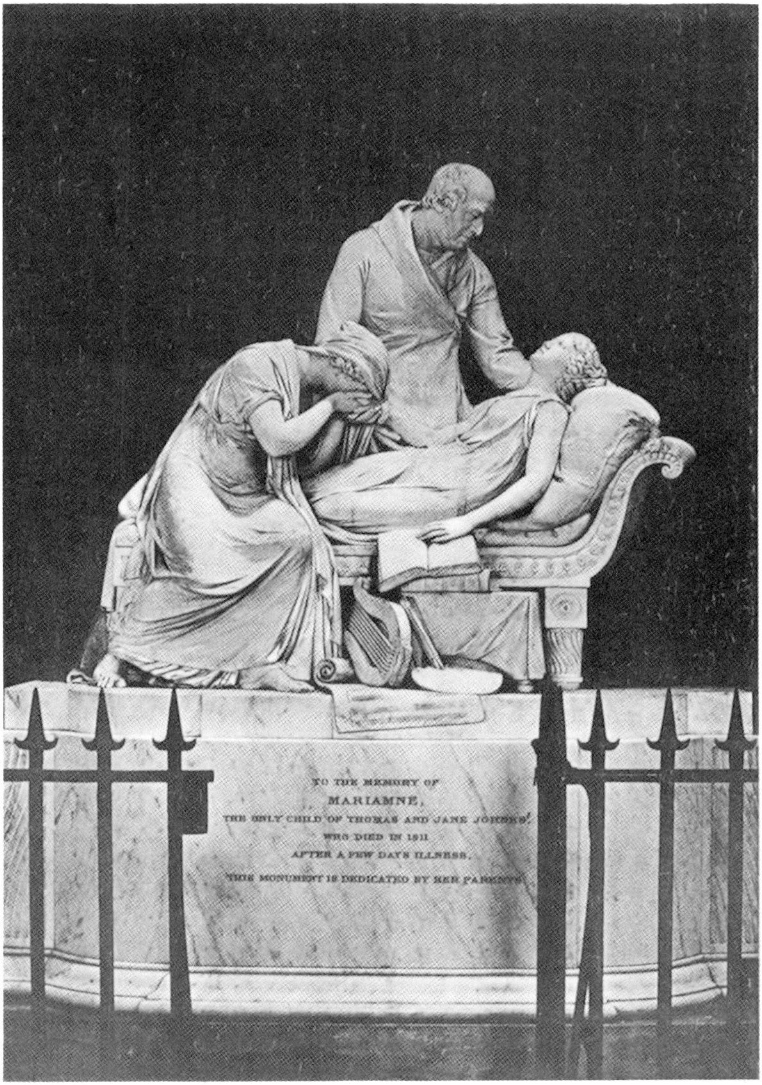

The monument to Mariamne by Sir Francis Chantrey

Rear view of Hafod (after enlargement) showing the library

Distant view of Hafod c. 1900

amusements. She had two gardens to attend to besides her music and drawing which she worked at assiduously. Her father's friends highly approved of this young blue-stocking, discreet and wise, who could listen attentively and speak with knowledge from a well-stored, highly cultivated mind. Her father's soul was bound up in her; more than ever she was the mainspring behind his every thought and fantasy. In her beautifully flowing script she corresponded with such eminent naturalists as Sir Joseph Banks and her ever-beloved Dr. Smith. The few surviving letters that she wrote to the latter are nearly all that we know of the adult Mariamne. A faint aroma of melancholy pervades them. It is impossible not to sense how hemmed in and constricted her life must have been in that lonely spot where the most trivial incidents seemed momentous. There was the occasion, for instance, when she and her Aunt Eliza, walking home from the Devil's Bridge one January day, were caught in a terrible blizzard of snow and nearly lost themselves and got soaked to the skin. Such an occurrence in her cosseted, sheltered life was clearly without parallel, though she escaped without even a cold. And her excitement when her Papa made her a present of 'a great deal of Manure' and allowed her an old man to work in her garden. . . . One's heart sinks for this caged bird though to many her bars must have looked bright enough.

Hafod occupied a unique position. As its Lord Lieutenant and Parliamentary representative, besides owning most of the county, Johnes was virtually king of Cardiganshire. A lenient, beneficent monarch who was never without some new plan for improving the welfare of his subjects. He had already achieved a great deal for them. Many of the benefits that he had striven to obtain had come to pass. Many more coaches now ran between Aberystwyth and England. There was a post-chaise to be hired in each of the principal towns and a daily delivery of letters was everywhere the rule. Large numbers of tourists came annually to this forgotten land which he had succeeded in bringing before the public. The inn which he had enlarged and equipped, at the

Devil's Bridge, putting it in charge of Mariamne's old nurse and her husband, was always crowded. Aberystwyth, as we have seen, had achieved that popularity which he had long ago prophesied for it. In the summer it literally overflowed: in 1805, he told Cumberland, the crowds were so great that many were forced to sleep in carriages. And he went on to say how 'they are going to erect a Theatre, and a self-appointed Master of the Ceremonies of the tribe of Levy means to commence his operations of Coupée and Borrée next summer.' There was a spicy whiff of illicit romance, as well, for it had become a favourite retreat for married ladies to elope to with their lovers. Each year new stucco houses were added to the crescent-shaped Marine Terrace that overlooked St. George's Channel, under the stark grey cliffs of Constitution Hill. From spring till autumn it was full of lively bustle, of military bands, bathing parties and smart little equipages carrying the fashionables along the sea-front. Picturesquely attired countrywomen came flocking down from the hills to the town laden with produce to sell to the foreign invaders, and fish-wives hawked their wares from door to door. Ships came sailing into the dangerous little harbour laden with coals and groceries, though at certain seasons the water was too low to permit them to enter. Even the sea contrived to make access to these desolate shores as difficult as possible. But despite all drawbacks the little town flourished and the Gothic palace up in the mountains, to which it owed most of its prosperity, was a favourite excursion for the visitors.

Really everywhere was improving at a great rate, it seemed to Johnes when he drove through the county, attending to his public duties and visiting his tenants. Thanks to his rewards and premiums, many farms presented a healthy and fruitful appearance; it could only be a question of time before the rest followed. He planned later on to hold annual sheep-shearings at Hafod, like those at Woburn and one or two other great houses. It would be an excellent means of bringing more people there, of a kind liable to be useful to the country. His faith was still unfaltering; all the abuse he had suffered, all his sacrifices, had been amply repaid.

Although he was fond of complaining that his circle of friends grew smaller every year he nearly always had people staying. Occasionally we catch a glimpse of an old friend among them: that parsimonious bachelor, Charles Greville, for example, promising to present Mrs. Johnes with a tree-peony. The fascinating Robert Fulke Greville had been married for some years now to his cousin and lifelong love, Louisa, Countess of Mansfield, and was living in splendour at her magnificent house of Ken Wood, which lay in a hollow between Hampstead and Highgate. It was one of Johnes's principal grumbles that few of his old friends troubled to visit him. It is not very surprising that the tedious, uncomfortable journey should have daunted their elderly hearts. They were all growing old. What had been a delightful adventure ten or more years ago was now nothing less than a bore. Most of them expended their time and strength on public works and careers and preferred, when they had the opportunity, to repose themselves in more accessible pleasances. There was that ambitious politician and connoisseur, for instance, Charles Long, whom Johnes found it hard to forgive for not returning to Hafod, for in the old days he had paid them several visits and had raved about its charms. On one occasion, in a fit of high spirits after a picnic dinner spread upon the rocky banks of a mountain torrent, he had risked life and limb leaping across the 'repulsive chasm'. But that was long ago. He, like many others, was stout now and middle aged, and had long since lost the careless exuberance of spirit which Johnes still managed to retain in abundance. Besides which, Long had his own fantastic Gothic house, which he had built at Bromley Hill in Kent, where he occupied his leisure in landscape gardening.

Even their dear Dr. Smith, in far-off Norwich, found it difficult to get away. He had moved there with his wife a few years after their marriage, taking the collections of Linnaeus with him and only spending a few weeks in London each spring to deliver his lectures. He was now *persona grata* at Holkham, the palatial residence of Thomas Coke, 'King Tom' of Norfolk, under whose vast roof all the great and good were welcomed. It was Smith who introduced the learned William Roscoe, the historian of the Medicis, at Holkham, who later carried out the enormous work of cataloguing its valuable library. Norfolk abounded with fine places, congenial company and magnificent collections, while the mountains of North Cardiganshire, enchanting though they were, seemed almost inaccessible.

It was the younger men who came most readily. An interesting couple who arrived to stay not very long after their marriage were the new Duke and Duchess of Bedford. He, as Lord John Russell, had been the younger brother of the ill-fated 'Loo', and the circumstances of his marriage had surprised and annoyed many of the late Duke's friends. Shortly before his death, Francis Bedford had created great consternation among the adoring Whig ladies of Devonshire House, by becoming engaged to the young daughter of the Tory Duchess of Gordon—a redoubtable Scotswoman of whom it was written:

The Duchess triumphs in a manly mien,
Loud is her accent and her phrase obscene.

Her husband had long since abandoned her for the more peaceful companionship of a humble mistress, while undismayed the Duchess pursued manifold political activities and found time, besides, to arrange great matches for her four daughters. She had already secured two dukes as sons-in-law, those of Richmond and Manchester, when Lady Georgiana became happily affianced to His Grace of Bedford.

Almost immediately Death plucked the prize away. As the unfortunate man lay dying, he begged his brother and heir to carry a lock of his hair over to Paris where his betrothed was staying with her mother. In due time this behest was faithfully performed. Lord John had only lately lost his own wife, thus a similitude in their sorrow may well have drawn him and Lady

Georgiana Gordon together. There was, moreover, the young lady's mother to be reckoned with, to whom one duke was as good as another, so long as he was free to wed. Be this as it may, the ladies in London who, with sighs and veiled satisfaction, had commiserated with the poor girl for losing Woburn and the strawberry leaves, were none too pleased to learn that she was to marry Loo's successor the following year.

Though he was a much lesser man than his brother, the new Duke was kindly and easy-going, and much addicted to farming and natural history. He and his host at Hafod were close friends and the visit was in every way successful. The grounds must have been beautifully illuminated by night in their honour, and the young Duchess enjoyed the novel experience of pulling a sheet of *Froissart's Chronicles* hot from the printing press. After their departure, she sent Mrs. Johnes a handsome present of two camellia trees from her conservatory at Woburn.

That dexterous conjuror, Hugh Smith, was there frequently, while another solicitor also assumed some importance in their lives. This time it was a literary one and a much younger man—John Hermon Merivale was a critic and minor poet, whose works were warmly praised by his friend, Lord Byron. This inevitably must have added to his interest, for Johnes ardently admired Byron's poems. Merivale was full of Byronic associations, his wife being a daughter of the headmaster of Harrow, to whom the poet paid the following tribute in a note to *Childe Harold*.

'My preceptor, the Rev. Joseph Drury, was the best and worthiest friend I ever possessed: whose warnings I have remembered but too well, though too late, when I have erred; and whose counsels I have but followed when I have done well or wisely.' And young Mrs. Merivale could relate to them how when she was a child walking with her mother, a boy lounging in the street at Harrow had been pointed out to her with the words: 'There goes Byron, like a ship in a storm, without rudder or compass.'

These new friends could never take the place of the old ones who had been part of the very fabric of his existence. Nothing could repair the loss of such a one as Lord Thurlow, for example, who, formidable in his dissolution as an emaciated old eagle, died at Brighton ministered to by his flock of illegitimate daughters in 1806. That was a sad springtime for Johnes, for only a few weeks earlier he had lost his beloved and faithful sister, Elizabeth Hanbury Williams. She and her husband had been constantly at Hafod; she had always been kind and approving and, childless herself, had loved Mariamne as her own. She was barely fifty-seven and the only member of his family left to him. Together they had suffered under their cruel mother who had treated her elder daughter as shamefully as she had treated him. And now poor Betsy was dead, while the Dowager was still alive and would continue to flourish all through the first decade of the century and beyond it. She had moved from Stratford Place to Portman Square, with Anne and the rich and prudent parson, Samuel, for whom treasure on earth was as much to be desired as a more problematical treasure hereafter. Although Johnes had not seen them for many years, they continually rankled in his mind as monsters of injustice who had robbed him of his dues and done their utmost to discredit him and bring him to the dust.

This corroding poison was ready to break out at the least opportunity. In these days he would be said to be suffering from persecution mania. In every untoward report or event he immediately discerned the shadow of his mother's hand. In spite of all her machinations, it was satisfactory to think that she had not succeeded in destroying him. He and Jenny had managed to found their ideal community, which would be safe for many a long year after their departure, under their child. What they had accomplished was praised everywhere and glowingly described in a number of books and publications. And during these years his own literary works were bringing additional recognition and fame. The three monumental volumes of Froissart had been duly followed by the Chronicles of de Joinville and those of de la Brocquière. All the world talked about them. There was evidence and to spare to provide a devastating retort to the wicked old woman in Portman Square who, he suspected, tirelessly schemed and plotted for his downfall.

CHAPTER XIII

'I Am Stunned but Not Knocked Down'

It was March 1807, with deepest winter still prevailing in the mountains. It was wretched weather for travelling and Johnes must have started for London in order to attend Parliament with even greater unwillingness than usual. It was extremely disagreeable to have to drag himself away from the manifold attractions of his warm, well-stocked citadel in order to face the rigours of the road and the blustering winds and rains of that inclement season. The beautiful painted glass that had come from Flemish churches, which now filled many of the windows, made Hafod seem more like a medieval fortress than ever, and a most fitting background for the translator of Froissart and Monstrelet.

A few months hence Johnes would be fifty-nine, the same age as his father, the Custos, had been at the time of his death. Not a thought of ill health or death had begun to trouble the vigorous son; nothing of that kind deterred him from making the long journey. He was as strong as ever and looked forward to many more active and useful years at Hafod. The worst part of leaving home was being torn from that trinity they formed, he and Jane and their child, apart from whom he was never really content. It seemed madness to desert the rarefied air of his home for the stench of a noisy city and jostling crowds bent on venal pursuits.

But he could postpone his departure no longer, for even the Member for Cardiganshire was expected to put in an occasional appearance at St. Stephen's.

It had been an uncommonly pleasant and interesting winter altogether. He had worked with such gusto at his translations that the printer had run out of paper, and he had been busy as well fitting up a small circular library for two very valuable purchases he had lately made. These awaited him in London; he must arrange for them to be packed and brought down to Hafod. One was the Pesaro Library that he had bought from a noble Venetian family of that name, while the other consisted of Caxtons and similar rarities which had formed part of the well-known collection of the late Stanesby Alchorne. While he was occupied with his books indoors, Jane had been busy attending to her flowers. The big conservatory opening out of the octagon library was now her particular interest, and many a happy hour they had spent loitering there together, enjoying its sweetness and warmth and the fine display of 'curious exotics' which had particularly delighted Sir Samuel Rush Meyrick, the historian of Cardiganshire, when he visited them a short while ago. Everywhere indoors there was so much colour and richness as to render them all quite insensible to the iron hand of winter. A perpetual creative flow enlivened the air. The pertinacity with which Mariamne had worked during the past months at her music and painting pleased him exceedingly. She was achieving wonders, painting miniatures now just as skilfully as a professional. As for her playing and singing, they entranced him more every day. He could listen for ever to his precious ewe lamb, his little Saint Cecilia. One song especially he loved to hear her sing, an air of Handel's with a refrain of lofty beauty that somehow seemed particularly to belong to her:

What tho' I trace each herb and flow'r,
That drink the morning dew,
Did I not own Jehovah's pow'r
How vain were all I knew!

Medievalism, flowers, music and the arts indoors; unremitting farming and planting outside; such a combination could not possibly be improved upon. Added to everything else, his good friend, Hugh Smith, continued most successfully to keep the wolf from the door, and at almost any moment Johnes might expect to receive an enormous sum of money for The Priory at Cardigan. The new Marquis of Lansdowne was on the very brink of buying it. He had decided to abandon Bowood and may have been drawn towards Wales by the early recollections of his wife, a lady said to be even fatter than Mrs. Fitzherbert, who had started life as the daughter of a Welsh parson and had been Lord Lansdowne's mistress for a number of years before their recent marriage. Johnes hoped to get the sale finally settled during his visit to town. It was by far the best bargain he had ever succeeded in making and he thought Lord Lansdowne, in spite of his increasing eccentricity, a very agreeable fellow.

At the beginning of the second week in March he drove regretfully away, having vowed to his dear ladies that he would be with them again in as short a time as possible. They were not left unattended. Eliza was staying at Hafod as well as John Hanbury Williams who had promised to remain until Johnes returned. It was now nearly a year since Mr. Williams had buried his wife, and William Shepherd had written the lugubrious verses that were placed on her tomb—a masterpiece of moroseness containing a dreadful message for all who paused to read that,

Here sad Remembrance fondly loves to dwell
And wrings with woe a widow'd husband's breast,
While aye she points to the dark narrow cell
Where the cold ashes of Eliza rest.

Stranger, or Friend! hast thou a partner dear?
Go, press her closer to thy aching heart,
With silent wing the moment hastens near,
The dreadful moment, when ye too must part!

At the time the widower's grief had been so overwhelming that it had quite looked as though it might only be a question of weeks before he joined his Betsy in that narrow cell, but since then he had succeeded in recovering his spirits wonderfully. He was particularly popular at Hafod just now, for he had announced his intention of making Mariamne his heiress. Although his extravagance and financial confusion were nearly as great as Johnes's, everybody was very much delighted by his decision.

Hafod without its master was never the same place, but all the same it was a very congenial little party that he left behind him. The busy days slipped by contentedly enough. A hard frost had set in, charming the mornings with a crystalline wonder that glimmered and sparkled over the grey fields and woods, and investing the evenings spent by a blazing fire behind closed curtains with a voluptuous satisfaction. Listening to it shivering and crackling outside made their comfortable rooms feel even more luxuriously snug. And so they sat on that memorable evening of Thursday, 12th March, the ladies with their books and sewing, warming themselves and talking in undertones, while the gentleman snored behind his paper. Although, as it turned out, it was an evening that none of them would ever forget, there was nothing outwardly to distinguish it from a hundred similar ones. It was simply a tiny segment of life's ordinary pattern—the snip of scissors and rustle of turned pages punctuating the quiet chatter, and perhaps a little music as well, for there was nearly always music wherever Mariamne was. At nine o'clock the usual pleasant break occurred when the tea and coffee equipages were brought in and probably something a little stronger for Mr. Williams. A quiet, homely evening rounding off a quiet, well-occupied day.

For none of them could guess what a heart-breaking, ghastly significance it was destined to assume for all of them. None of them could suspect that every chance word that was spoken that night, each look that was exchanged, would be feverishly sought for afterwards and seized and fitted into the tattered remnants that they strove to piece together, to rebuild the vanished scene. Memories would strain to breaking point in their efforts to re-create this drawing-room where they sat, a room that resembled a glowing flower border with its tapestries, exquisitely painted china and other choice ornaments. Had they but known it, their eyes were resting on many of these things for the last time, whilst others when they saw them again would be so defaced and mutilated that it would have been almost better if they had been totally destroyed. Yet, when at ten o'clock they rose as usual to light their candles and climb the stairs to bed, they were untouched by even the faintest apprehension of disaster. It was quite beyond the bounds of possibility that anything could alter —at least not for many years to come. Everything would go on exactly the same, for none of them could wish it otherwise. The only difference would be that the dear, familiar rooms would constantly be improved as new and beautiful objects found their way there. As they sleepily mounted the stairs towards the gallery above, they little suspected that for years to come they would still be recalling and grieving over their lost treasures. 'If only . . .' they would sigh. 'What a pity it was not saved. But there was no time.' For that was the most dreadful part of it. There was no time at all. The scorching wings of the fiery angel swept across their sky with devastating speed.

It was Jane, always a light and restless sleeper, who was the one who awoke at a quarter past three on the morning of Friday, 13th March—a date already cursed by every inauspicious portent. Strange and ominous sounds made her start up and listen. Then she detected the dreaded smell of smoke growing more potent every instant as the roaring noise drew nearer. She sprang up and rushed next door to waken Mariamne, and scarcely had she roused her and hurried her from the room than the ceiling came crashing down. Fire had broken out in the attic; a warming pan in the housekeeper's bedroom was afterwards believed to have caused it; and already it had made such progress that the upper regions were cut off.

The frosty night was their worst enemy. Wells and springs were frozen fast while the fire-sprites leapt and multiplied unhindered in the dry air. There was a fire-engine, but not a man on the place knew how to work it, and the labourers' cottages were too far away from the house for their occupants to reach it in time to be of any help. Jane, fearless and resolute as she always was when faced with danger, took command. Before anything else was done, she insisted that every life must be saved. Maid-servants, scorched and screaming, were trapped on the roof and much precious time was spent bringing them down with ropes and ladders. By the time they were all accounted for the house was doomed. Already half of it was a raging, roaring inferno, with walls and beams crashing into the swirling flames; but, undismayed, Jane was determined that her husband's books should be saved. Although it was in imminent danger, she rushed to the octagon library with Mariamne and Eliza and started emptying the shelves. Then she remembered the priceless, irreplaceable old French manuscripts up in the gallery. Without a thought for her own safety she sped up the little stairway and started to fling them down, but the flames were racing her, heralding their approach with huge gusts of smoke that nearly choked her. She would not give in without resisting for as long as she could, for these most precious possessions of her beloved Mr. Johnes, his priceless manuscripts and notes, the labours of a lifetime, must at all costs be saved. She struggled bravely on, pulling down armfuls of ancient vellums and casting them below, while the fearful noise and heat grew ever more oppressive. At last, stifled and blackened by smoke, she could do no more and fell unconscious to the ground. As she was brought into safety the flames broke in and drove them out of the room and out of the house for ever. Showers of lead from the roof fed the great blaze that lit up the mountains and stained the sky a lurid crimson that could be seen for miles around. The force of the fire was such that it carried the burning books high into the sky and tossed them all over the mountains. By the time this fearful conflagration brought helpers running from all directions, no aid could avail the charred skeleton that was all that remained of Hafod.

Throughout this dreadful night Mr. Hanbury Williams had not spared himself, though, according to the report later published in the *Gentleman's Magazine*, he must have cut an extraordinary figure. For it described how 'Mr. Hanbury Williams . . . naked, and a few men-servants, by wonderful exertions, at the hazard of their lives, succeeded in saving most of the valuable plate, china and a quantity of inferior furniture; the wine, the linen, Mrs. Johnes's apparel, trinkets, etc. and the principal furniture, magnificent glasses etc. were all lost . . . at 6 (excepting the three turrets at the corners of the mansion and the Conservatory) only the bare walls remained, a melancholy memento of the former splendour of the place.' And at six, with nothing left to them but their night shifts, Jane, Mariamne and Eliza were sheltering in the gardener's cottage. Now that everything was over they were shivering and sick with terror and the stifling stink of the charred and smoking ruins of all they had prized and loved, that was carried to their retreat by a mocking little wind.

Thus the disaster his mother foresaw had overtaken him, though in a different guise from what she had anticipated. Nearly all his possessions, his choicest books, his pictures and other beautiful things had perished, and what remained was for the most part badly damaged. The disaster was further increased by the fact that the house was insured for much less than half what it was worth. From every point of view the calamity was a crushing one, but Johnes met it with stoical courage. Not a word of complaint or recrimination seems to have passed his lips; nothing but thankfulness that his family had not suffered. Even when confronted by the hideous ruins the grandeur of his bearing did not diminish. Throughout the whole distressing business he displayed a calm dignity that carried him shoulder-high and amazed his friends.

Even under the first shock of the news, when it reached him

in London on 16th March, he had not faltered. 'My dear Sir,' he wrote that day to a friend. 'I shall begin with good news. I came here last Thursday, very well. My wife and child are very well. I have sold the Priory well.—Now the reverse of the medal is, that Hafod was burnt down last Friday. No lives lost. Thank God it was not worse. Today I set out for the ruins—I must renew the fable of the Phoenix.'

Ten days later, from the Devil's Bridge, where they were staying before setting out for London and Hugh Smith's house in Bloomsbury Square, the same high spirit is reflected in his letter to Cumberland: 'In three short hours, the exertions of nearly thirty years [have been destroyed]; but I am thankful to God it was not worse, that my family escaped unhurt, and that they are all well.' And to Dr. Robert Anderson he said: 'I am stunned, but not knocked down.'

In spite of having declared that another Hafod should rise like a Phoenix from the flames, for some little while he seemed quite unable to make up his mind what course to take. He talked of buying a fine house in London and building a modest cottage at Hafod for occasional visits. Then he thought he might move away altogether and settle in Norfolk where he would buy Lord Orford's palatial seat, Houghton, which had been offered to him. The old resilience had lost none of its elasticity; on his own admission he was quite carried away by the many exciting possibilities open to him. But the mountains had no intention of allowing their prisoner to escape. While he wavered and built his airy castles, the spirits set to work, exerting every wile of light and shadow, of breeze and tempest, to recapture his allegiance. The plantations never looked more flourishing, the fields as green, the cascades more splendid. The influence spread to the human element to complete its work. Wherever he went his people swarmed round him, with tears entreating him not to forsake them. His deeply implanted sense of responsibility towards the natives and the land reasserted itself and threw out the dreams and fantasies. The notion of abandoning this beloved place was suddenly insupportable to all of them. Another house must immediately be built, more beautiful, more commodious in every way, than its forerunner. The fable of the Phoenix *should* be renewed.

Accordingly, they rented a small place within a few miles of Aberystwyth, known as Castle Hill, where they would live during the rebuilding. Baldwin of Bath was again engaged as the architect, for the outer walls of the house were still standing, though all Nash's additions had disappeared. On the 1st September that same year, Johnes's birthday, the building was begun. To celebrate both events the family stayed at the Devil's Bridge in order to spend the day at Hafod watching Baldwin and his builders commencing their great task. But at the last moment Mariamne refused to go; the ordeal of revisiting Hafod, of seeing it all disfigured and desolate, was more than she could bear. So she and her Aunt Eliza stayed at the inn and found plenty to amuse them in watching the traffic of sightseers coming and going to the famous waterfalls. And they fortified themselves with the reflection that it would surely not be long before the house was finished, for under the pain of heavy penalties the contractors had promised to have it roofed in by Christmas.

It would not only be quickly finished but furnished as sumptuously as before. Already this September a wonderful opportunity for acquiring all kinds of magnificent embellishments presented itself. In Wiltshire that erudite eccentric, William Beckford of Fonthill, was on the point of demolishing the Palladian mansion, known by some as Fonthill Splendens, which his father had built at great cost in order to inhabit the romantic abbey on a hill in the park that Wyatt had originally designed as an interesting ruin. All the splendid contents of old Alderman Beckford's classical mansion were to be sold. Having seen the start made at Hafod, Johnes hastened down to his brother-in-law's at Bath and together they attended the Fonthill sale. Thanks to Lord Lansdowne having bought The Priory, there was no check or limit to what Johnes might spend. Alderman Beckford's

Hafod Church c. 1910 (designed by James Wyatt, 1803)

Hafod Church—the interior c. 1900

The monument to Mariamne after the fire

taste accorded with his own. Among many other things he acquired some of the beautiful French glasses that he loved to have in his rooms as well as a number of chimney-pieces. One of these, sculptured by Banks and representing two somewhat incongruously allied couples—Pan and Iris and Penelope and Ulysses—cost 1,400 guineas, and he paid seven and eight hundred for others. The birth of the Phoenix was to be attended with every magnificence.

While the mountains once more echoed the thud and clangour of hammers and picks, screeching pulleys and rattling wheels, still another proof was given to the world that Johnes's energies were in no wise impaired by misfortune. The following spring the first volume of the *Chronicles of Monstrelet* was published by the Hafod Press. It was prefaced by a dedicatory letter addressed to John, Duke of Bedford, which, with a fine defiance, was dated from Castle Hill on 13th March 1808—the first anniversary of the fatal fire.

CHAPTER XIV

'I Shall Never Again Bear Music'

In spite of threats and promises the rebuilding of Hafod was a limping business that went dragging on for three interminable years. Like a man suffering from concussion when his first burst of energy and resolve had spent itself, Johnes succumbed to a great weariness. What he had undertaken was a formidable task for a man verging on sixty. It was late in the day to start his life's work all over again. If it had not been for Mariamne, he probably never would have carried it through. The prospect had entirely altered since his early pioneering days, when he and Jenny had been as wildly in love with Hafod as they were with one another. Then it had been a brilliant Maytime: now, autumn was fast declining into winter. The wheels were running slowly, made slower than ever by the relaxing climate of the valley, almost at sea-level, which Castle Hill overlooked from the lower slopes of a wooded hillside. There was nothing to incite him in this gentle landscape of green pastures with the Ystwyth gliding smoothly between them on the last stages of its journey to the sea. The drowsy air sapped him. It made him feel unequal to facing the long, ten-mile drive to Hafod, uphill almost all the way. While the *idea* of the new house continued to be resplendent, he could only manage to drag himself there to watch its progress at longer and longer intervals. He had not got it in him now to accelerate the efforts of the workmen, to resolve their difficulties and sweep away their objections. The ostrich-like tendencies that he had always yielded to, had now taken entire charge—he felt too tired to combat them. He hated the thought of seeing the place in the state it was in; the house a shambles, the outhouses stuffed with the things that had been saved from the fire. The statues, pictures and all the other objects he had prized so highly, were jumbled up anyhow in the damp, cobwebby sheds. For his peace of mind it was better to keep away from there . . . better to forget them until the house was finished.

Except for the builders, and often for weeks they were absent and work at a standstill, everything at Hafod stagnated. All the different departments of that once busy and populous settlement were closed, and with all the rest the little school which the family had taken such a special pride in. Indeed, the school had provided them with another of those shattering disillusionments with which their long association with Hafod abounded. Some time during 1807 a fearful scandal had been brought to light, on the strength of which it had been immediately shut. There is nothing to tell what happened, only Johnes's own assertion that the twelve girls and small boys had 'all turned out bad—whores and liars and all through the worthlessness of the master and mistress'. Once again his generous plans had gone agley through the untrustworthiness of those in whom he had believed. It was impossible after having suffered so many disappointments for the same sense of rapture to inspire them which a quarter of a century ago had made the future look as bright as the inexhaustible supplies of gold which then had implemented their plans. Money was another matter that now it was just as well for his peace of mind not to dwell upon.

It was safer to remain in the valley with his books and translations to occupy him, and always new catalogues, of course, to peruse and mark. For he went on buying on an enormous scale, for the glory of the new house. Even his trusty squire, the lawyer

Hugh Smith, was hard put to it sometimes to conjure anything out of the empty bag. For another terrible reverse had befallen Johnes—at the last moment Lord Lansdowne had failed to complete his purchase of The Priory, having decided to reside in a 'whimsical tower' at Southampton instead. Johnes, who had already spent some of the money he was expecting to receive was thrown into a desperate dilemma by this 'dirty conduct'. The building was proving a constant drain on him. He had only received £26,000 from the insurance brokers and another lawsuit against his mother was rumbling on. In short, for his own comfort, it was best to forget about business, although it was not possible to ignore it entirely. Before very long he was forced to sell some of his timber at Hafod—trees which he had planted soon after he had seen it first, in a vain attempt to meet his obligations. Under the smart of the sacrifice, 'I *will* clear myself and be contented', he declared, though even as he wrote the words he must have known that the incurable itch to spend, the insatiable hunger for possessions, made contentment of that sort quite impossible for him.

It was not only that the air of the valley disagreed with him, but his general health was not nearly as good as it used to be. His girth had increased to such vast dimensions that in 1809 a report was current in London that he was in a confirmed dropsy and impatiently awaiting the tapper to arrive from town to relieve him. The beloved friend of his youth, William Windham, on hearing of it was greatly distressed and wrote at once to condole with him, an attention that pleased Johnes immeasurably. All his life he had never ceased to regret his lost intimacy with Windham—one of the most fascinating and fundamentally unsatisfactory of men. Undoubtedly he had something that made it impossible to forget him, for 'Weathercock' Windham's vacillating affections had an exacerbating effect on men and women alike for years after that talented, unstable man had discarded them. His letter to Johnes was very soon to acquire a melancholy significance which made it all the more precious, for

Windham died not many months later. Fire, which had ruined Johnes, was the cause of his death, for he sustained an injury while helping to rescue books from a friend's burning library, from which he never recovered.

Although in many respects these years were dull and savourless, weighted with lassitude of mind and body that the cloying, clogging climate aggravated, they were not by any means unhappy. With his wife and child Johnes would have been contented in a far less agreeable spot than their quiet retreat. To both her parents Mariamne was a perpetual source of joy. Her many charming accomplishments filled the quiet, plain house with melody and colour that rippled continuously throughout the long, sleepy days. To her elders it may often have resembled the magic light and music which plunges its enraptured captives into forgetfulness of earthly life. Certainly, however, it had quite the opposite effect upon the young lady. For a great change had come over Mariamne: not only was her appearance rosier and plumper, but she was also far less satisfied with a retired country life than formerly. Like all young things, as her father said, she was eager to see and be seen. At the cost of we know not what struggles and heartburnings she had come to terms with herself. It was necessary no longer to choke back her burning eagerness to see the world, behind a mask of feigned indifference. In 1808 she was twenty-four. She was no longer a nervous young girl shrinking from pleasures and experiences which she feared could bring her nothing but mortification and heartache. All that had been got over. Now, poised and expectant, she was ready to emerge and take her place in society as the erudite Miss Johnes of Hafod, who counted among her friends several eminent men of science and letters. She could watch the great world with amused detachment while indulging her capacity for enjoying splendid scenes and occasions that she had inherited from her father.

Accordingly, from 1808 onwards, a house in London was rented for the season and Mariamne played her part in the social scene with zest. 'My young one is like a bird escaped from a cage,' Johnes reported, and indeed the resplendent background of Regency London must have been particularly dazzling to those young eyes, trained to the grey-green solitudes of her native hills. The interiors of the great houses surpassed one another in their superb and fantastic decorations, while the crowds that thronged them at these summer festivals had in their own way the same exotic brilliance. Among the rank and fashion Mariamne might see the Teutonic-looking English princes with their voluptuously proportioned ladies, and exiled European royalties covered with ribbons and stars. Waves of rich odours wafted through the warm rooms, the ladies in their clinging, jewel-encrusted gowns smelling quite as sultry-sweet as the massed-up banks and swinging garlands of tuberoses and orchids. The beaux and the bucks in their wonderfully embroidered shirt-fronts, exuded strong wafts of patchouli as they leaned against the walls, chattering together and ogling the pretty misses through their spy-glasses. Mariamne could watch their antics unperturbed as she talked with the more staid and elderly gentlemen who greeted her parents. It was almost impossible to hear the band that played somewhere not far off through all the noise and babble, but she had many other opportunities of listening to fine music. There was the opera and concerts in plenty to attend, while Mr. Viganoni regularly came to their house to sing with her. There were all kinds of pleasures in London; quieter gatherings with their old friends; moonlit excursions on the river to Vauxhall and Greenwich, and drives into the country to dine at such temples of taste and culture as Ken Wood and Bromley Hill. . . .

In the summer of 1810 the Johnes family were not to be seen in London, for at last Johnes had been driven into taking firm measures with his lazy builders. All three were heartily sick of Castle Hill and longing to be back at home. The previous autumn they had returned from a tour in Scotland expecting to find the house finished and ready for them to move back into. Greatly to their annoyance, the contractor had again failed to fulfil his promise. The place was still so far from being completed as to be quite uninhabitable and any prospect of returning there looked extremely distant. Then, to his dismay, Johnes found that many of his valuable things had been stolen from the outhouses, while others were ruined by the rats and the rain. If they hoped to get back at all, or have anything left, it was quite plain that he must exert himself. All through the winter they drove there each week to hurry on the men and make arrangements for their return, with the result that this took place the following June. Even then they were not free of a number of annoyances, for in every department the work had been carelessly done and something was wrong. Before they had been there three weeks the staircase cracked, and the masons had to be sent for post-haste from London. Then there was all the work and agitation of arranging the rooms and getting the furniture into place. The strain he endured watching his labourers heaving and groaning under the stupendous weight of his colossal statues affected Johnes to such a degree that it brought on an attack of haemorrhage. Fortunately the labourers, who literally had borne the burden and the heat, came through their ordeal unharmed.

But these little mishaps were trifles that soon were forgotten. His spirits were as good as they used to be before the fire, now he was home again. The new house was his pride and joy, a most wonderful improvement on the other. As he walked slowly up and down outside, surveying it, his heart swelled with gratification. There it was, this proud and splendid Phoenix, with its pinnacles, domes and pavilions looking finer than ever, in eloquent proof of the indomitable spirit which had triumphed over annihilation. Thirty-three years ago he had walked like this in the garden contemplating with equal pride the first edition of the same house then just finished. Only then the path looked new and raw, like the recently-laid lawns, the newly planted shrubs and the house itself. At that time he was still a youngish man, fair-haired and sturdy, ready at the least excuse to rush up a mountainside or wade waist-deep in the river. Now the garden and the landscape beyond it, which he had fabricated, had grown mellow through the years which had wrought even greater changes in his own appearance. His hair was quite grey now and his body such a size that it was not to be wondered at if the gossips in town declared him to be dropsical. But his heart was as young as ever, his belief in Hafod's destiny undimmed by apprehensions. The first house, whose weathered walls enshrined the present one, had been built for himself and Jenny. This time it was for Mariamne. Everything it contained, every purchase he had made, was for her. Though, of course, for many years to come the three of them would continue to enjoy it together.

It was remarkable how everything had flourished during his long absence. His trees had grown to such a size that he hardly knew them again and it was difficult to recognize parts of his own walks. He had never seen them in such beauty, though a dozen new improvements instantly suggested themselves. Along with the old buoyancy came all the old foibles and fantasies in force. He was scarcely in the house a few days before they were echoing in his wild excitement over a wonderful clay that had been found on one of his farms which would surely prove most valuable. All the old warmth and conviction glowed in his declaration that this was only another instance proving what riches the mountains contained. He was not particularly annoyed when he received a most discouraging report from the eminent geologist to whom he had sent a specimen for, of course, none of the geologists knew very much; as a science it was still in its infancy.

All summer long the house was in a state of pandemonium, with workmen all over it, raising clouds of dust as they hammered and sawed away, finishing off the rooms. Although none of the spare bedrooms were ready, it did not prevent Johnes from inviting his friends to come. He could not control his eagerness to show off his new things and to hear their enthusiastic congratulations and praise. And Hafod, which long ago had cast a spell upon them, drew them back there, one after another. Almost the first arrival was William Shepherd, who celebrated the occasion with one of the earnest, heavy-footed lucubrations in verse which his visits there generally resulted in. Mariamne usually provided the excuse (twice it had been her birthday, another time her garden), but this year it was to the Phoenix that he sang.

But lo! as raised by magic wile,
Dear Hafod, thy majestic pile
The traveller sees with gladden'd eyes,
In renovated beauty rise.
Again the crowd, with mute amaze,
Around thy glittering splendours gaze;
Again the cultured eye reviews
Thy wonders of the graphic muse;
With beating heart and longing sigh,
Tier upon tier upraised on high,
Again beneath yon lightsome dome,
The scholar marks the curious tome;
Again with cheerful smile, thy lord
Graces his hospitable board.
And, as she eyes the list'ning guest,
With joy dilates the mother's breast;
While, duly still, at twilight grey,
Trills Mariamne's dulcet lay.

His letters to his wife at Gateacre afford a glimpse of what it was like during those first months. Temporary beds were set up in any convenient corner and little sleep was to be expected after daybreak when the masons and carpenters began to get busy again. On entering the house the new arrival was faced with two mammoth figures—a bronze torch-bearer and a marble Bacchus—which doubtless caused him to exclaim almost before he was inside. He had scarcely arrived before Johnes hurried him off on a tour of inspection; the triumphant exuberance with which he displayed his new acquisitions and arrangements was impossible to resist. 'A very grand painting by Rubens' hung in the dining-room, in the panel that the Romney group, lost in the fire, used to fill, and in the new octagon library was one of the splendid chimney-pieces from Fonthill. There were no less than three different libraries, each one overflowing with the books amassed during the past three years. And in case of another conflagration all the family had their apartments on the ground floor. Mariamne's dressing-room occupied one of the pavilions and afforded a peaceful refuge from the turmoil prevailing elsewhere, to Shepherd and others whom she favoured with an invitation.

It may have been some time about now that Fuseli came there, for he is said to have decorated the walls of the entrance hall with scenes from Froissart *en grisaille*, though no account has been left of it. It is certain, however, that later on this summer Stothard arrived to fill eight panels on the upper part of the octagon library, immediately below the dome, with chivalrous scenes from Monstrelet in the same medium. The house already owed a good deal to Stothard's advice and plans, for Johnes had consulted him continually about its interior arrangement and finish. He remained there hard at work for nearly three months, under somewhat trying conditions, it would seem, from the following undated letter to Mrs. Stothard.

'*Hafod.*

'My dear Rebecca,

'Since your first letter I have been very unhappy in reading your account of yourself. I had no resource from the unpleasant thoughts you made me entertain, but to apply still more closely (if possible) to my engagements here, and to return as soon as possible home. You have not an idea how my time is filled up. . . . I have no exercise but what the pencil affords me, and sometimes running from one part of the house to the other. Sometimes I get an hour out of doors to get a little air. The small room I paint in affords me none; filled, as it is, with eight canvases, with my colours, oils and turpentines, etc. All the family here, without exception, are very solicitous to administer to my convenience; and I have some difficulty to resist the repeated requests of Mr. Johnes that I should go out more for my health's sake. I mention this to convince you that I might be happy enough with my situation here, if yours and the children's welfare did not solely possess me. If I wish to succeed well with the subjects I am painting, to gain credit and future engagements, it is for your sake, and the care of my health for the same reason, that I may undertake what better may insure it. This, my dear, believe is from my heart, with which compliment has nothing to do.'

These murals were a fitting apotheosis to Johnes's literary career. The Hafod Press had just issued the fifth and last volume of Monstrelet and was about to print an amended edition of Froissart's Life. Thereafter it would be closed, the type and press furniture would be scattered and the cottage which had housed it restored to its original use and shelter a poor woman and her family. Johnes had announced that he had sheathed his pen, and in future intended to 'draw his plough-share into active service'. All his energies would be concentrated upon improving his estate. He had finished with experimental farming. His big home-farm had been sold up in 1806 and his plan for the future was to reclaim wastes and take over from his tenants the management of badly cultivated farms. At the same time more and more trees would be planted, until finally the whole estate would be one vast forest. Fresh walks would have to be constructed, leading to the new farms and plantations. The only thing that worried him was that even should he live to be ninety he still would not have done. By the autumn he was already hard at work transforming a bog into a valuable farm.

With all their old occupations and charitable enterprises once more engrossing them the family settled down happily to enjoy the winter months. But it was not long before, once again, the precariousness of human projects was sharply brought home to them. The adverse fate that had singled Johnes out as its quarry had not finished with him yet by a long way. Scarcely was the winter begun than he fell seriously ill, and even after he recovered many months were spoiled by the malaise and langour with which it left him. He was too unwell to take pleasure in any indoor occupation, not even in his books. He could only stand and gaze longingly through the windows at his favourite walks and the high, windswept places where he longed to ride. And as one pictures him standing there in rueful contemplation of the mountains whither he is temporarily too feeble to go, his shaggy, deep-jowled head thrust forward, his shoulders humped under the folds of his dressing-gown, one is again irresistibly reminded of one of the wild mountain cattle—though now it is of an old, sick ox that has been brought into captivity.

He had recovered completely by the spring, and towards the end of April they set out for London, where he had again taken a house, 15 Harley Street, for the season. After eighteen months spent in Wales, Mariamne was eagerly looking forward to enjoying the gaieties and interesting encounters of the forthcoming months. In London friends of all degrees were invited to their breakfasts and dinners, and among them there was always a good sprinkling of artists and literary folk whose conversation she enjoyed quite as much as her father did. This year they were hoping to see something of a new acquaintance, a bibliophile clergyman named Thomas Dibdin, who acted as Lord Spencer's librarian at Althorp and was also the author of several literary works. In his recently published *Bibliomania* there had been not only a flattering allusion to Colonel Johnes and his octagon library but one to Mariamne as well, who, said the author, already evinced 'the true spirit of a female bibliomaniac'.

They had not been many days in London before Johnes, dropping in one morning at Longman's the publishers, met his old friend, Dr. James Smith. Smith was paying his annual visit to the capital, spending six weeks or so there, attending conferences and lecturing, while his wife remained quietly at Norwich. The doctor now moved in most exalted circles where his opinions were respectfully sought and his judgments deferred to, but this made no difference at all to his affection for the Hafod family, to whom he had been bound for so long by peculiarly intimate ties. He gladly accepted an invitation to dine with them a few days later and at the time appointed duly presented himself at their house.

An exceedingly pleased little party must have sat down to their dinner that day in the shadowy Harley Street dining-room, the elaborately draped curtains of the period and the steep façades of the houses across the cobbled street, modifying the late afternoon light as it fell softly upon the richly laden table. It was a long while since the doctor had seen them and he thought they all looked remarkably well and the two ladies 'as free and kind as ever'. There was much to hear and to tell, and the savoury smell of roasted joints and birds mingling with the genial gurgitation of the decanters must surely have encouraged expansiveness. He had to hear all about the new house at Hafod and all their plans for the season in town, and especially Mariamne's, for she was the heroine of the occasion. As he affectionately watched her, what a host of old memories must have haunted him. Of early morning rambles through the sun-speckled woodlands with a diminutive little girl who listened with rapt attention, and was as sensitively aware as he was of the flow and rhythm of life all round them, even in each tiny particle of twig and beech-mast that crackled under their feet. . . . Of a rugged path winding upwards through sheer sublimity and a blaze of noontide glory, above dizzy precipices and foaming torrents, sunshine and shadows sweeping over the pale mountains and fearful rocks in waves of indigo and gold. And suddenly the child's plangent notes thrilling through the airy spaces, completing his ecstatic delight. . . . But darkness blotted out the glowing picture and another took its place. This time the scene was drab and stifling—a crowded coach, lurching and rumbling through a rainy evening. His head ached and he felt sick and uneasy, but this urgent, desperate journey from London to Hafod had to be made and as fast as possible, despite the cold wet weather. He had refused to listen to his friends' warnings, gladly risking his own precarious health for the sake of his beloved little friend of the glades and mountains who now lay at death's door. . . . And so it went on, in a never-ending stream flowing across the background of his thoughts as he observed with pleasure her animation and the glow in her cheeks. He had nursed her, taught her, had taken endless pains to please and instruct her. To-day he was still her valued counsellor and dear friend. It was gratifying to know that her air of good health and well-trained mind owed at least something to himself. Very touching, too, was her smallness and deformity, which gave her an indefinable air of reserve and apartness, for all her very evident pleasure at being once more in town.

One other meeting that he had with her this spring in London, which may well have been their last, is on record. On the evening of 19th May, as he wrote to his 'Dear Pleasy', he dressed himself in his evening clothes to attend a small and select party that was being given by a rich widow, a certain Mrs. Weddell, at her house in Brook Street. Her house was well known for its fine pictures and beautiful contents which had been collected by her late husband, and it was always open to the inspection of all who furnished suitable credentials. When Smith was ushered into the widow's drawing-room he found her sitting alone with the fascinating, auburn-haired novelist, Amelia Opie, whom Smith knew well. Mrs. Opie was the daughter of a Norwich doctor, and as a brilliant and exuberant girl had been surrounded by a number of eligible suitors. To the horror and astonishment of her friends she chose instead to become engaged to a humbly-born artist, John Opie, who, thanks to the patronage of Thomas Coke of Holkham, was just beginning to be known. The marriage had proved an immense success and, largely due to his clever and charming wife, Opie's reputation had soared. Possibly he was another of the artists who stayed at Hafod, for a painting he had made of Johnes's favourite Newfoundland dog used to hang there, until, like many others, it was burned in the fire.

Assuredly on this Thursday evening in May the President of the Linnaean Society was warmly welcomed by the two ladies, who made him sit down between them and engaged him in 'some very pleasant chat' until they were interrupted by the arrival of a large crowd of guests. Many old acquaintances were among them, most of whom had at some time or another been to Hafod. There was Sir Thomas Frankland and his lady, the Roger Wilbrahams, and the rich and talented wife of Charles Long, herself an expert designer of gardens. Presently, unaccompanied by her parents, Miss Johnes appeared. The instant Smith caught sight of her he went up to her, for he was charmed to see her; her arrival clearly made his evening. They spent a long time together talking, and he was much diverted by her. 'She was very free and funny with me, just like she used to be,' he told his wife, to whom Mariamne sent 'her most particular and kind compliments'. Later, who should come sweeping in to join the assembly but the famous and formidable Mrs. Siddons, and it amused Smith to tease Mariamne by threatening to make her speak to the great actress. Although Mariamne confessed that she knew her, she was really alarmed at his suggestion, and protested that she 'durst not approach her'. And in the end Smith gave in and contented himself with introducing her to other friends of his, less famous and formidable, and carried back with him that night happy recollections of a delightful evening and a captivating and courageous young woman who had wonderfully succeeded in surmounting a cruel affliction.

That was on the 19th May. There was still time for Mariamne to enjoy a few more parties and to sing a few more songs with Mr. Viganoni, before the doom that pursued this unhappy family descended upon her. Exactly three weeks later she was lying ill with a 'strong nervous affection'. The two doctors who were attending her assured her parents that there was no danger, but as poor Johnes gazed at her helpless form the fearful conviction that they were wrong assailed him. All through that month she lay in bed and instead of improving under the drastic treatment prescribed by the doctors she grew worse every day. And on the 4th July, four days after her twenty-seventh birthday, Mariamne died. 'She had the look of an angel, and so quietly did her spirit depart that it had I believe some hours fled before those who sate beside her knew of it. She appeared in a sweet and smiling sleep,' Johnes wrote with shaking hands to William Shepherd.

This ultimate blow had broken him. What the fire that had devoured his home and most of his possessions had failed in achieving was accomplished by the treacherous blast that slew his ewe lamb and laid the future waste.

They brought her back to Hafod and laid her to rest in the elegant Gothic church, though they could not endure to remain there and fled back at once to England and Hugh Smith's country house in Surrey. But during the first weeks of August they tremblingly went back again, for where else could they go? Whilst they still dreaded them, they ached for the familiar scenes and occupations which alone might assuage their agony. Ghosts would be lurking everywhere, in every chamber of the scarcely finished house which still smelt raw with paint and plaster. Wherever they walked they would expect at every turn to catch sight of that beloved, bent little figure hurrying along, armed with basket and trowel, towards her usual ploys. Everywhere there would be echoes; in the wind ruffling the tree-tops, in the waters dashing and splashing over the rocks, they would hear her name. And as they approached the house there would be the overwhelming recollection of that spring morning when the three of them had driven away, all agog and cheerful, at the thought of the summer season in London. It had proved, instead, 'to be the dreariest of winters'. Going back to the house they had rebuilt for Mariamne demanded all the fortitude they could

Hafod Church—the interior after the fire, 1932

Mariamne's dressing-room at Hafod (probably by Mariamne Johnes)

Hafod in 1955 being dismantled and demolished

muster, for the opulent domes and graceful spires mockingly adorned the mausoleum of all their hopes and joys.

Their woods and mountains did not fail them. The green tranquillity and soul-reviving heights, always the same and always changing with the hours and climate, soothed their hearts. Here they would remain doing all the good they could. The necessity of doing good, which had driven Johnes all his life, was now more urgent than ever, for only thus could they look forward with certainty to being some day reunited with their treasure. At Hafod, their old roots would be kept alive by memories, while they justified their continued existence by ceaseless endeavours to help their poor people. This was all that was left for them to do. Otherwise everything was emptiness and silence—the silence indoors especially was terrible. Once music and song had filled it with delight, but now only their echoes disturbed the sleepless darkness of the nights. . . . 'I never saw this place in such beauty,' Johnes wrote to Dr. Smith a week after his return, and at the end of his grief-stricken, uncomplaining letter, like a cry of agony, came the impulsively dashed off postscript: 'I do not think I shall ever again bear music.'

There was still one last service that he could render her, and that was to place a memorial in the church. There was solace to be found in planning how to make this as perfect and complete as possible, in discussing it and inviting suggestions from those who had loved and admired her. Stothard was consulted, and before very long arrived at Hafod, bringing with him a promising young sculptor named Francis Chantrey. At that time his work was only just beginning to be noticed, but Johnes had a high opinion of his abilities and hoped that this monument would 'establish his Character for a first rate Sculptor'. And this it is said to have done when a year or two later it was exhibited at Spring Gardens.

It was Stothard who made the drawing of the supremely moving group, portraying the little family together for the last time; the dying girl stretched upon her couch attended by her mourning parents. At her side were all the objects that she had delighted in: her palette and brushes, her books, and her lyre reposing upon a scroll bearing the words and music of that favourite song: 'What tho' I trace each bird and flower that drinks the morning dew. . . .'

Like everything else that owed its existence to Johnes's imagination, this statuary group was conceived on an heroic scale. When it was finished, it proved to be much too large to be taken inside the Royal Academy. Nevertheless, it was Johnes's intention to have it placed above the altar, and his young lawyer friend, Merivale, when he came to stay with them that first autumn, composed the verses that were to be engraved on it.

When at the holy altar's foot is given
The blushing maiden to the enamoured youth
Whose long tried honour, constancy, and truth,
Yield the fair promise of an earthly heaven,
Though to far distant friends and country led,
Fond parents triumph 'mid the tears they shed.

Shall we then grieve, that a celestial spouse
Hath borne this virgin treasure from our sight,
To share the glories of the eternal light,
The end of all our prayers and all our vows?
We should rejoice—but cannot as we ought—
Great God! Forgive the involuntary fault.

Other tried friends, as well, came to cheer them, for Johnes craved for the company of those he cared for to mitigate the fearful emptiness. But there was one who came to Hafod that September whom he refused to see and turned away from the door, and this was his kinsman, Samuel Rogers.

Rogers and his sister Sarah were making a little tour in Wales and had arrived at Aberystwyth where they were spending a few days. One fine morning they set out to visit their cousins at

Hafod. It made a pleasant excursion and Rogers, with his passionate curiosity about other people's business, was no doubt quite as eager to see how the poor Johneses were bearing up under their heavy affliction as he was to look over the new house. They had, therefore, an interesting treat to look forward to at the end of the long, beautiful, though somewhat fatiguing drive. It was a memorable excursion, or would have been if things had worked out as Rogers expected.

At the end of about three hours their chaise drew up in front of the house, and while they waited for the servants to answer the bell the prospect of rest and perhaps a good dinner must inevitably have titillated their imaginations. But when the door was opened, by a man-servant arrayed in deep mourning, they were informed that Mr. Johnes could not receive them. As the man waited for them to drive off again Rogers made one more bid. In that case, perhaps Mr. Johnes would allow them to visit the pensile garden before they went? for no doubt he was anxious to see the vase with his verses to the robin, and show it to his sister. No request could possibly have been more unfortunate. The pensile garden was now thrice-hallowed, its gate jealously locked and everything within its precincts kept exactly as if Mariamne were still alive and caring for it. The key to it was only given to one or two highly privileged friends. Certainly no prying eyes were permitted, and least of all Rogers's, whose tongue could be as cruel as his eyes were sharp. Once more the answer was no! and the frustrated sightseers were left with no further choice than to turn the chaise round and depart, unrested, unrefreshed, whence they had come.

Back in London again, Rogers lost no time in spreading the tale of Johnes's churlish behaviour to him. Among others to whom he repeated it was George Cumberland, who found it sufficiently interesting to make a note of it in his pocket-book.

CHAPTER XV

The Scene in Chiaroscuro

There were still another five years of life for Johnes to get through after his daughter's death; five years in which to goad and drive his numbed faculties and cumbersome, exhausted limbs, along the threadbare track of useful activity. The lights had gone out for ever on that fatal 4th July; the light of their lives and the light that for more than a quarter of a century Hafod had shed across Wales and beyond it. Light and colour had fled away. Indoors it seemed as if the sombre tints of the grisailles by Stothard and Fuseli had come creeping down from wall and ceiling in malevolent, fog-like emanations, suffusing the whole house in a sad, perpetual twilight.

Except for visits from the faithful Eliza, he and Jane were all alone now at Hafod, which had been instrumental in separating them from nearly all their kindred. Life went on much as usual; farming, planting, looking after the poor people—who needed it more than ever that terrible winter of 1811. It had been a shocking year for the whole of Cardiganshire. Months of incessant deluges and floods had ruined the harvests and raised once again the grisly spectre of famine. Hundreds were thrown out of employment, and to save them from starvation Johnes took on as many as possible to make a new drive and a few more walks. On the coast the fisher-folk were also in dire distress, for the herring fishery had failed and they must be succoured as well; a permanent fund must be started immediately for the benefit of the widows and orphans. Wherever he looked, much cried out to be done and there was only himself to do it. That his benevolent projects continued to meet with little encouragement no longer mattered. His own partial failure was, moreover, painfully apparent; for ever since the premiums and money awards he had offered for good farming had been discontinued some years ago there had been a general back-sliding into the old bad habits. As he had not succeeded in teaching his poor countrymen how to help themselves, it behoved him to mitigate the dire results of their indolence; his back was strong enough still to carry them unaided. There was enough work at Hafod to keep hundreds of poor wretches employed for years, and if the other landowners were not willing to help with his philanthropic schemes, it merely meant that he must bear the whole burden himself.

Another perpetual anxiety was the thriftlessness of the servant class. It worried him to death, and at home he was unremitting in his efforts to persuade his domestics to put their money safely by. It was deplorable the way they seemed to spend every penny they earned. It was almost impossible to make them see how important it was to practise economy and save up for their old age. He talked of establishing a savings bank for servants in Aberystwyth, though he was probably discouraged from pursuing the plan when he saw how little his own household were inclined to act upon his good advice. He had tirelessly preached thrift and economy for more years than he could count, but feared he had succeeded in making very little headway. It was extraordinary how the lower classes appeared incapable of understanding how much happier and more contented they would be if only they would practise these excellent qualities. . . .

As for his own finances, they were going from bad to worse. With all his ingenuity, his jiggling and juggling, Hugh Smith was no longer able to stay their headlong descent towards ruin. Johnes was compelled to sell more of his timber and, as usual, made a bad bargain. Samuel Rogers, at one of his famous breakfasts at St. James's Place, told Cumberland about it and that Johnes had lost £2,000 on the deal. Rogers also declared that Johnes's total income was now reduced to £900 a year. He may well have been right, for certainly the poor old Khan of Hafod was ready to sell almost anything. He parted with some of his books, the Alchorne collection which had formed the nucleus of his new octagon library, for after all, as he said with a sigh, who should he keep them for? Through Thomas Dibdin the collection was offered to Lord Spencer at three times the figure Johnes had paid for it. When Dibdin's letter to his patron announcing these important tidings arrived, his lordship was on the point of stepping into his travelling carriage on his way to visit the Duke of Bedford at Woburn, whither he most certainly carried the news of the sorry straits poor Johnes was in. The purchase was duly made, but once again it all turned out very differently from what Johnes hoped. When the books arrived at Althorp they were found to be not only dirty and defective, but many of the Caxtons were duplicates. 'It was necessary', said Dibdin, 'that the trenching or pruning knife should be exercised in "mitigation" of "pecuniary" punishment; and I will do Mr. Johnes the justice to say that he underwent the amputating process with the unflinching intrepidity of a martyr.'

He had suffered too many similar martyrdoms throughout his life not to be inured to them by this time. Nothing mattered much now in any case. The best he and Jane could hope for was to go patiently on from one dark day to the next, doing what good they could. Doing good, unfortunately, was proving exceedingly expensive; there was that army of workmen to pay for one thing. Matters reached such a pass that in the winter of 1813 he was forced to play out his last trump card. The reversion of Hafod was offered for sale; it would be a grand speculation, said Johnes, for some rich man of taste to make. It had not been on the market long before a purchaser presented himself in the shape of a Mr. Claughton, who wonderfully cleared the black financial skies by paying down a large sum on the spot, a second payment to be made after Johnes's death.

Did the Dowager, dying at last at Portman Square, live to hear of this final expedient to which her once beloved elder son had been driven? Assuredly she did, for it was not until the winter that she died, and long before then the news must have reached the ears of her daughter Anne, who, like the Reverend Samuel, never forgave Johnes for throwing away his fortune. The tidings may well have sent the old woman's wandering thoughts back to that long-ago winter at Croft Castle when her husband had invited his little countrified niece to stay with them. Mrs. Johnes herself had taken quite a fancy to the pretty hussy, for a hussy, and worse, that ungrateful girl had proved. Jane undoubtedly had been at the root of all their troubles and sorrows . . . her poor son had always been too good-natured and easily swayed by a pretty face. . . . Jane's bright eyes and who knows what besides, had been his downfall. The scheming baggage had forced him to marry her . . . she had done all she could to bring about his ruin by encouraging his wild plans and setting him against his poor mother. . . . Well, they had been punished. That crippled girl of theirs was dead and now his total ruin was nearly accomplished. . . . What a host of ancient memories and hurts twitched and muttered among the curtains of her bed, while the old, old woman died.

It was several days before the news reached Johnes, for none of his relations, not even a servant, wrote to inform him. In fact, he learnt it from an upholsterer in Grosvenor Street, at whose shop he chanced to call, a circumstance that deeply offended him. For more than a quarter of a century Jane had been awaiting the event with impatience, but now that it had come at last it was too late to help her husband. Or perhaps after all it was not? For the Dowager had not been dead many months before Johnes was instituting proceedings against his brother and sister for the return of heirlooms which he claimed his mother had wrongfully removed from Croft thirty years before, though 'heirlooms' sounds too grandiose a title for the useful furniture and forks and teaspoons he sought to recover. He had reached the pitch when he could not leave them alone; when he was determined to prove by every means in his power that he was still very far from being an extinct volcano. . . .

It had taken two years before he could bring himself to return o London, which would ever be a hated spot, the scene of his life's great tragedy. He had no spirits now for company, and in any case most of his old friends were dead or had faded away from him. But there were still his parliamentary duties, and Chantrey's studio, too, to visit this winter, to see how the monument had progressed. Although it had been exhibited in 1812 it was still not quite completed. Johnes, when he saw it, was very much pleased with it; he had never seen anything, he said, 'more simple or more pathetick', though he shuddered to think of the day when it would be set up in their little church. How were they ever going to endure witnessing that poignant scene, Sunday after Sunday; the three together, perpetuated for all time in that hour of agony, in marble cold as death. He could not guess that he tormented himself in vain; that this was a trial that none of them would be called upon to face.

From Chantrey's studio in Salisbury Street it was not very far to go to Soho Square, where, in a house at the opposite end from that of their old friend Sir Joseph Banks, Payne Knight had been living for several years. One of the largest rooms in Knight's house was used as a private museum, where his exquisite bronzes, his intaglios, jewels and coins were to be seen against a sublime background of fine paintings—the savage splendour of Salvator Rosas, the shimmering repose of Claudes, the dark glitter of Rembrandts, arousing in the sensitive observer all the delicious sensations of picturesque ecstasy. This winter of 1813 Knight was sixty-four, some eighteen months younger than his cousin, Johnes, and altogether in much better case. In spite of his extravagant tastes and his open-handed generosity to struggling artists, he had inherited enough of the Knight prudence to restrain him from running through his fortune. His castle in Herefordshire reared its mock fortifications as proudly as it had ever done above his romantic valley and ideal landscapes, while to his house in Soho Square flocked all the brightest, most accomplished spirits of the age. Payne Knight was an influential and important figure. The principles which he and Uvedale Price had laid down would continue to influence popular taste until the 1830's, when the romantic movement would displace them. In spite of the high reputation his opinions enjoyed, in 1816 Knight nevertheless committed a serious error of judgment, when before a Select Committee of the House of Commons he strongly opposed the purchase of the Elgin Marbles on the score that they were not good enough to be bought by the Nation. His attitude in this matter was marked by his usual high-handed self-assurance, and when the Committee inquired whether he had, in fact, seen the marbles which Lord Elgin had brought to England, he replied with icy hauteur: 'Yes, I have looked them over.'

In spite of friends, fortune and the position he had made for himself, his latter years were not destined to be happy. His remarkably keen powers of enjoyment gave way more and more to moods of despondency and inertia out of which it became increasingly difficult to rouse himself, until in the end he was left with what he described as 'a perfect tedium vitae'. He, who formerly had never had enough of it, simply did not know how to get rid of his time as he wandered disconsolately about the streets from the house of one friend to another. He died in 1824, it was said of an apoplectic affection; but many years later Samuel Rogers had a very different, a far more sinister, tale to tell. When a younger acquaintance asked the poet whether he had known Payne Knight, Rogers replied: 'Yes! he was a relation of mine. He poisoned himself with prussic acid—his nerves were destroyed by *women*.'

Six months prior to Knight's death, Uvedale Price had seen

him 'full of blue pills and blue devils', so perhaps Rogers's story was true. Uvedale Price in his old age was quite the reverse, still as active and cheerful as ever. He and Lady Caroline continued to pay occasional visits to their house in Aberystwyth—to the end the only couple among all Johnes's acquaintances who had planted a stake in Cardiganshire. Wordsworth has left a thumbnail sketch of 'Uvedale Price striding up the steep sides of his wood-crowned hills, with his hacker, i.e. his silver hangar, slung from his shoulder, like Robin Hood's bow. He is 77 years of age.' The year before his death he was made a baronet.

Certainly after that unfortunate episode of the pensile garden, Johnes, on his return to London in 1813, would not have called at Rogers's beautiful house in St. James's Place. He would have nothing more to say to Rogers nor could he approve of him from any point of view. 'I am not that great admirer of Rogers's poetry you seem to be,' he wrote about this time to Cumberland. 'He polishes and polishes until the Steel wears away, as an acquaintance of his said. . . . [He] has no heart—and I can give you proofs enough of it without ascending the rugged hill of Parnassus to look for them.' It would have delighted him to hear Carlyle many years later saying of the poet: 'Oh! that poor old man with his starry eyes and crystallised speeches! It makes me melancholy to think of him for days afterwards.'

Perhaps this was the last occasion when Johnes took that dreaded journey to London, for he had not been back at home very long before he fell seriously ill from a neglected cold. His health was steadily deteriorating, and the sadness and wet weather at Hafod made it difficult to recover. His doctors advised him to winter for the future in a warmer climate, and so in the spring, from Weymouth where he had gone to recuperate, he made an excursion into Devon and bought a small property near Dawlish known as Langstone Cliff Cottage.

The excitement of buying a house did him a world of good; there was a distinct echo of the old high spirits in his enthusiasm for the beauties and advantages of Devon and the delightful possibilities of his new acquisition, which, of course, later on he would have to rebuild in a superior style. For the present he contented himself with making a few improvements outside. It was like a breath of new life, an ideal escape from the cares of Hafod which had become altogether too heavy for his aching old shoulders. And at Langstone there were no reminders of happier days to fret him: no little phantom to glide out of the shadows to follow him wherever he went. No, in this pretty cradle, rocked gently by the balmy breezes, he and Jane would find a contentment and peace of mind they could never know at home. There would be congenial neighbours close at hand, among whom was Dr. Drury, the former headmaster of Harrow, who had retired to his estate near Dawlish where he was leading the life of a country gentleman. The Merivales were very often there, and the doctor's brilliant son, Henry, an ardent collector and bibliophile whom Johnes had known for some long while. Great things were always expected of this young man, whose fine intellect was consistently sacrificed to his indolent habits and extravagant tastes, which so far exceeded the income he earned as Master of the Lower School at Harrow that they finally landed him in the bankruptcy court.

Johnes eagerly looked forward to returning to Devon early in the winter, but when the time came it found him instead lying dangerously ill at Hafod, with what he later described as 'water on the chest'. It was a winter of Russian severity and the house was snow-bound for many weeks. It was not until May that he was well enough to travel to Devon, but, once there, the fine air of Dawlish quickly restored him. It was with the utmost regret that he left it in June, to spend the next three months at home. But he vowed he would not remain at Hafod for a single day after the 1st of October.

He did not want to go back there now, for at last its hold had dwindled right away. Instead of strengthening and exhilarating him as they had done of old, his mountains weighed him down like lead. As for all his works there—where did they lead, those paths his slothful labourers were for ever hacking out of the rough moorland? They only added fresh intricacies to the giant maze in which he had mislaid everything he had. Though the hills were a living green with summer foliage, he must be careful not to look where the finest trees had all been felled and carried off. But it was difficult to avoid seeing the denuded areas for the sheets of rose-red willow-herb that had rushed up from the earth to hide the bleeding stumps. And indoors, too, in the octagon library, there were many black gaps in the shelves where books had been taken down and sold. . . . At Hafod, wherever he turned, there was nothing but sadness. And now he had just heard from Chantrey that the monument was ready, and all that was required were his instructions for its packing and despatch. If it was sent off fairly soon it might be placed in the church by the anniversary of her death. But he could not bring himself to write to Chantrey about it. It would have to remain a little longer at the studio . . . another year, and Johnes would be feeling stronger; better able to bear the strain. . : . After all, there was plenty of time.

When Dibdin arrived at Hafod in July Johnes made no secret of his impatience for the 1st of October to dawn, so that he could hurry away from what the parson elegantly described as 'his paradise blooming in the wild'. Dibdin, who was ready to admire everything he saw there, was particularly pleased with the house, declaring that the 'hall, diningroom and suite of libraries are doubtless among the most beautiful and striking in the kingdom'. And Stothard's scenes from Monstrelet in the octagon library were in his opinion far finer than the coloured compositions the artist had done for Lord Exeter at Burleigh House, and were 'unquestionably very much beyond what a foreign artist has previously effected in the same chiaroscuro style, on the sides of the entrance hall at Hafod, from Froissart's Chronicles. . . . Everything *without* this matchless room is grand, quiet and impressive; mountainous scenery feathered nearly to the summit by larches; . . . cascades and mountain streamlets . . . vastly striking and exhilarating.' But Johnes's undisguised dissatisfaction with the place, his anxiety to return to Langstone, were such that Dibdin was constrained to indulge in pious reflections upon the discontent inherent in human nature, to the extent that 'Man never is, but always to be, blest'.

If only time would hurry! Johnes was feeling the effects of his illness again; he would never be able to shake it off properly until he was back in Devon. Nothing seemed able to raise his spirits, not even the chance of a visit from a very distinguished and high-minded acquaintance of his who had been his contemporary at Eton and for whom he had always felt a most particular admiration—Thomas Coke of Holkham. That September Sir James Smith (for the doctor had been knighted in 1814) was travelling in grandeur through England with Mr. Coke, stopping at a number of great houses on their way to Sir Watkin Williams-Wynn's agricultural meeting at Wynnstay in Flintshire. Smith was most anxious to introduce his friend to the unforgettable beauties of Hafod, and the plan that they should go there was all arranged when Coke discovered that to travel there and back from Flintshire would take up a whole week which he could ill afford to spare, owing to the badness of the roads. At the last moment the visit was cancelled, but it made little difference to Johnes, for nothing seemed very real or important now except his desperate longing to get back to the life-giving airs of Devon. Later on his good Sir James must visit them at Langstone.

At last the long-awaited morning came when he could turn his back upon Hafod and hasten towards the south. Even the glory of the autumnal colouring, as their carriage bowled down the drive, could not stir a flicker of regret. The only thing now that mattered was haste; they must travel as fast as they could. At every stage fresh horses were ready waiting to carry them on again, for they only paused at night, and even the nights were cut as short as they could be. Eliza, who went with them, much regretted this uncomfortable hurry, for she would have enjoyed seeing something of the interesting towns they went clattering through at a fearful rate, for Mr. Johnes would not hear of pausing. Nothing must delay their arrival at Dawlish. On they went, day after day, on that breakneck journey, and when at last they arrived at Langstone much to Eliza's astonishment it turned out not to be a cottage at all but 'a handsome house, elegantly furnished'. Knowing her brother-in-law as well as she did, it is a little strange that she had not guessed that before.

'Man never is, but always to be, blest.' Once more the truth of Dibdin's aphorism was proved, for that winter the climate at Dawlish was very far from genial. It was quite as cold as it was in Wales and they lived nearly as quietly, for it was generally too bad for Johnes to venture out. A few morning calls, a few dinners, broke the monotony of the winter, while all they looked forward to impatiently was the spring and warmer weather. But when spring came at last, and better things might be looked for, Johnes fell ill again, and for the last time, with a return of his old complaint. He lingered on through the first three weeks of April, and on the 20th of that month we catch a final glimpse of him, enjoying a bottle of champagne with Henry Drury while they talked of Alduses. It was plain, then, that he was sinking rapidly and at four o'clock in the afternoon of the 23rd he breathed his last.

It was Dibdin who wrote his epitaph in the *Bibliographical Decameron* which was published the following year. In accordance with a favourite literary device, two imaginary figures, Lysander and Almansa, were preparing to discuss the merits of several collectors whom death had lately removed from their ranks.

LYSANDER: And first for dear Mr. Johnes.

ALMANSA You notice him very affectionately methinks.

LYSANDER: I do: nor without reason. He had his foibles and his faults—for who is without them? but he had great goodness of heart—a general love of mankind—and no moderate warmth of regard towards those who were dear to him from marriage and other ties. And then his love of *Books*, of pictures, of architecture, of grots, waterfalls and rivers, and of all the grand and soul-reviving features of mountainous landscape. How intensely did this passion possess him! Some twenty years before his death he was in the plenitude of his book-wealth—and some ten years agone he was doomed to undergo one of the greatest vicissitudes which a collector could experience, in the loss, by fire, of a portion of his library. Yet, believe me, Hafod at this moment contains a library worthy of the taste, spirit and perseverance of him whose presence so lately gave it interest and animation.

After that last sad journey, when she brought her husband home and left him with their child, Jane went back to Devonshire and never saw Hafod or Wales again. She continued to live at Langstone Cliff Cottage for a number of years before moving into a smaller house in Exeter, where she remained until her death in 1833. She lived a very retired life, a few old friends staying with her now and again, and Martha and Fanny Harley always spending the summer months with her. Otherwise she was entirely alone, parted even from Eliza by some bitter dispute which alienated her finally from every member of her family. It is not difficult to guess its cause. 'Money—the root of all evil,' wrote the widow of John Johnes at the back of an old letter from Mr. Johnes of Hafod before she folded it away. The debts to John Johnes were still unpaid at the time of his death in 1815, and his young son who succeeded to an impoverished estate had little hope of obtaining any redress. Johnes had left a mountain of debt behind him and scarcely any money.

Jane nevertheless contrived to live very comfortably. She kept her carriage and her rooms were filled with the beautiful things she had brought away from Hafod. She lived very quietly and was as actively charitable to her poor neighbours as she had always been. 'A heart torn as mine is', she once wrote sadly to Cumberland, 'cannot mix much in society, but I find amusements in my books and plants, and I thank my God that I am able to do it.' The Cumberland family, who had been living in Bristol for many years, were a source of great pleasure to her. One of the daughters, Eliza, a girl in her twenties who loved painting and music, was a particular favourite of Jane's and used to stay with her every year. 'She is quite like a mother to me,' Eliza said, when she paid her first visit to Langstone in 1820, carried away by admiration for the gracious, ageing lady, the fine style in which she lived, and her background of grandeur and tragedy. They drove about the deep lanes together, and in the evenings, after they had dined 'in great form', sat with their needlework, the girl listening entranced to Jane's endless stories of Hafod and its glories. She never tired of describing all they used to do there, the dreadful fire and all about Mariamne. She brought out Mariamne's things to show Eliza Cumberland, as well as all her drawings and paintings. And Jane, always generous and giving, presented Eliza with Mariamne's colours—a signal honour, for, said Eliza: 'She cannot bear to part with anything that was hers.'

All through those long years of exile Jane's thoughts hovered perpetually over Hafod which, throughout the seventeen years of her widowhood, was standing shuttered up and uninhabited. Claughton had further complicated the appalling confusion of Johnes's affairs by getting out of his purchase. The place had been thrown into chancery, where it remained until 1832. Everything in the house was just the same as it had been when Jane left it, getting dustier and damper every year. All the furniture spoiling in the rooms; her beloved husband's books mouldering on the shelves of the libraries; his wines still in the cellars. Outside, their beautiful walks were getting more and more entangled and boggy, their gardens a desert of weeds. And the lawns sloping down to the river, where in happier days the peacocks had paraded their jewelled fans, had reverted to rough grass browsed by sheep off the mountains that pushed their way into the garden through the broken fences. The little school had

The library just prior to demolition

long been closed and nobody cared for the poor people or minded what became of them, now that her beloved Mr. Johnes was dead. Such goodness of heart as his was unequalled, yet no man ever met with greater ingratitude. Even in his last hours he was thinking of new employments for the poor people of Cardiganshire, although they had never exerted themselves to profit from all he had done for them.

Thoughts such as these were ever in her mind, and another chafing anxiety was the monument which had never been brought to Hafod church. It was still at the studio in London, for it could not be paid for. There seemed to be no possibility of it ever being paid for and the trustees had warned her not to meddle, or she might find herself made liable for all the debts and entirely ruined. Jane worried and fretted worse than ever now she was growing old. Round and round went the nagging memories of old sorrows and injustices, until sometimes she could scarcely bear it. Then she would seek comfort in recalling an air that Mariamne used to sing, promising joy in the end: 'Brighter scenes I seek above, in the realms of peace and love.' Jane had loved much all her life long, from the time when she was the elder sister at home looking after her darling brother and the three little girls. For years she had sacrificed herself to them, and so later on had Mr. Johnes, sharing his home with them, giving them everything they could possibly wish for. Yet see how cruelly they had behaved; how ungratefully they had treated them. . . . And then her beloved husband and child—what inexpressible devotion, this—yet one after the other they were snatched away. . . . Yes, no one had loved more ardently than had Jane, though somehow there had never been very much peace. And there was little peace to be gained now, with her mind dwelling eternally on the past with its happiness spoiled by the wrongs they had suffered and the forlorn splendour of poor Hafod left alone among the mountains, under a stormy sky.

Epilogue

In November 1854, George Borrow, in the course of a tramp through Wales, put up at the inn at the Devil's Bridge whilst he explored the surrounding country. It was not the little hostelry which Johnes had added to and equipped with his own beds and wine, for that had been pulled down many years before and replaced by an imposing stone building that Borrow described as an immense, lofty cottage containing a stately staircase and a gallery. It had been erected at great expense by the late Duke of Newcastle.

In September 1832, Hafod with all its contents and the estate had been sold under an order of the Court of Chancery at the Auction Mart in London. The Duke had bought it for £70,000 and took possession of it twelve months later, only a few days before Jane Johnes died at Exeter. For the next twelve years he made it his principal residence.

Henry, 4th Duke of Newcastle, was then an elderly widower and one of the most unpopular men in the country, detested by the public for his arrogant, autocratic character and conduct. On several occasions his actions provoked such indignation that his property was destroyed and his safety endangered. Perhaps, therefore, Hafod's remote situation and excellent natural defences of bogs and mountains may have appeared particularly attractive. Only a year before he bought it he had met with great abuse for causing tenants on his Nottinghamshire estates to be forcibly ejected from their homes. Questions had been asked in Parliament, and the speech he made in reply, with his famous retort: 'Is it not lawful for me to do what I please with my own?' had so much enraged the people of Nottingham that they burned his castle there to the ground. In London, feeling against him was just as strong, the windows of his house in Portland Place were smashed by the mob, while Clumber had to be strongly fortified against possible attacks. With all these unpleasant incidents and possibilities seething along his horizon, the mountains of North Cardiganshire may have assumed an additional charm, promising a peaceful haven where he could spend a large part of the year without much danger of being interfered with.

He made many alterations at Hafod, both in and out of doors, and is said to have spent £20,000 on it. His bad reputation as a landlord boded ill for the tenants, though according to what Borrow heard he proved kind and philanthropic. Borrow was told a great deal by a loquacious old mining captain whom he encountered on one of his rambles. This John Greaves was a native of Durham, employed by a company of north country men who, as the Rheidol United, had been profitably working the lead mines for the past thirty-five years.

The name of Johnes meant little to Greaves—the family had died away, he said vaguely. But he had counted the Duke of Newcastle as his dearest friend, and many was the 'pleasant chat and discourse' they had had for hours and hours together. 'His Grace', said Greaves, 'had not a bit of pride', or at least showed none to him, and he had done a wonderful amount of good at Hafod. He had farmed on a large scale, reclaiming thousands of acres of waste land, just as Johnes had done, and building capital farms and offices for his tenants. 'His grand feat, however,' said Greaves, 'was bringing the Durham bull into this country, which formed a capital cross with the Welsh cows.' His attempt to import north country sheep, on the other hand, had been a failure, as Greaves had warned him all along it would be. 'Says

I to the Duke: "It won't do, your Grace, to bring the north country sheep here: because why? the hills are too wet and cold for their constitutions"; but his Grace, who had sometimes a will of his own, persisted and brought the north country sheep to these parts, and it turned out as I said—the sheep caught the disease. . . .'

Thereupon Greaves had told the Duke of a wonderful salve made of bran, butter and oil, which might yet save them. 'The Duke listened to me, and the salve was made by these very hands; but when it was made, what do you think? the foolish Welsh would not put it on, saying it was against their laws and statties and religion to use it, and talked about the Devil's salves and the Witch of Endor, and the sin against the Holy Ghost, and such-like nonsense. So to prevent a regular rebellion, the Duke gave up the salve, and the poor sheep pined away and died, till at last there was not one left.'

But the Duke had been gone from Hafod for nearly a decade and had died. When he left the place he carried back with him to Clumber nearly everything of value, including the fine sculptured fireplaces and the ornate glasses that Johnes had bought at Fonthill. With these he had a link, for his eldest son had married the great-granddaughter of old Alderman Beckford. When Borrow inquired who was the present owner, the mining captain replied that it was a great gentleman from Lancashire who did not take the same pleasure in it that the Duke had done, or spend so much money on it.

Thus Borrow was well versed in its recent history when he set out to walk there early one morning on his way southwards. He knew scarcely anything about Johnes, though he was particularly anxious to see the monument to Miss Johnes in the church, which was considered one of Chantrey's greatest works. For at long last it had arrived there, thanks to the generosity of the Duke of Newcastle, who, seeing it one day at the sculptor's studio, had bought it and had it brought down. And later that morning Borrow beheld it placed beneath a stained-glass window. Deeply moved, he gazed long at 'the truly affecting scene: a lady and gentleman . . . standing over a dying girl of angelic beauty . . . extended on a couch, from whose hand a volume, the Book of Life, is falling.'

After presenting a trifle to the woman who had unlocked the church for him, Borrow descended the hill that led through the park. Like many and many another one before him, he was amazed by the scenery—the bright green valley with the Ystwyth brawling through it, sometimes hidden among groves, sometimes showing long stretches of water; and the noble, richly wooded mountains. The farther he proceeded the more beautiful it became. At last, turning a corner, he beheld the house, standing on rising ground with a range of mountains behind it. 'A truly fairy place it looked, beautiful but fantastic, in the building of which three styles of architecture seemed to have been employed. At the southern end was a Gothic tower; at the northern an Indian pagoda; the middle part had much the appearance of a Grecian villa. The walls were of resplendent whiteness, and the windows, which were numerous, shone with beautiful gilding.' After looking at it for about a quarter of an hour, his feelings divided between admiration and laughter, he went on down the road and out of the story.

Although the great Lancashire gentleman, Sir Henry de Hoghton, may not have spent much money on the estate, he certainly spent a great deal on the house. He pulled down a large part of it and with the assistance of Salvin built another in the Italian style with projecting roofs, terraces and a campanile (Borrow's Gothic tower). What remained of Johnes's charming abode continued to cling against Salvin's formidable structure like a wisp of lace caught against an ugly cliff. When the Italian villa was completed the intention, no doubt, was to sweep away every vestige of the original. But it never was finished. According to the local legend, the baronet's lady ran away from him, which so much disgusted him that his projects were abandoned and Hafod was once more put up for sale. From then onwards his addition remained exactly as it was. Roofed and glazed, it is true, though behind the dead eye-slits was a dismal warren of unfinished rooms and passages. As time advanced the unplastered walls grew shaggy with horrid excrescences, and since floors and ceilings were missing almost everywhere, an endless vista presented itself of rotting beams and transoms. A nightmare-like confusion that reached from cellar to attic, permeated by a peculiar stale smell all its own.

A Llanelly speculator was not deterred from buying it from Sir Henry. He broke up and sold large portions of the property, himself with his family living in the Gothic house. At first he is said to have lived in great style, driving large parties over the mountains behind six horses. Extravagance may have been his downfall, for he died bankrupt. A macabre interest is attached to this event, for the bailiffs foreclosed on his body as it lay at Hafod, just as they had done a century earlier on the wicked Sir Herbert's—it is said to have been the last occasion when this desperate measure was resorted to in Cardiganshire.

This brings us to about 1870. Hafod now became the property of a young man of good fortune and studious habits, whose naturally retiring disposition was further accentuated by his deafness. And there he remained, in peace and charity, for more than fifty years, pursuing his recondite studies (their nature was never quite clear) in the small circular library where many of Johnes's books still occupied the shelves. A locked door divided it from the octagon library beyond it, for this had been gutted; perhaps by Salvin's men prior to demolition, and only the shell remained, surmounted by its glaucous dome. As time advanced well into the present century and the memory of the present writer, the appearance of this learned recluse perfectly matched his strange surroundings—a slight, black-clad figure with a skull cap on his white locks and a little pointed beard, his fine-drawn, etiolated countenance stamped with amiable remoteness. By then little was left at Hafod to suggest the glories of the past. The walks had all been lost in the woods and coppices for many

Endpiece: Drinking fountain in the garden 1955

long years, and the temples, statues, bridges and pagodas had long since crumbled to decay. But 'Miss Johnes's Garden', in the thicket above the great rock, was still an important feature. Up the steep path visitors would be taken on summer evenings after tea to see the vase to the robin-redbreast, pausing on their way to admire the elegant obelisk to the Duke of Bedford. Indoors, an inferior residue of Johnes's pictures were still on the walls, one to which special attention was always drawn being that of Miss Johnes's music master. It was a portrait of Viganoni by Pellegrini which the singer had given to his patron long ago.

Hafod had an uncomfortable reputation. Inevitably, of course, it was said to be haunted, and it really did look as if the poltergeist which Paynter had paid the wizard from Breconshire £100 to lay, must have come to life again. The furniture was reputed to have a way of moving about at night and rearranging itself. Music, too, was sometimes to be heard; the strains of an old-fashioned instrument—a harpsichord, perhaps, or a lyre—plaintively drifting through the empty chambers. A lady might be seen at dusk walking in the garden or along the gallery upstairs. In the end it was impossible to persuade servants to come to such an out-of-the-way, creepy old place, with the result that in the period between the two wars the venerable owner was compelled to leave his home, and for the second time in its history Hafod stood for years furnished and uninhabited.

The adverse fate that had pursued Johnes and his works was active still. In 1932, his elegant church was destroyed by fire and Chantrey's great monument defaced beyond repair. For five years after that it hovered darkly above the lonely house among its woods, waiting to complete its task of destruction. Then, when the owner's death released it, it descended vulture-like upon its prey and picked it clean. First the house was stripped and then the mountains, of their proud and splendid cloak of green whose first strands were woven on a fine summer's day in 1780, when Thomas Johnes came riding up the valley and, spell-bound, vowed that here was Paradise.

Bibliography

Anderson, William: *The Scottish Nation*. 1865.

Annual Biography and Obituary. 1817.

Bell, C. F.: *Annals of Thomas Banks*. 1938.

Borrow, George: *Wild Wales*. Ed. 1901.

Bradley, A. G.: *Highways and Byways in South Wales*. 1903.

Bray, A. E.: *Life of Thomas Stothard*. 1851

Campbell, Lord: *Lives of the Lord Chancellors*. 1869.

Clay, Rotha M.: *Julius Caesar Ibbetson, 1759–1817*. 1948.

Clayden, Peter W.: *Rogers and his Contemporaries*. 1889.

Coleridge, Samuel Taylor: *Miscellaneous Criticism*. Edited by T. M. Raysor. 1930.

Cumberland Papers: British Museum, Add. MSS. 36491–36516.

Davies, D. J.: *Economic History of S. Wales prior to 1800*. 1933.

Davies, Walter: *General View of the Agriculture of S. Wales*. 1814.

Dibdin, T. F.: *Bibliomania*. 1809. *The Bibliographical Decameron, 1817*.

Dolaucothi papers: National Library of Wales.

Edwards, Edward: *Lives of the Founders of the British Museum*. 1870.

Evans, George Eyre: *Cardiganshire, its Antiquities*. 1901. *Lampeter*. 1904.

Evans, John: *Letters written during a Tour through S. Wales*. 1804.

Fenton, R.: *Tours in Wales, 1804–1813*. 1917.

Finberg, A. J.: *Life of J. M. W. Turner*. 1939.

Fry, Katherine, and R. E. Cresswell: *Memoirs of the Life of Elizabeth Fry*. 1847.

Gentleman's Magazine. 1807.

George, R. H.: *History of the Herefordshire Borderland.* 1914.

Greville, Robert Fulke: *The Diaries of the Hon. Robert Fulke Greville.* Edited by F. McKno Bladon. 1930.

Hucks, John: *A Pedestrian Tour through North Wales.* 1795.

Hussey, Christopher: *The Picturesque.* 1927.

Hutton, Catherine: *Reminiscences of a Gentlewoman of the Last Century.* 1891.

Ibbetson, J. C.: *Painting in Oil and Watercolours, with a Memoir.* 1828.

Jones, G.: *Sir Francis Chantrey, R.A.* 1849.

Jones, T. Gwynn: *Welsh Folklore and Folk Custom.* 1930.

Lipscomb, George: *Journey into S. Wales.* 1802.

Lloyd, T., and Turnor: *General View of the Agriculture of the County of Cardigan.* 1794.

Malkin, Benjamin Heath: *Scenery, Antiquities and Biography of South Wales.* 1807.

Merivale, Anna W.: *Family Memorials.* 1884.

Merivale, John Hermon: *Poems, original and translated.* 1828.

Meyrick, Sir Samuel Rush: *History of Cardiganshire.* 1810.

Mitford, Rev. J. W.: *Commonplace Books and Recollections of the Rev. J. W. Mitford.* British Museum, Add. MSS. 32559–32575.

Nichols, John: *Illustrations of the Literary History of the Eighteenth Century.* 8 vols. 1817–1858.

Owen, Hugh: *Additional Letters of the Morrises of Anglesey.*

Roberts, Ellis: *Samuel Rogers and his Circle.* 1910.

Robinson, C. J.: *History of the Castles of Herefordshire and their Lords.* 1869.

Romney, John: *Memoirs of the Life and Works of George Romney.* 1830.

Shepherd, William: *Poems, original and translated.* 1829.

Smith, Sir James E.: *Tour to Hafod.* 1810. *Unpublished Correspondence:* Linnean Society Library.

Smith, Lady (Pleasance): *Memoir of Sir J. E. Smith.* 1832.

Bibliography

Stirling, A. M.: *Coke of Norfolk and his Friends.* 1908.

Summerson, John: *John Nash, Architect to King George IV.* 1935.

Thomas, D. Lleufer: *Lewis Morris in Cardiganshire.* Y Cymmrodor, Vol. XV, 1901.

Trevelyan, G. M.: *English Social History.* 1944.

Vaughan, Herbert M.: *The South Wales Squires.* 1926. *The Hafod Press.* 1912.

Waring, Elijah: *Recollections and anecdotes of E. Williams.* 1850.

Whitley, William T.: *Artists and their Friends in England.* 1928.

Wyndham, Henry P.: *A Tour through Monmouthshire and Wales.* 1781.

Index

Index

Index

Index